IMAGES
of America

OHIO LIGHTHOUSES

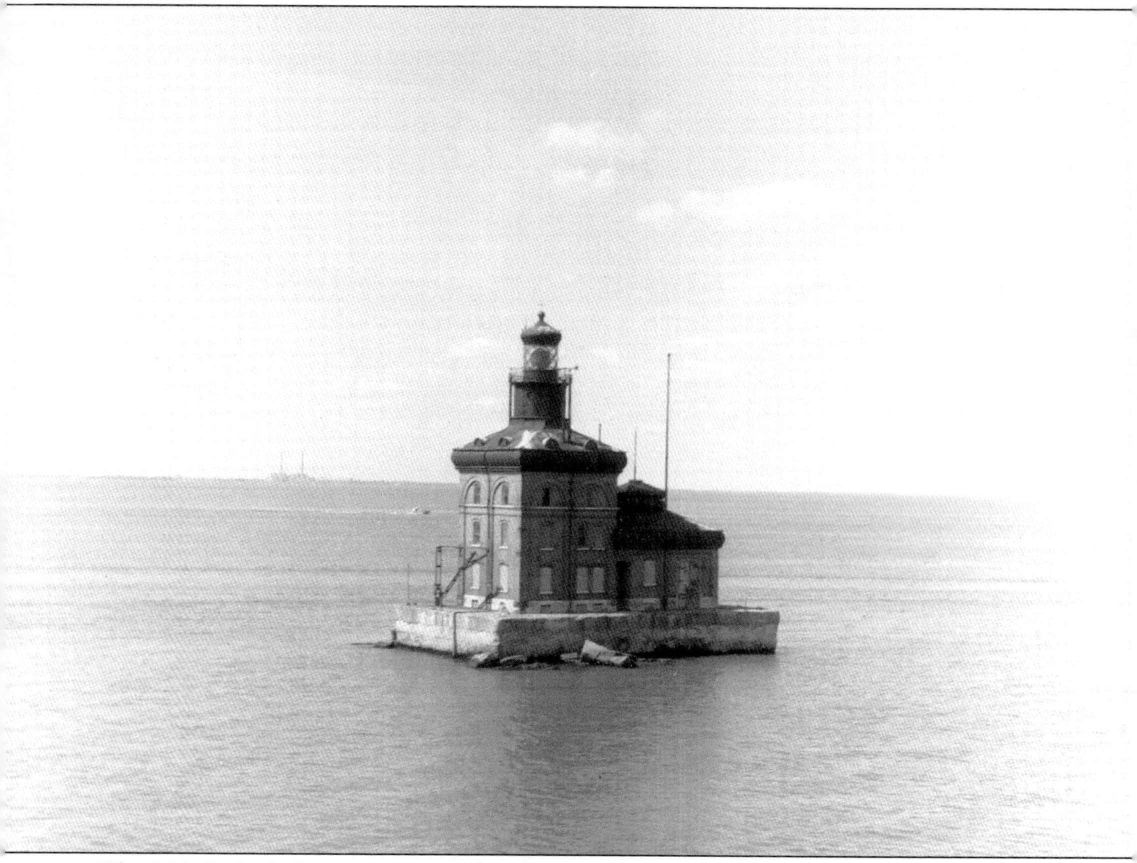

The Toledo Lighthouse was completed in 1904 and stands 64 feet high. (Bowling Green State University.)

On the Cover: Marblehead Lighthouse with Charles "Cap" Hunter, keeper (right), and Edward Herman, assistant keeper (far left). (Sandusky Library and Follett House Museum.)

IMAGES *of America*

OHIO LIGHTHOUSES

Wil and Pat O'Connell

ARCADIA PUBLISHING

ISBN 978-0-7385-8332-7

Published by Arcadia Publishing
Charleston, South Carolina

Printed in the United States of America

Library of Congress Control Number: 2010943217

For all general information, please contact Arcadia Publishing:
Telephone 843-853-2070
Fax 843-853-0044
E-mail sales@arcadiapublishing.com
For customer service and orders:
Toll-Free 1-888-313-2665

Visit us on the Internet at www.arcadiapublishing.com

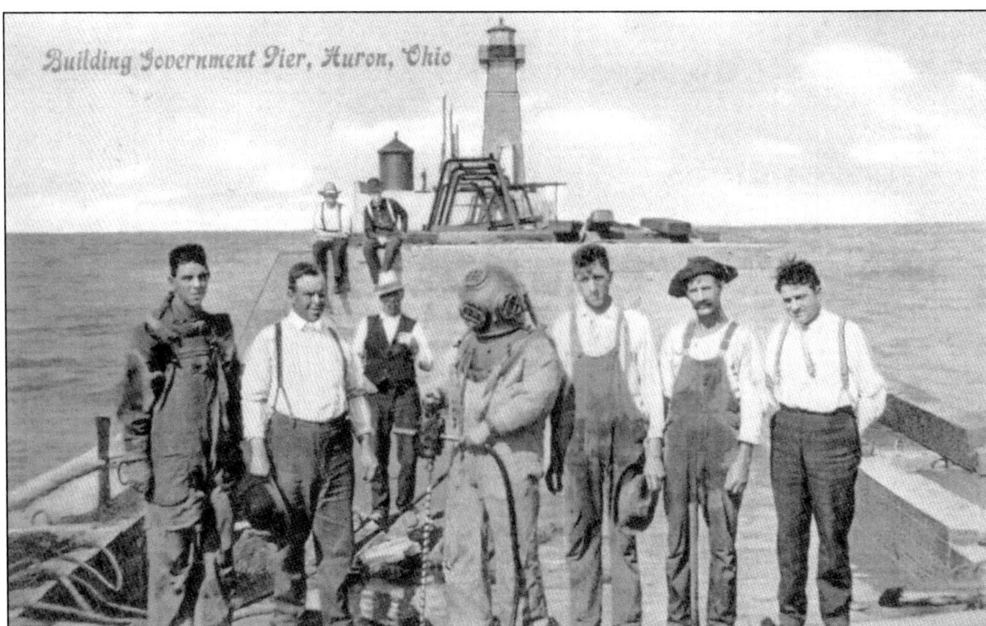

Men building the government pier, including one still suited in his diving outfit, pose around 1909 with the Huron Lighthouse in the background. (AC.)

Contents

Acknowledgments 6

Introduction 7

1. The Disappearing Island Lighthouse 9
2. World Famous Ship Wrecks near the Lighthouse 23
3. Fire Destroys the Lighthouse 29
4. Slightly Sinful Island Lighthouses 35
5. From Ugly Duckling to Beautiful Swan 47
6. Lighthouses at Famous Cedar Point 63
7. Mystery of the Lost Lighthouse 83
8. The Most Beloved Lighthouse 93
9. Heroes at Cleveland Lighthouses 101
10. A Haunted Lighthouse and Entombed Keepers 113

ACKNOWLEDGMENTS

The pictures in this book are from the following organizations, and we wish to thank the following people in these organizations and many others who made this book possible: Jim and Nancy Reid of Galion, Ohio; Philip and Joyce Edwards of Marblehead; Sharon A. Leis-Scagnetti of Ottawa Trader in Marblehead; Carolyn and Frank Sipkovsky of the Black River Historical Society in Lorain; Lynn Lay, Ohio State University librarian; Curtis Lay, computer expert, Columbus; Sarah Clifford, Mansfield; Mary Alice Gladding, Fairport Harbor Museum; Melissa Basilone, senior acquisitions editor, Arcadia Publishing; Ron Davidson, archivist, Sandusky Library and Follett House Museum (SL); Mike Speer, archivist, Conneaut Library (CL); Robert Graham, archivist, Bowling Green State University (BGSU); Christopher Gillcrist, Great Lakes Historical Society (GLHS); Mary Ilario, Still Picture Reference Team, National Archives and Records Administration (NARA); Irene Martin, historian, Toledo Library (TL); Peggy Debien, curator, Ottawa County Historical Museum (OCHM); and Bob Hartman, president of the Marblehead Lighthouse Historical Society. Pictures from the author's collection are coded AC.

Introduction

True but hard-to-believe tales give accounts of Ohio lighthouses and the people who depended on their lights, including a few slightly sinful boaters. Lighthouses inspire images of protection and guidance, but behind every flashing beacon are a story and a secret to be revealed.

A deceased lighthouse keeper left a trunk with a clue that solved a 64-year-old lighthouse mystery. The Lake Erie Fishing Club, located next to the Middle Island Lighthouse, had nothing to do with catching fish. The huge freighter *Bayton* hit the lighthouse twice. Why was the freighter severely damaged, when the lighthouse only needed minor repairs? Why did the government pour money into a disappearing island and sinking lighthouse?

A haunted lighthouse became famous for its ghosts, but who were the "spirits that did not represent people"? Under what circumstances did an old Australian prison ship sink near an Ohio lighthouse? How did an Ohio lighthouse keeper become the only person to win two gold medals for bravery from the government?

A lighthouse is a silent communication like no other—a signal, a message between two people far apart. They are strangers in the night, but lighthouse keeper and sailor have a common goal: to get the ship safely to its destination.

In *Ohio Lighthouses* are true tales of keepers' lives at the lighthouses and the sailors who relied on them and their beacons warning of danger. Each is alone—one on the water, and the other in an isolated lighthouse. There is comfort for the sailor in knowing that the keeper is there to stave off hazards, and the keeper derives satisfaction from knowing that his efforts help the sailor.

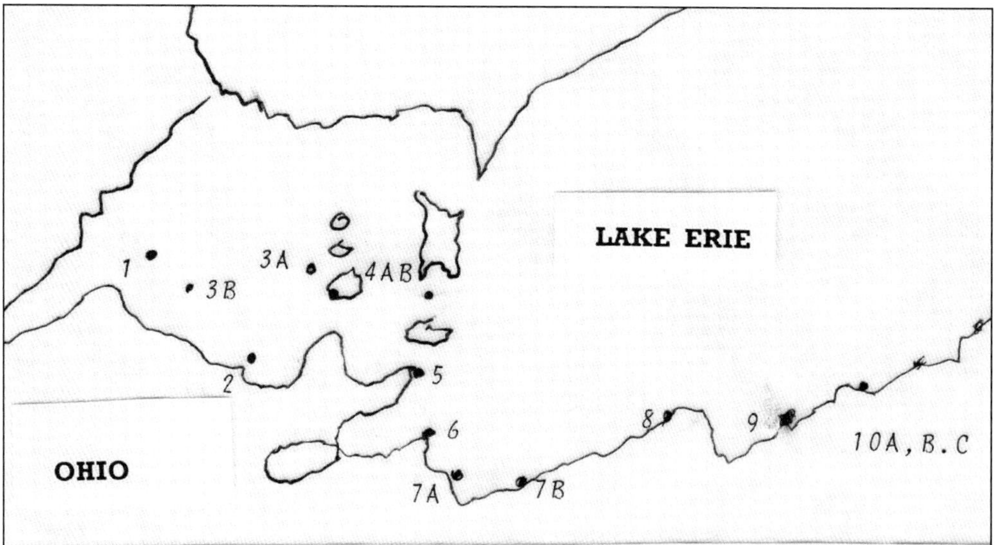

1. **Toledo, Turtle Island, Maumee Crib, Manhattan Range and Stoddard Range Lighthouses**
2. **Port Clinton Lighthouse**
3. **Green Island (3A) and West Sister Island (3B) Lighthouses**
4. **Middle Island (4A) and South Bass Island (4B) Lighthouses**
5. **Marblehead Lighthouse**
6. **Cedar Point and Sandusky Bay Lighthouses**
7. **Vermilion (7B) and Huron (7A) Lighthouses**
8. **Lorain Lighthouse**
9. **Cleveland Lighthouses**
10. **Ashtabula (10B), Fairport Harbor (10A), and Conneaut (10C) Lighthouses**

The locations of the 10 Lake Erie lighthouses that are focused on in this book are on this map.

One

The Disappearing Island Lighthouse

In 1832, no one realized that the lighthouse guiding ships into Toledo Harbor was built on a disappearing Lake Erie island made of mud, not stone—namely, Turtle Island. The Toledo Lighthouse's 44-foot conical tower held eight white, fixed lamps with reflectors. The lighthouse was replaced in 1866 with a schoolhouse-type structure, although the island, once 6.68 acres, had shrunk to only an acre. The government built a retaining wall around the sinking lighthouse to save it. In 1904, a new lighthouse, built at the end of an eight-mile-long Toledo channel into the lake, replaced it. Today, water laps at the doors of the old lighthouse and nearly covers the retaining wall erected to protect it. One day, the island, the lighthouse, the retaining wall, and the Ohio-Michigan boundary marker on the island will disappear under the waters of the lake, like the fabled city of Atlantis sinking into the ocean.

The 1904 Toledo Harbor Light is unique. Placed on a crib in 21 feet of water eight miles from shore, the lighthouse seems out of place in Lake Erie. When viewed from a boat 50 feet away, its huge size is intimidating, and the unusual architectural style is a blend of Moorish and Romanesque styles.

People say the Toledo Lighthouse is haunted, its ghost called the Phantom of the Light. When boaters and fishermen seek shelter in the lee of the Toledo Lighthouse during a storm, lightning reveals the phantom in the window. The US Coast Guard does not deny that there might be ghosts haunting the lighthouse, but some believe that the Phantom of the Light is actually a male mannequin dressed by members of the Coast Guard in one of their uniforms to keep vandals away.

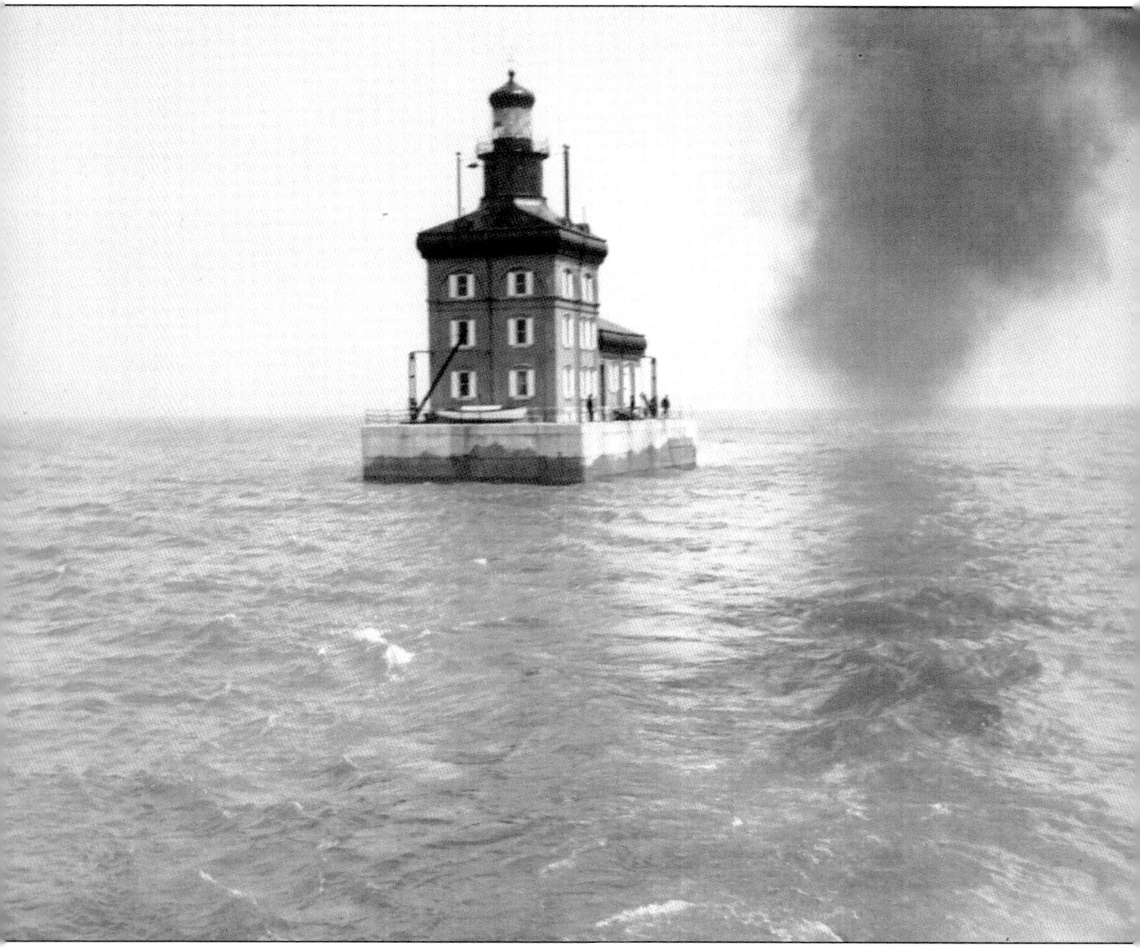

Legendary tempests on the Great Lakes have sunk huge freighters. When fierce storms come rolling through, it must be unnerving for a lighthouse's inhabitants. If it were to collapse, there would be no means of escape. A massive crib, 86 feet long and 48 feet wide, supports the heavy lighthouse. Below the water level, hemlock timbers and oak planks were bolted together. Then, a combination of stone, sand, gravel, concrete blocks, and poured cement brought the crib 12 feet above the water level. In 1904, an article praised the new Toledo Lighthouse as being the most modern lighthouse and fog-signal station in the world. Major Symons, engineer at the 10th Lighthouse District, said the Toledo light was a model of perfection. (NARA.)

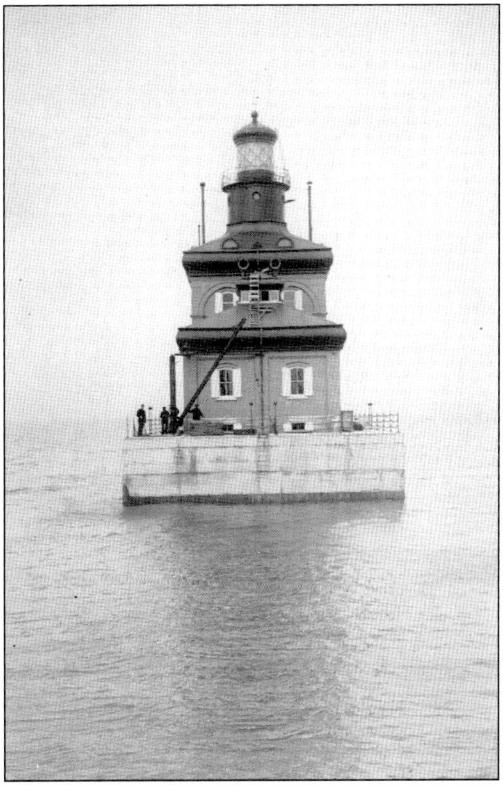

In 1904, the light was widely praised as the "best beacon on Lake Erie." Inside the 54 panes of curved glass is a third-order lightning flash lens resembling a large bull's-eye. Oil for the lamp inside the lens is forced to the burner by compressed air. Weights cause the lens to rotate on ball bearings every 30 seconds and send three flashes, two white and one red, produced by the ruby glass inside the bull's-eye. (NARA.)

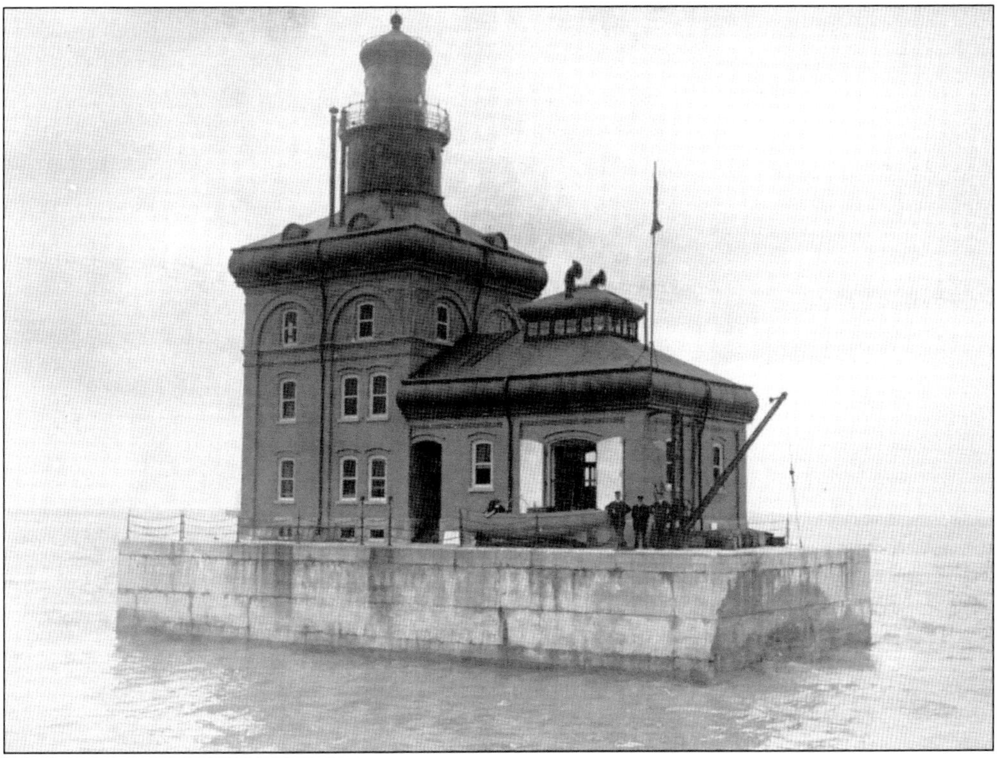

If the lighthouse were for sale today, the advertisement might read, "Spectacular lakefront views from every window." According to a 1904 article, it has all the amenities possible for two families. A cellar has the furnace and oil storage. The other three floors contain an engine and power room, an office, two kitchens, sitting rooms, bedrooms, bathrooms, hot and cold running water, polished brass and bronze plumbing fixtures, oak trim, and maple floors. The first keeper at Toledo Lighthouse was Dell Hayden from West Sister Island. His assistant was Edward Reicherd. (NARA.)

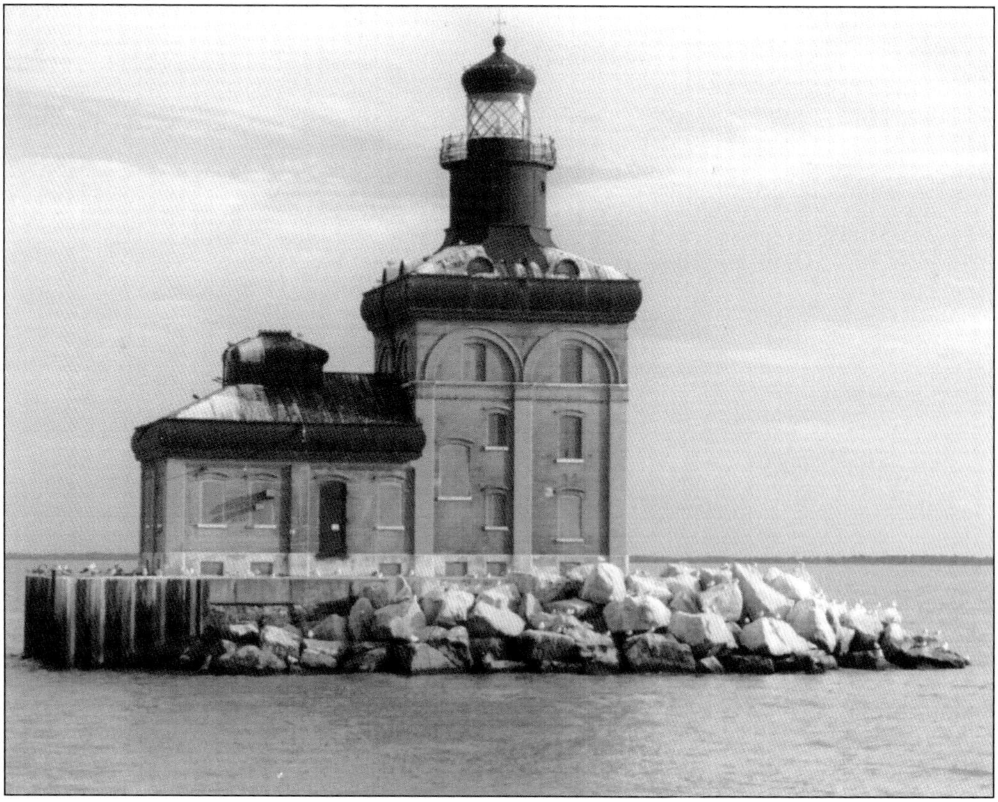

The lens for the Toledo Lighthouse was imported from Paris and cost $5,000. (AC.)

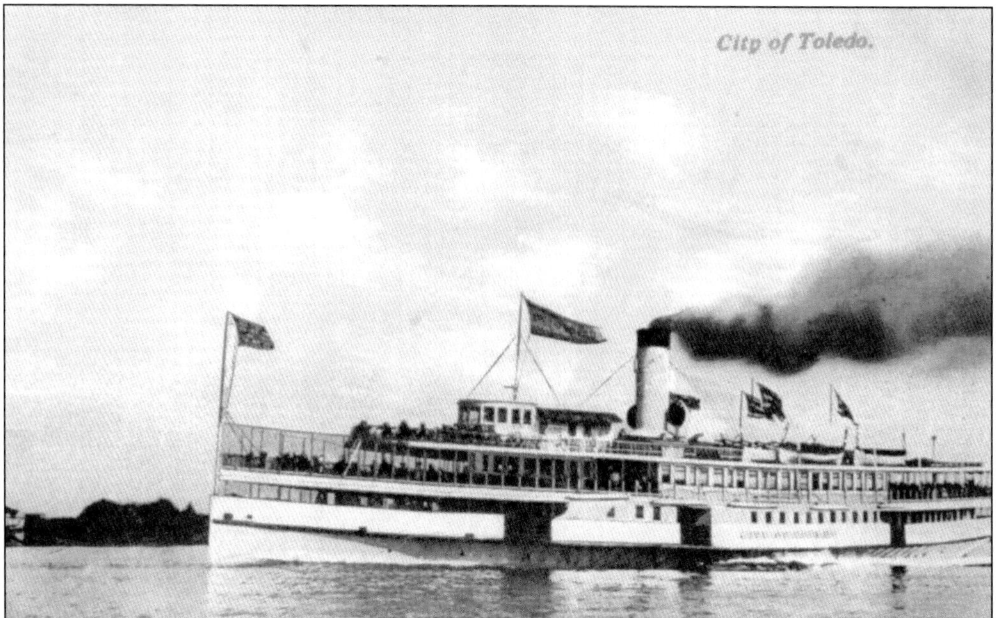

The *City of Toledo* excursion steamer was 212 feet long and built in 1891 by Craig Ship Building Company of Toledo and plied the waters of the Great Lakes. (AC.)

A long time ago, colorful character and short-term lighthouse keeper August "Gus" Gramer was physically removed from the lighthouse by heavily armed men for insubordination and quarreling with his assistant and superiors. He was instructed to leave but refused, so he was carried away. He had the last word, however. When he reached shore and newspaper reporters were nearby, he yelled, "You guys can't fire me. I quit!" (AC.)

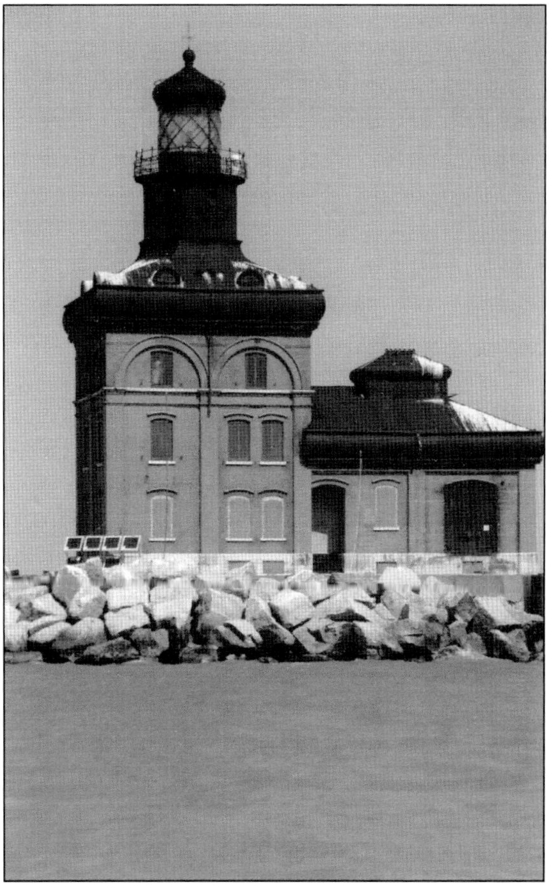

The fancy Toledo Yacht Club's unusual architecture can be appreciated in this photograph from 1909. (AC.)

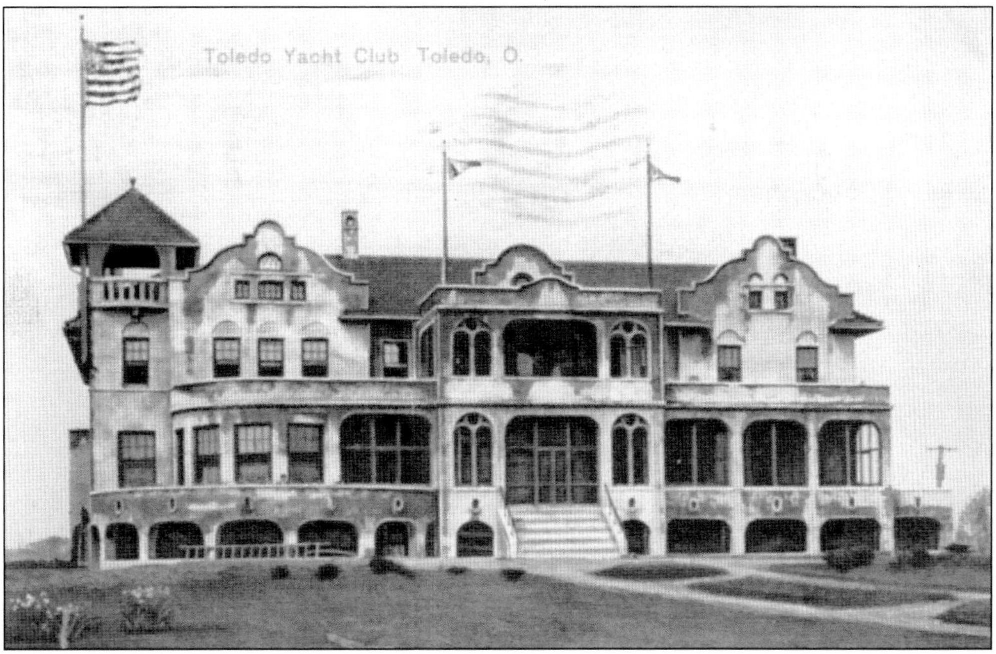

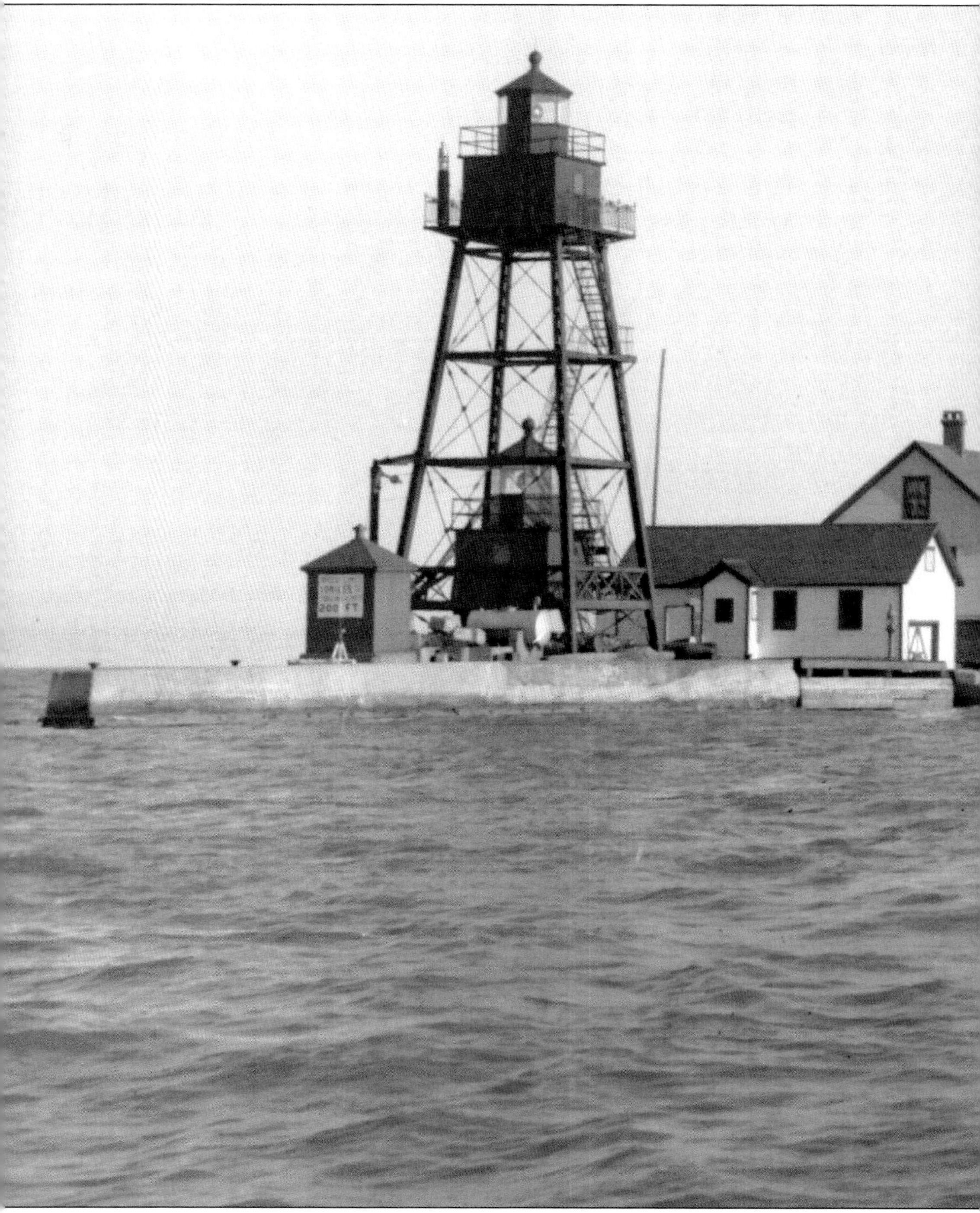

It was a funeral of sorts—a showing of respect and a display of affection. Congress approved funding for the removal of the Toledo Crib Lights, pictured here around 1930. On June 30, 1957, nine hundred yachtsmen anchored their boats off the crib lights for a ceremony bidding farewell to the familiar landmark. Flags were dipped, horns were sounded in salute, and crewmen from an Ottawa River Yacht Club cruiser placed a wreath on the southeast corner of the crib. Life would

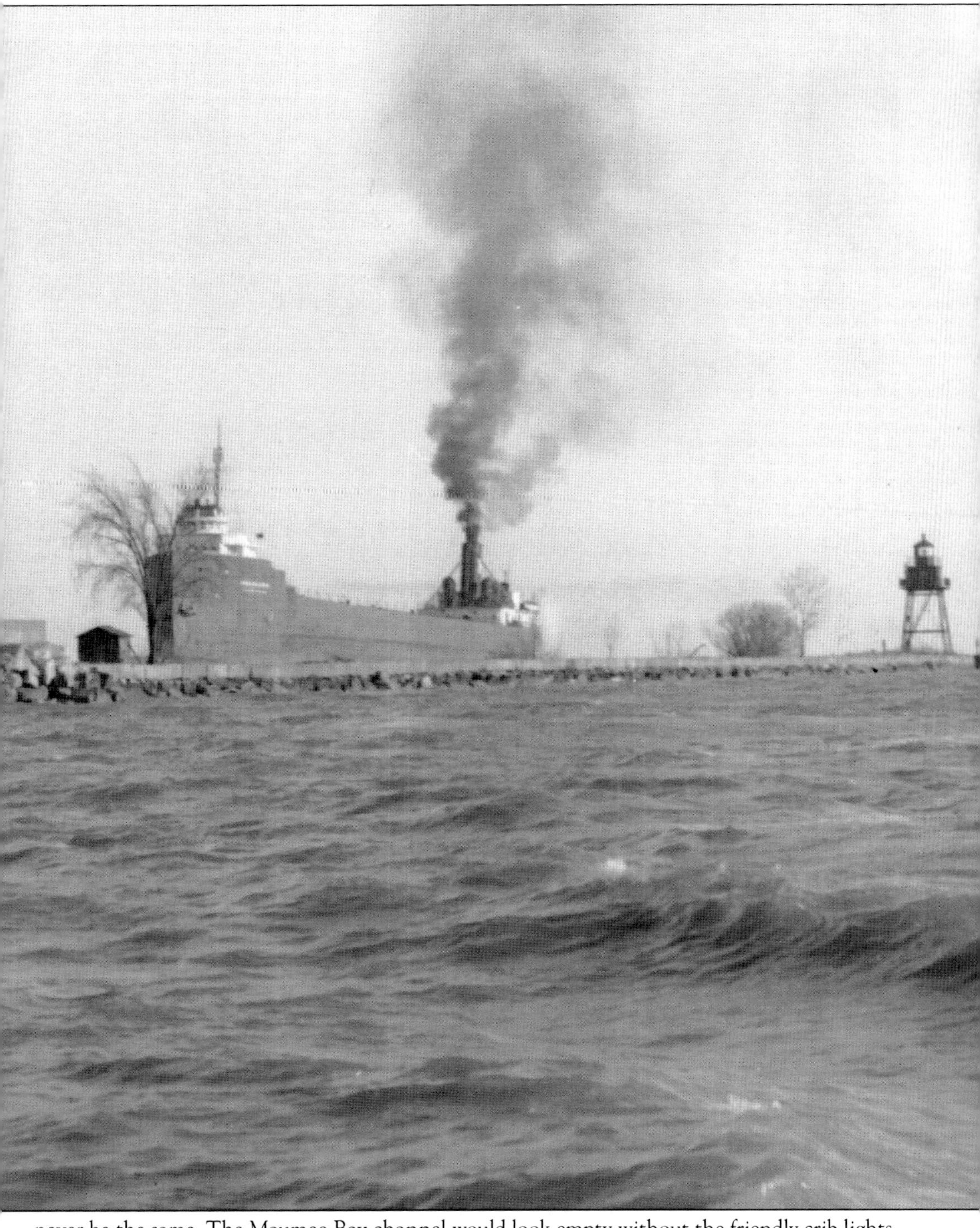

never be the same. The Maumee Bay channel would look empty without the friendly crib lights to guide the boats. The life of the structure began May 3, 1899, when the government ordered the building of the Maumee Bay Range Lights, nicknamed the "Toledo Crib Lights." Three years later, two wooden towers were completed, 1,300 feet apart. In 1907, the two lights were connected with stone, and in 1918, steel towers replaced the wooden towers. (GLHS.)

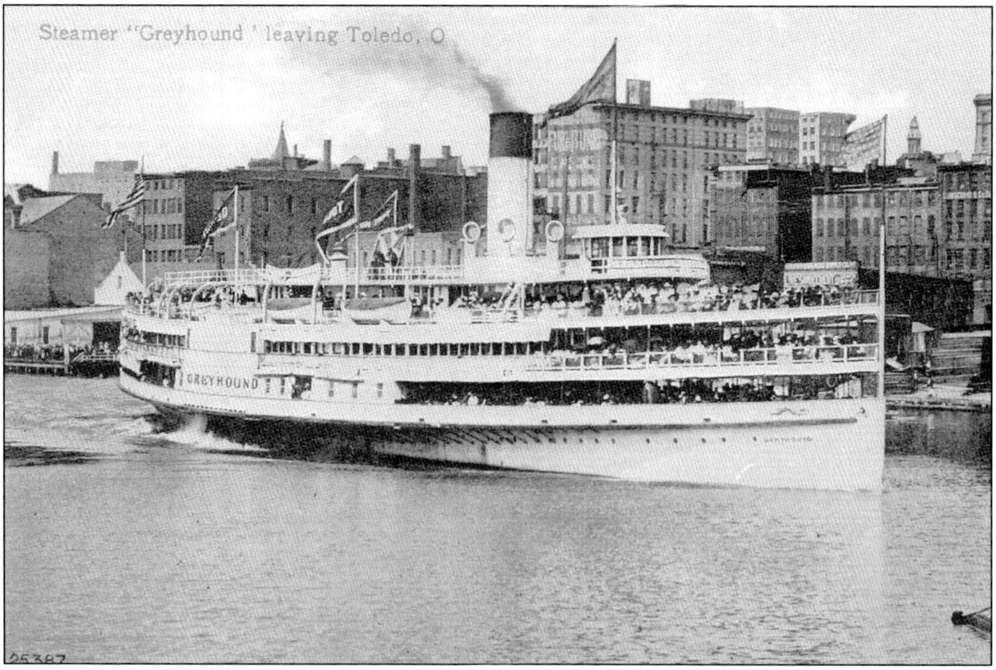

The popular excursion boat *Greyhound*, built in 1902 at Wyandotte, Michigan, is pictured leaving Toledo with passengers. (AC.)

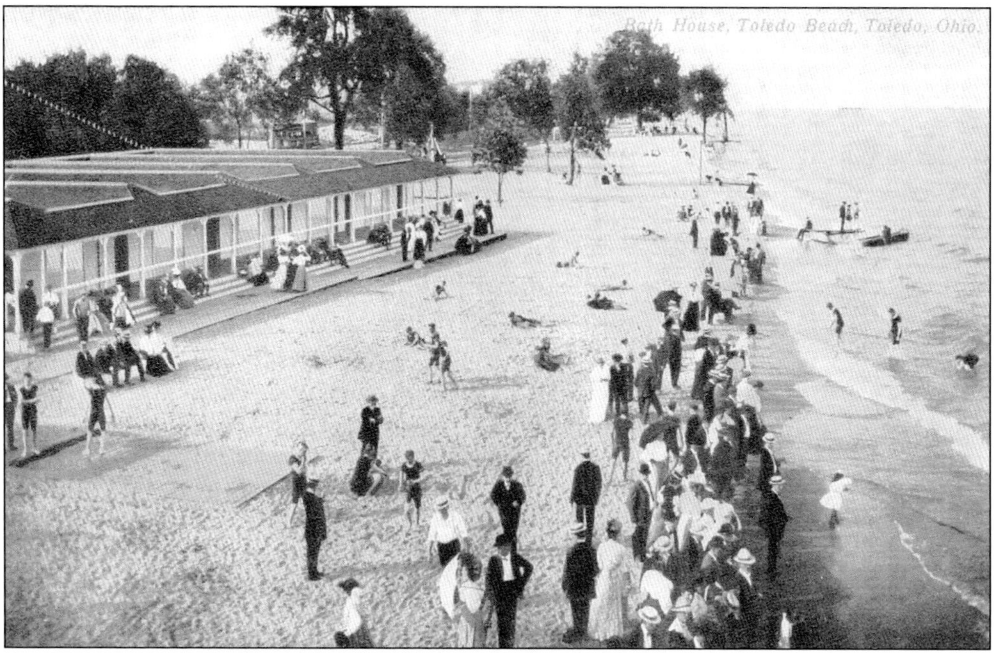

On a warm day in 1910, people visit the Bath House and stroll on the Toledo beach. (AC.)

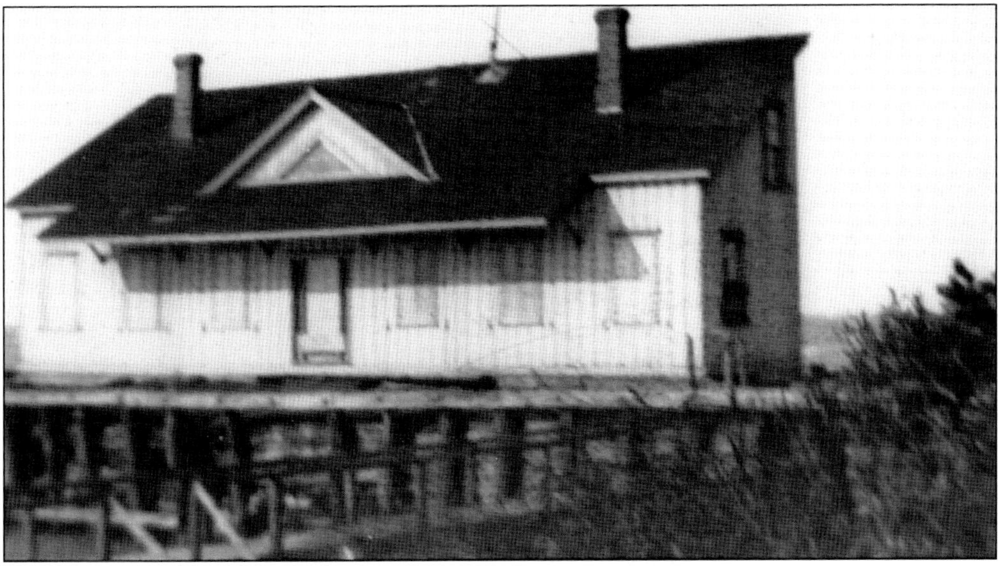

This Cedar Point Range Light is an identical twin to the Stoddard Range Light pictured in the *Toledo Times* on March 13, 1923, and the *Toledo Blade* on February 8, 1929. Capt. George Stoddard lived in and operated the lighthouse in Toledo from 1868 to 1905. Captains used the range lights to guide their ships through the crooked channel into Toledo. In later years, Toledo motorists driving by this structure, which appears to be only half a house, speculated on the oddly shaped building, but few guessed the structure was originally a lighthouse. It was 60 feet across and only 15 feet wide and was demolished in 1953. (Read more about this lighthouse in chapter six.) (SL.)

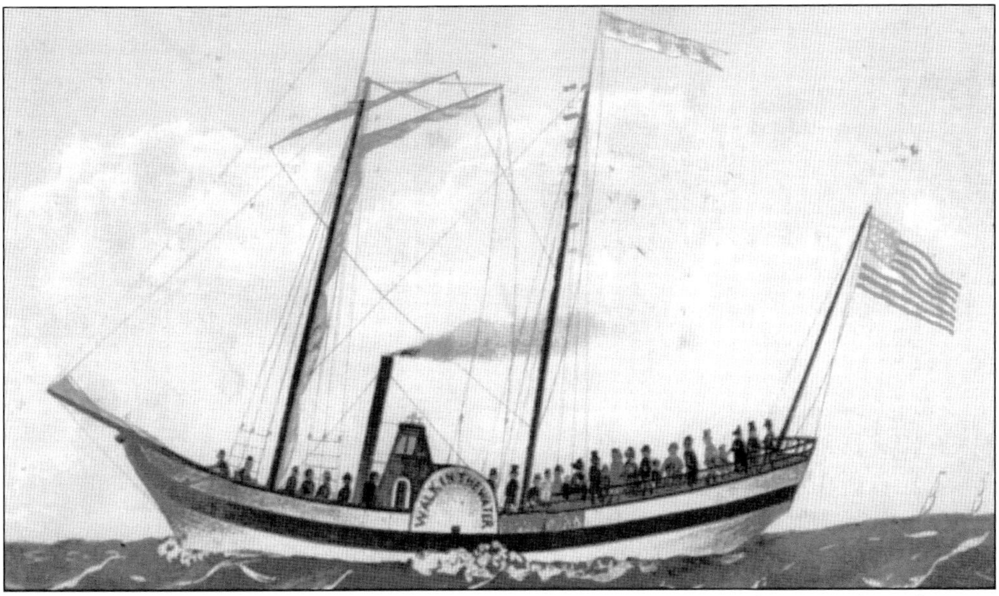

Walk-in-the-Water was the first steamship to sail on Lake Erie. Notice the masts for sails; even the builders were skeptical and wanted a backup plan. Built in 1818, it transported passengers between Buffalo and Detroit weekly, stopping at Kelleys Island, then named Cunningham's Island, for firewood. In November 1821, when nearing the port of Buffalo, it ran onto a beach, splitting the keel and smashing the hull. All on board were saved, thanks to the quick thinking of the lighthouse keeper who came to their assistance. (AC.)

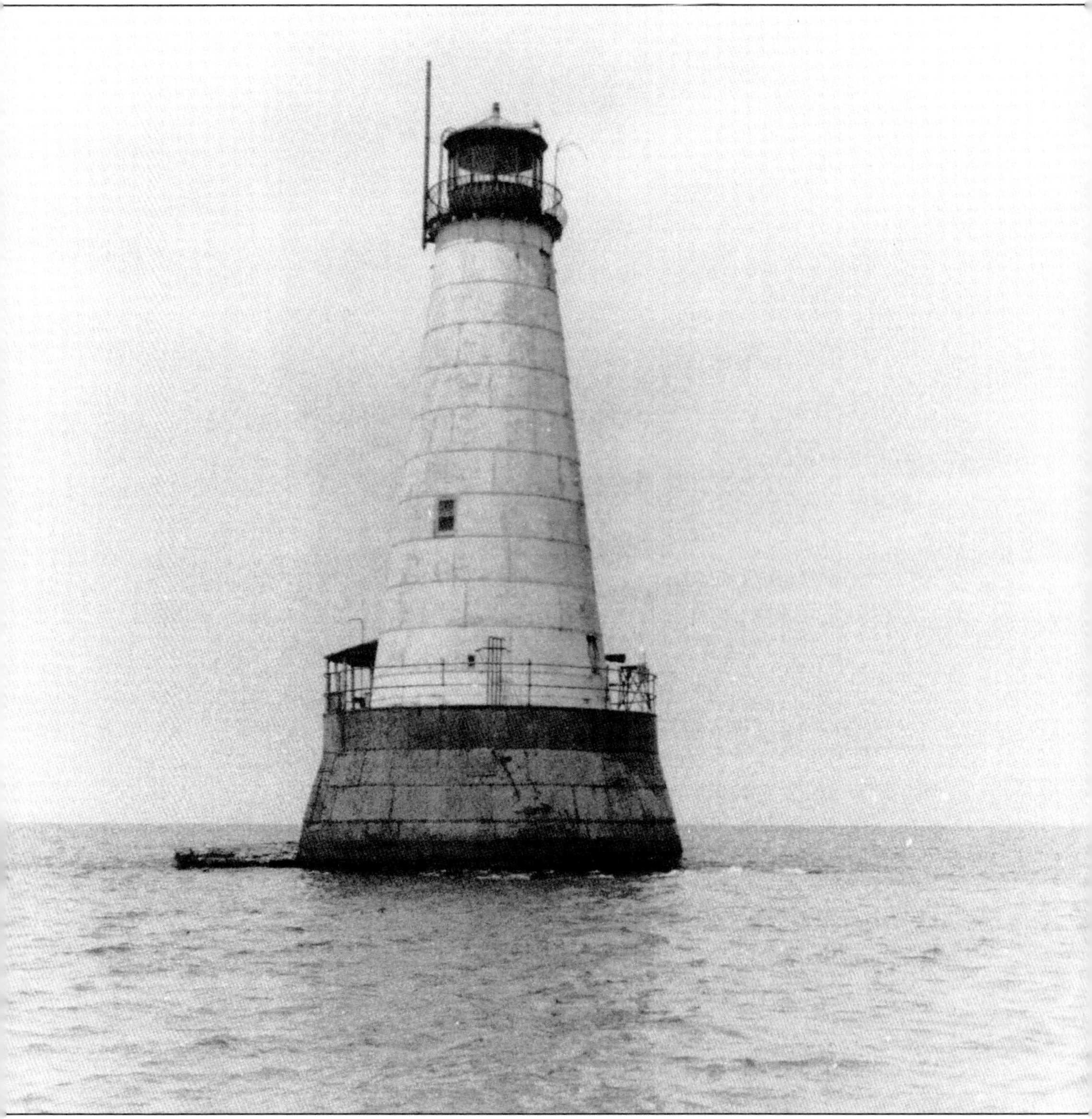

A crew member on the rum boat *The Barrel* tells a story of running whiskey during Prohibition (1920–1933): "We began in March and ran 180 trips delivering whiskey to Toledo without trouble. Then on December 23, 1928, we left Toledo for Canada, dodging drifting ice and traveling in daylight, since all the Coast Guard boats were dry-docked for the winter. Reaching Canada, we loaded and returned past the Pelee Lighthouse on Christmas Day. All went well until we were about one mile from Toledo. We ran into a solid sheet of ice an inch thick a mile from shore. Believing that we could cut through it, we ran into it for about 100 feet and could go no further. We were stuck. The next day, we walked ashore, found a phone, and called the boys, telling them to come and bring sleds. When the boys arrived, we carried 250 cases of liquor over the ice to shore and loaded it on the sleds. We left the rum boat in the ice all winter. In spring, after the ice broke up, we ran *The Barrel* to Port Clinton, where we put her on a lift and checked for any damage to the hull. There was none. Her berth in the ice didn't hurt her a bit." Pelee Passage Lighthouse, built in 1901 on a reef north of Pelee Island, guided ships until 1976. (GLHS.)

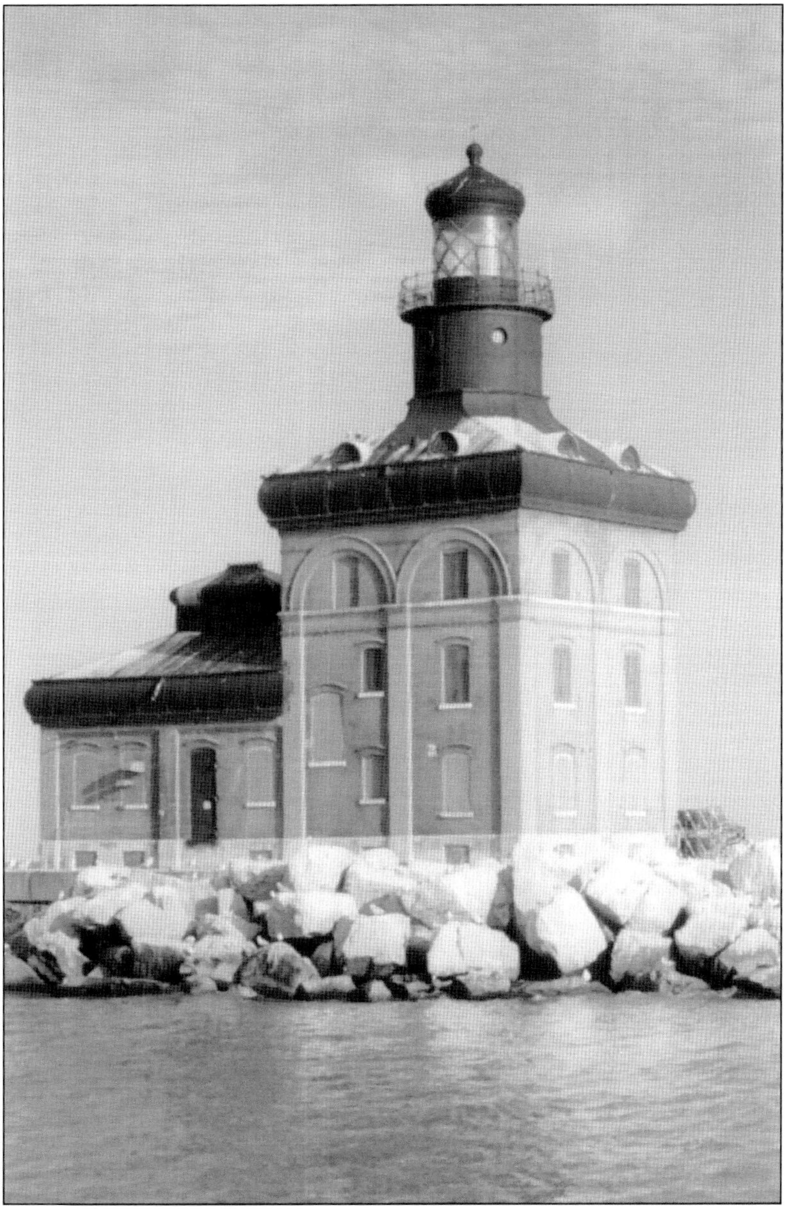

The Toledo Lighthouse guided ships and slightly sinful boats alike. During Prohibition, bringing liquor from Canada was illegal. One dark night, Smith, the young skipper of the *Blue Goose*, left Amherstburg, Ontario, for a small fishing village near the Toledo Lighthouse. Loaded with whiskey and running without lights, he and his father-in-law were soon passing the Toledo Lighthouse. Two miles from shore, the skipper saw the running lights of another vessel. His story runs as follows: "I looked around and there was the Coast Guard cutter astern and gaining. I knew I couldn't outrun it, so I went below looking for the life preservers, which happened to be buried underneath cases of liquor. I knew that I didn't have time to dig them out, so I went topside expecting at any moment to hear the roar of the Coast Guard's gun as the vessel got closer. Only thing to do was jump into the water. I asked my father-in-law if he could swim, and he said 'no.' 'Well, then,' I told him, 'this is where you learn.' " And he did. (AC.)

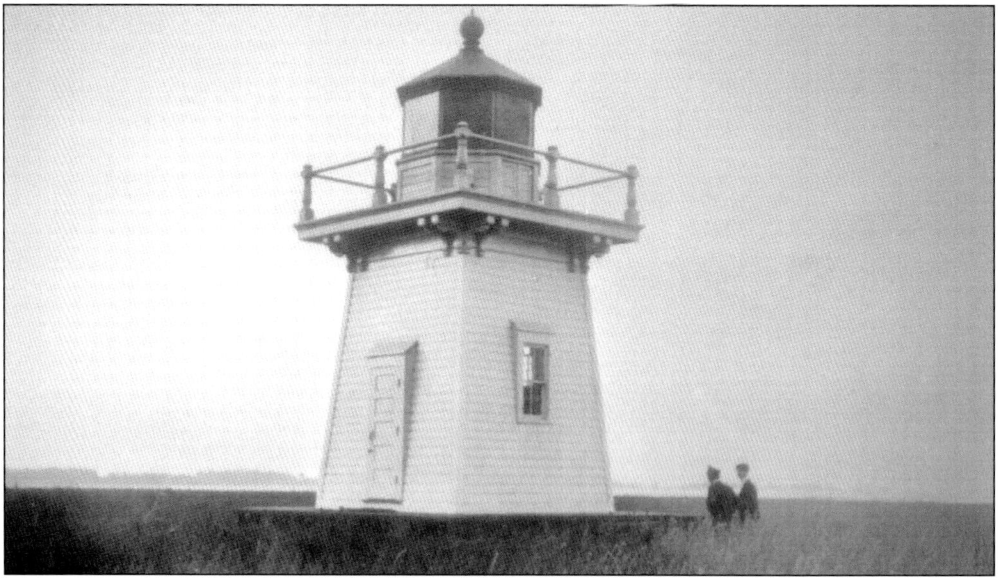

The Manhattan Range Lights were built in 1895 to mark the middle of the new straight channel into the Toledo Harbor. The short front-range light stood on an artificial island with a walkway connecting it to shore. A sixth-order lens displayed a fixed red light for 8.5 miles. Built on a riverbank, the taller rear-range light displayed a similar red light with a 53-foot focal plane. At some point in time, the wooden towers were replaced by skeletal metal towers. Both lights were discontinued at an unknown date. The light keepers were as follows: Harvey Dayan (1895–1903), Edward Ahart (1905–1926), and David Sutherland. (Both, NARA.)

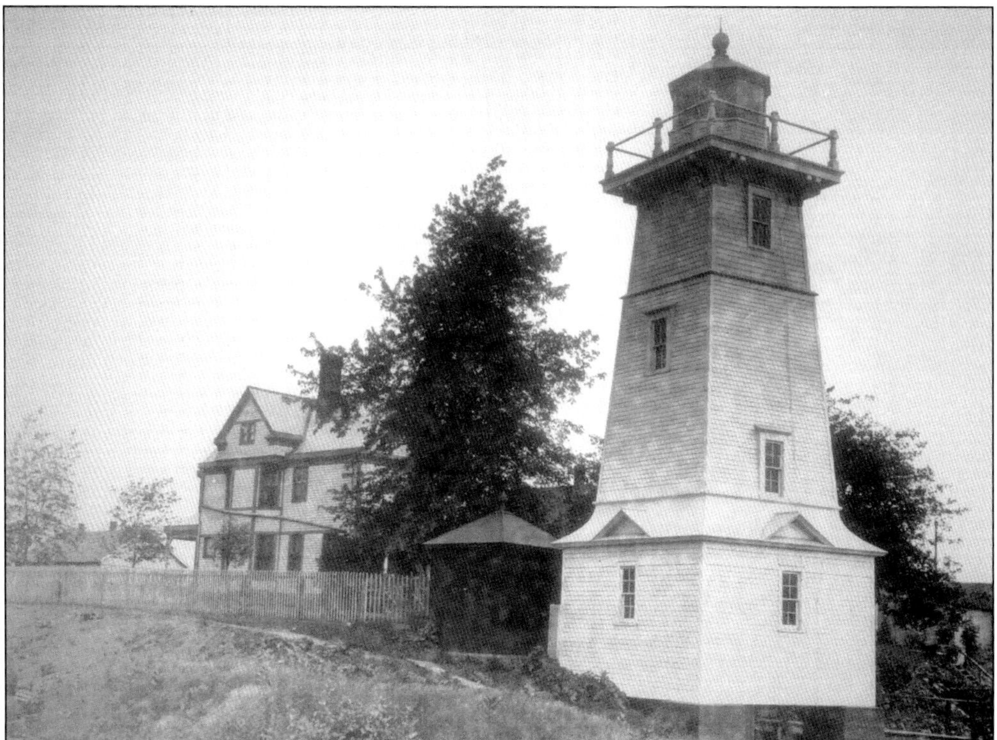

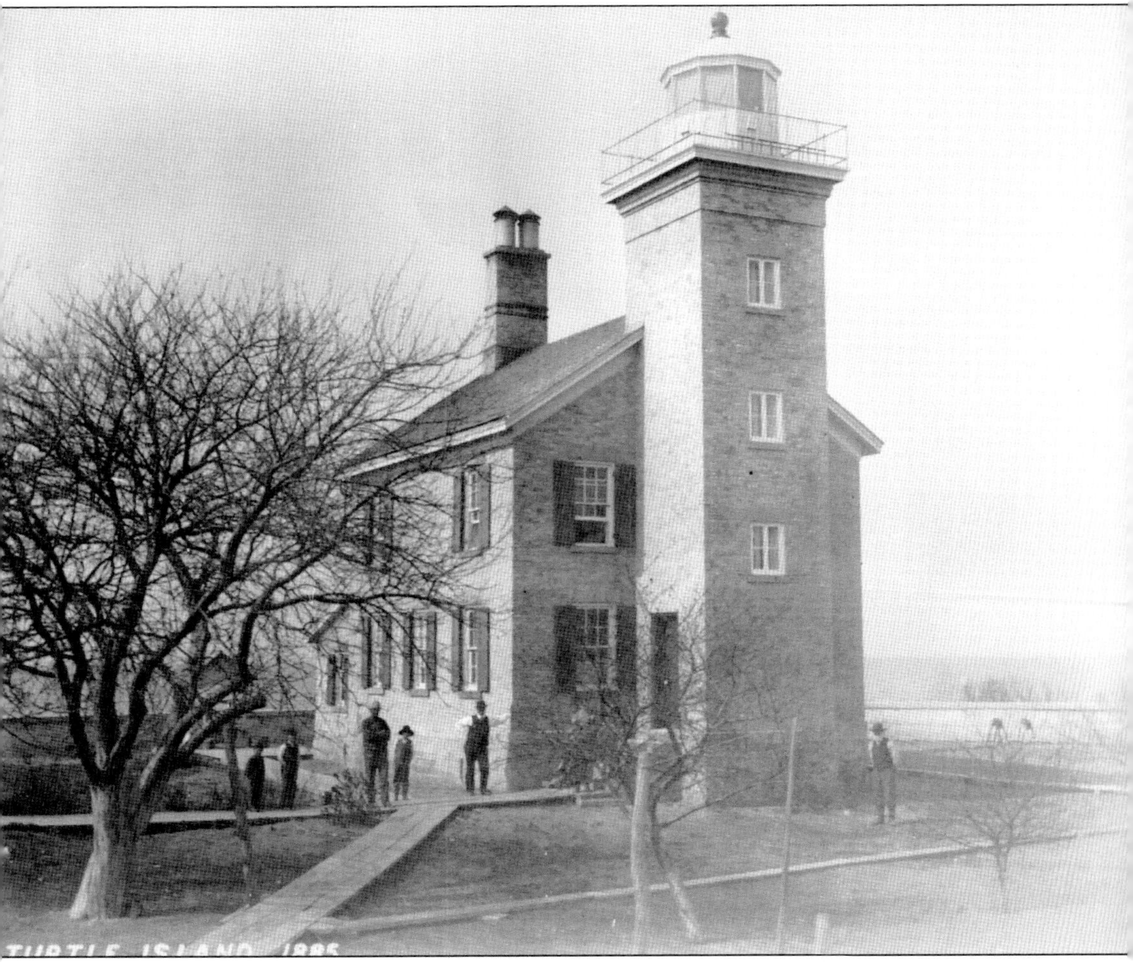

If there were another bad storm, the Turtle Island Lighthouse would disappear into the lake. It was 1882, and the sinking island left water lapping at the door of the lighthouse. Turtle Island, named after prominent Miami Indian chief Little Turtle, was once 6.68 acres, when Fort Turtle safeguarded the entrance to the Toledo Harbor. The fort was abandoned in 1827. The government built the first lighthouse in 1831 and replaced it in 1866 using Milwaukee brick (pictured). By 1883, it became apparent that this lighthouse was going to disappear, and the government realized the importance of a beacon at this location and built a large retaining wall around the light. This wall, finished in 1884, saved the structure. During a span of 72 years, Turtle Island Lighthouse had 15 main keepers. William Haynes, keeper from 1875 to 1904, is on the right. (NARA.)

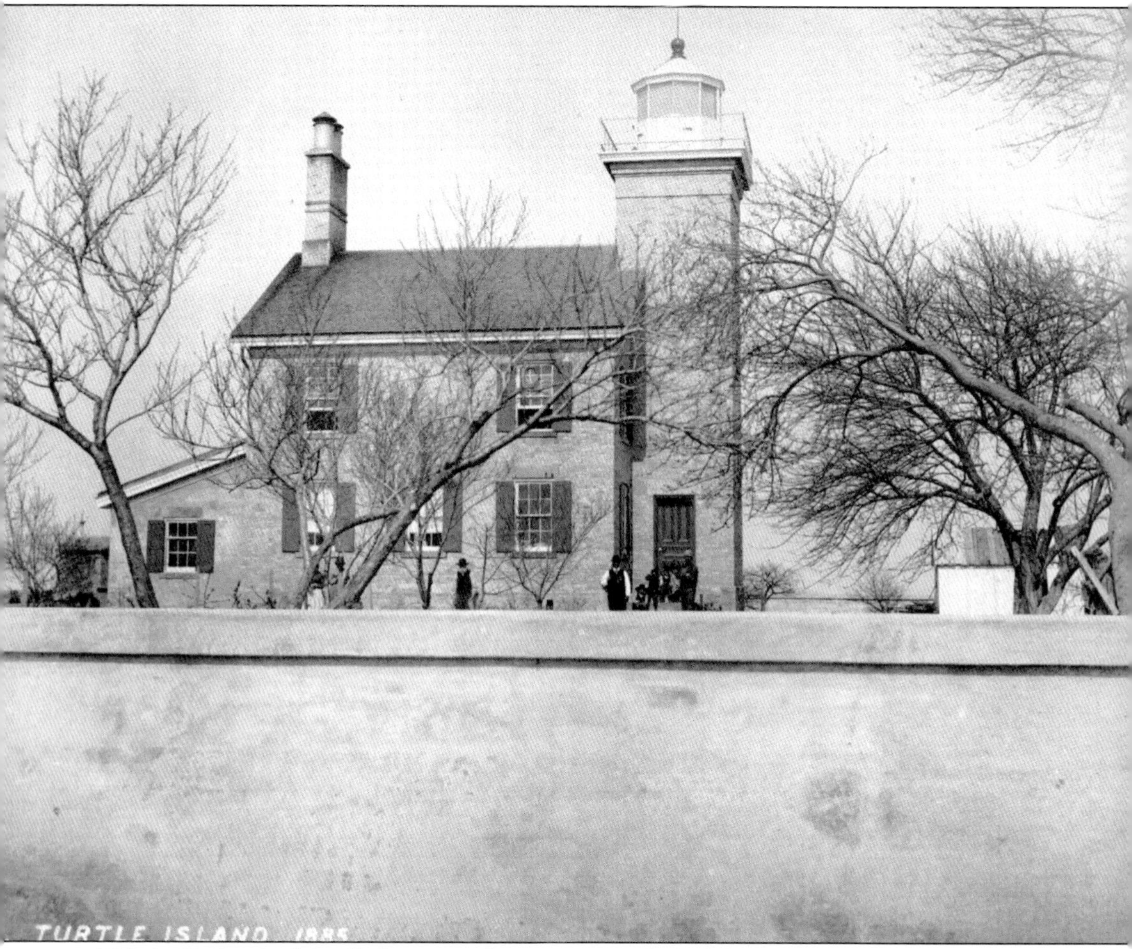

Toledo Harbor had finally become what many people had dreamed—a deepwater port with a 12-mile channel into the lake allowing the largest freighters to enter. By 1904, a 72-foot steel-framed, brick-covered Romanesque-style lighthouse was completed at the beginning of the channel. Turtle Island Lighthouse, pictured in 1885, was no longer needed, so the island was sold and the lighthouse abandoned. After years of dispute, it was determined that the Ohio and Michigan state boundary line runs through the center of this one-acre island. In 1945, a boundary marker was carved on the retaining wall circling the island. Someday, Turtle Island, the lighthouse, the boundary marker, and the retaining wall will disappear underneath the waves of Lake Erie. (NARA.)

Two

World Famous Ship Wrecks near the Lighthouse

The ship *Success* was special from the very beginning. Narratives vary, and the following is but one version of the boat's history. According to this account, *Success* was built in the mid-1800s at Moulmein, Burma, from large teak trees. Skilled craftsmen carved beautiful scenes and scrolls throughout the teak interior. Its passengers traveled in luxury from Great Britain to Australia. In the 1850s, a shortage of prisons prompted the Australian government to purchase older ships, like the *Success*, and outfit them as temporary prisons. They were then anchored in Sydney Harbor. Allegedly, the prisoners were treated badly by their captors—neglected, abused, and even tortured—and this well-kept secret was hidden from the public. When prisoners murdered the captain of the *Success*, Captain Price, the secret torture was exposed, and people were outraged. The inhumane conditions shocked and disgusted citizens.

Said to be embarrassed, the Australian government ordered all prison ships destroyed in order to remove any memory of the prisoners' mistreatment from the minds of concerned citizens. But fate protected the *Success*. It was not scrapped but is said to have later sunk in the Sydney Harbor. *Success*, however, had a destiny, and the ship was to survive. This was no ordinary boat but one bound for great things.

This narrative vein maintains that after being submerged in saltwater for five years, the ship was raised from the depths of the harbor to float again. Its tough teakwood hull was as sound as a bell, and it was outfitted as an exhibition boat. Prison relics were put on display. Articles of torture from the ship's dark past were fascinating to the public, and people paid good money to see how the prisoners were mistreated. The *Success* toured ports for years—first in Australia, then in Great Britain, Ireland, and the United States.

Success was a true entertainer to the end. In 1946, spectators on the beach celebrating the Fourth of July near the Port Clinton Pier Lighthouse watched the ship's final act with awe. Possibly the work of arsonists, fire erupted on the deck. Burning to the water's edge, *Success* sank on the spot. A noble, beloved ship and a world celebrity, it had stirred the imaginations of millions.

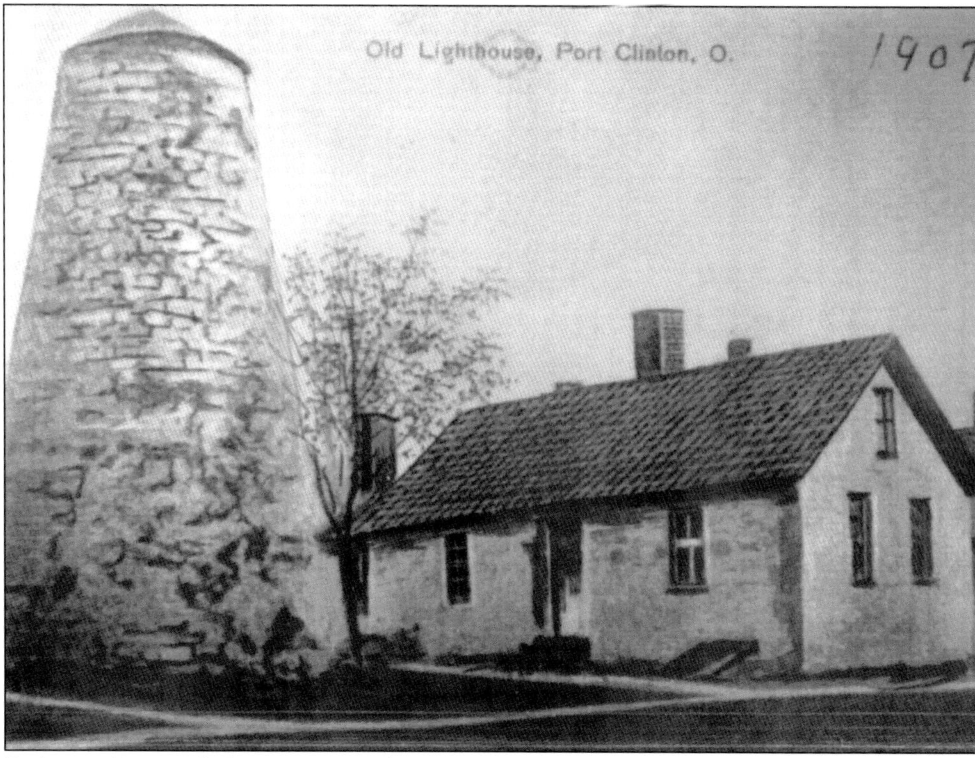

Built in 1833 to mark the entrance to the Portage River, the 40-foot Port Clinton Stone Lighthouse had a black lantern room at the top. By 1838, eight lamps and bright reflectors were used. Whale oil lit the lamp; it cost 50¢ a gallon in 1833 and soared to $2.55 a gallon by 1855 due to the near extinction of the sperm whale. The lighthouse was demolished in 1899. (OCHM.)

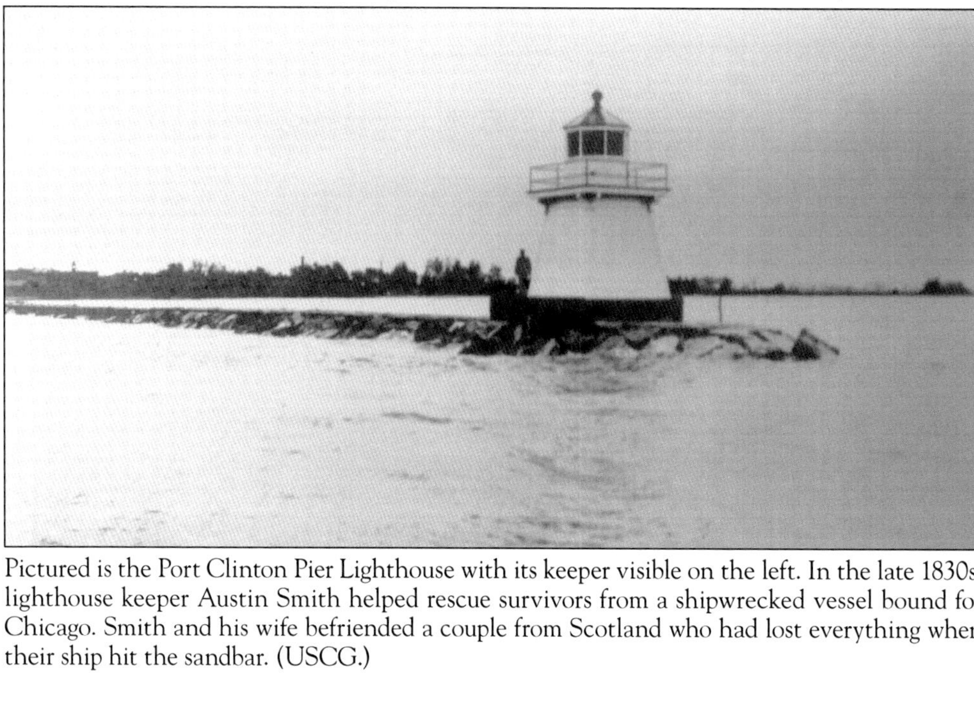

Pictured is the Port Clinton Pier Lighthouse with its keeper visible on the left. In the late 1830s, lighthouse keeper Austin Smith helped rescue survivors from a shipwrecked vessel bound for Chicago. Smith and his wife befriended a couple from Scotland who had lost everything when their ship hit the sandbar. (USCG.)

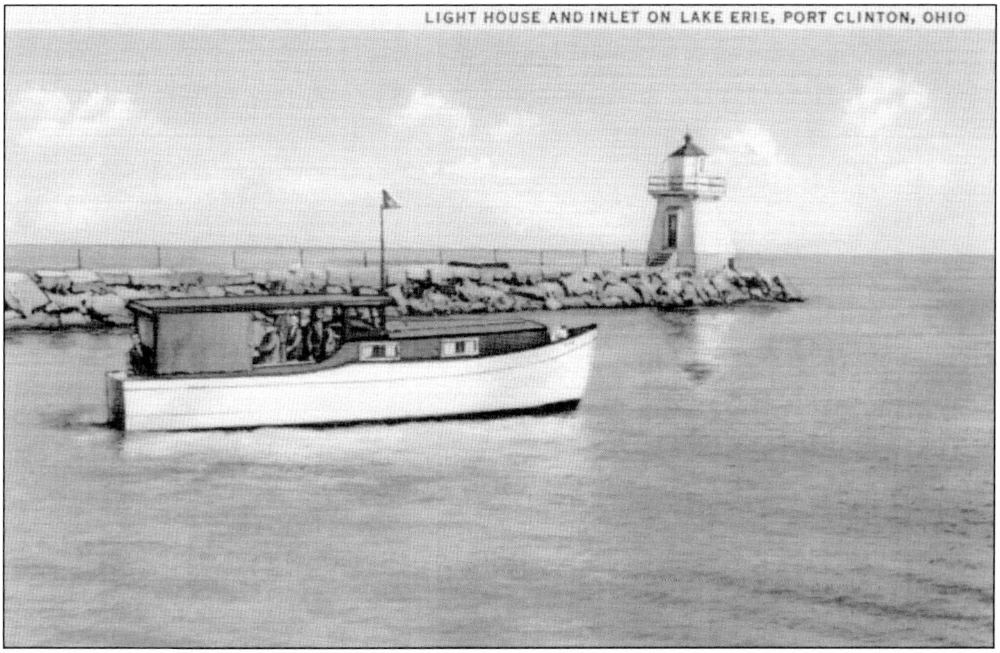

A 1930s Matthews boat, built in Port Clinton, moves by the 1896 Port Clinton Pier Lighthouse at the entrance to the Portage River. A kerosene lantern provided a light that could be seen for six miles. In 1964, the light was moved to Port Clinton, and in the late 1970s, it was purchased by Brands Dry Dock Marina in Port Clinton. That company maintains it today. (AC.)

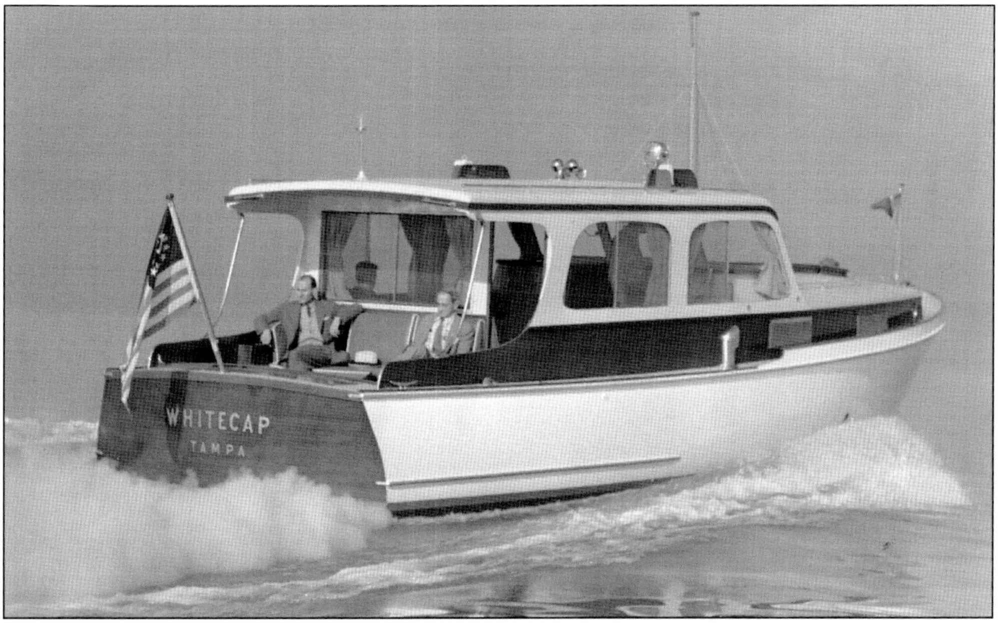

Pictured is a popular 42-foot Matthews wooden luxury yacht built in Port Clinton. Owners of various models of the large Matthews boats included celebrities, such as bandleader Guy Lombardo, entertainer Arthur Godfrey, and John Ringling, a partner in the Ringling Bros. and Barnum & Bailey Circus. Founded in the 1800s by Scott Jeremiah Matthews in Bascom, the company moved to Port Clinton in 1906. (OCHM.)

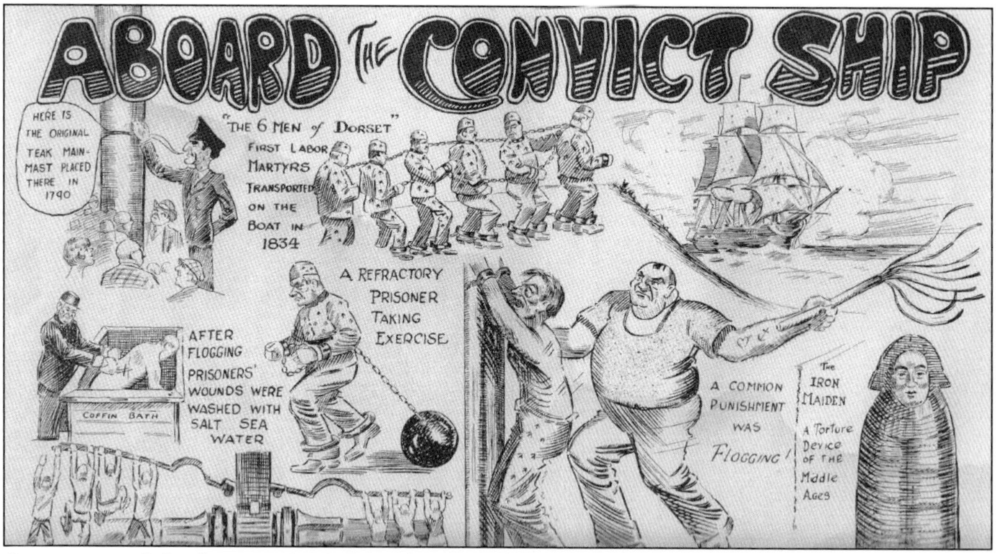

One owner of the *Success*, Capt. David H. Smith, said the ship grossed $450,000 in 1925. The *Success* certainly lived up to its name for Smith. Some of the torture devices people paid good money to see are depicted in this drawing, including flogging whips with strands of rawhide and brass wiring. Afterward, the prisoners' wounds were washed with seawater. Prisoners were compelled to trail a punishment ball up and down the upper deck for one hour each day. An iron maiden, a torture device of the middle ages, was kept on the poop deck. Pictured is a *Success* brochure from when the ship toured as an entertainment vessel in Cleveland. (OCHM.)

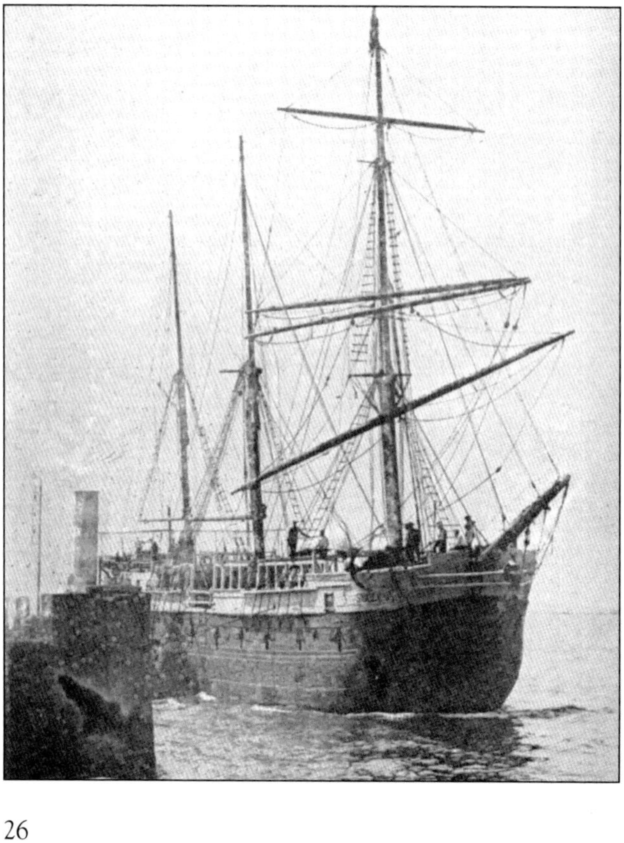

The *Success* is seen here tied to the dock. (AC.)

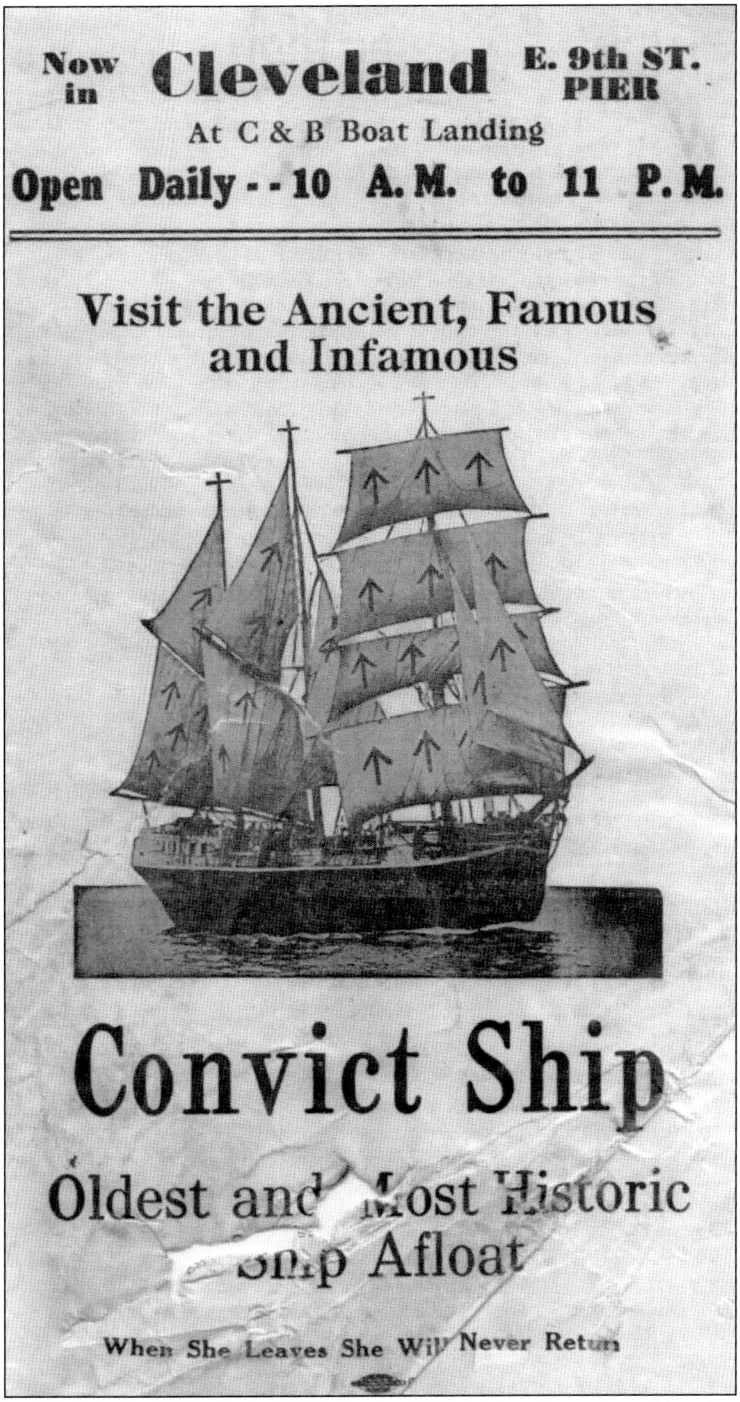

Why Captain Price of the prison ship *Success* took such a seemingly undesirable job may never be known. The ship was permanently anchored in Sydney Harbor, so any navigational skills he might have had were never needed. The prisoners blamed Captain Price for their torture. Desperate and with nothing to lose, they overpowered the captain and murdered him. An investigation followed, and the secret torture, neglect, and abuse of the prisoners were exposed. (OCHM.)

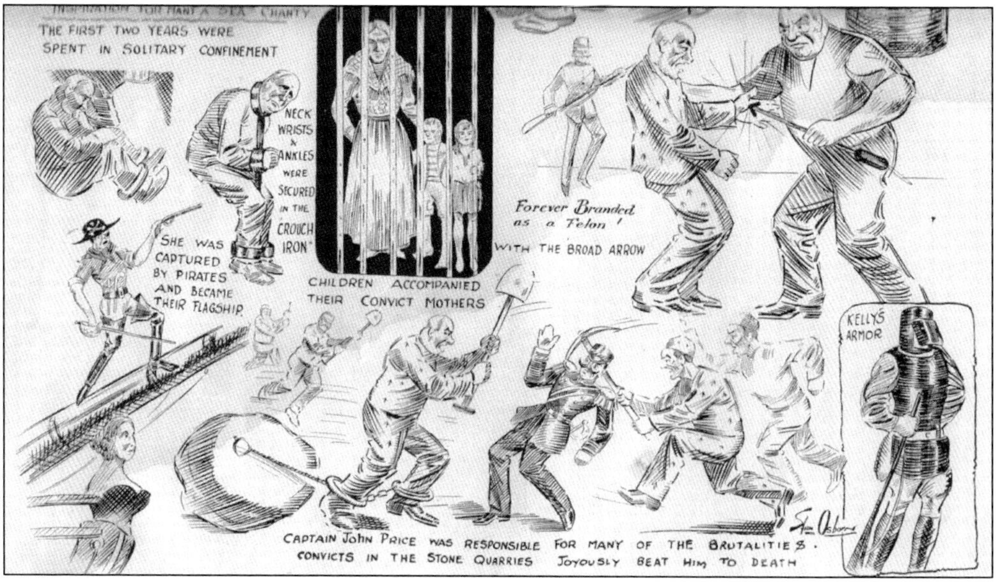

The drawings from this brochure depict the murder of Captain Price, killed for the many brutalities for which the prisoners believed him responsible. Also shown are some of the ship's forms of torture, such as securing the neck, wrists, and ankles in the "crouch iron" position, leg irons weighing 56 pounds, branding, and how prisoners were shackled to stones weighing up to 2,000 pounds. (OCHM.)

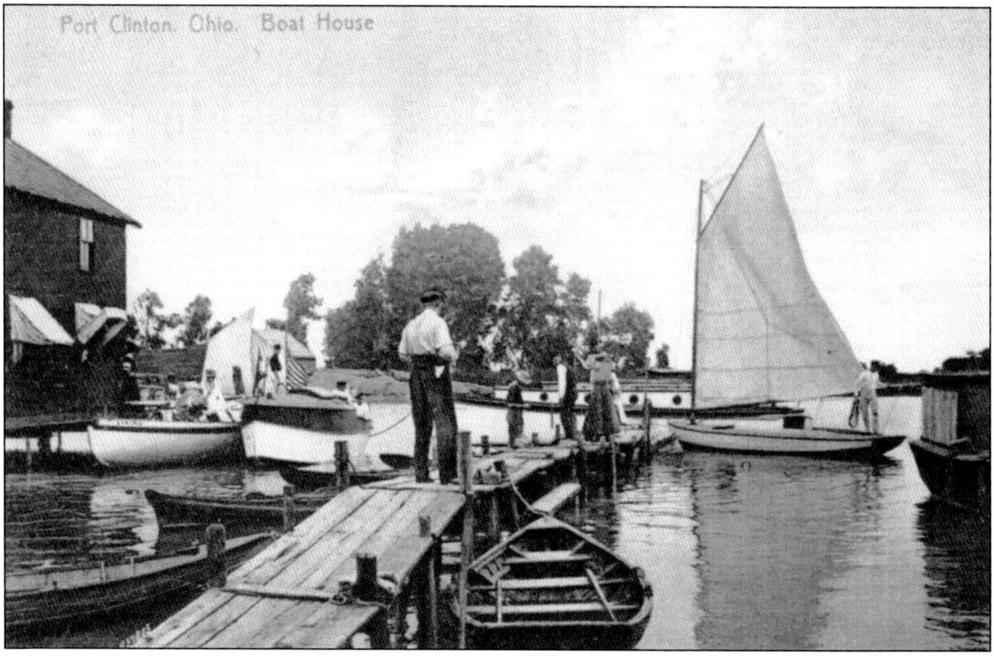

Summertime activity outside the boathouse at Port Clinton is shown around 1908. (AC.)

Three

Fire Destroys the Lighthouse

In August 1898, when their large sailboat overturned in the stormy night, five men were tossed into the lake. As the sailboat sank to the bottom in 30 feet of water, its 40-foot mast protruded 10 feet above the surface; the wooden pole was a strange sight in the open water. One man who could not swim grabbed a life preserver. Two other men struggled in the cresting waves. They seized lines trailing from the top of the mast and fought to keep their heads above water in the violent gale. Hours later, the sky lightened, the storm subsided, and the angry waves changed into peaceful, rolling swells.

Nearby, Mr. Gibeaut, Green Island Lighthouse's keeper, rose from his nap after tending the light all night. He saw two men in the water near the mast. With no boats nearby, he realized that he must save them himself or they would drown. He launched his boat, a small naphtha craft named *Twilight*, and started out to meet them. Waves covered the men at intervals. Each time Gibeaut lost sight of them, he wondered if he could reach them in time. He approached them and, with great difficulty, pulled each man into the boat. They told him that Mr. Bolles, the man with the life preserver, was floating toward South Bass Island when last seen. Wanting to save him if he could, Gibeaut turned the launch toward the island.

Bolles weighed 290 pounds and could not swim, so it was luck that he was able to grab a life preserver before the boat sank. Although unable to fasten it, he held the preserver together with one hand and with the other hand managed to hold a handkerchief over his mouth and nose to keep from drowning.

Two young boys on South Bass Island saw Bolles and wanted to rescue him, so they began to row is his direction. Gibeaut and the boys met, and Bolles was pulled into the boys' boat with Gibeaut's help. Later, Bolles recovered. He never forgot the boys or the keeper who saved his life and showered them with gifts during his lifetime.

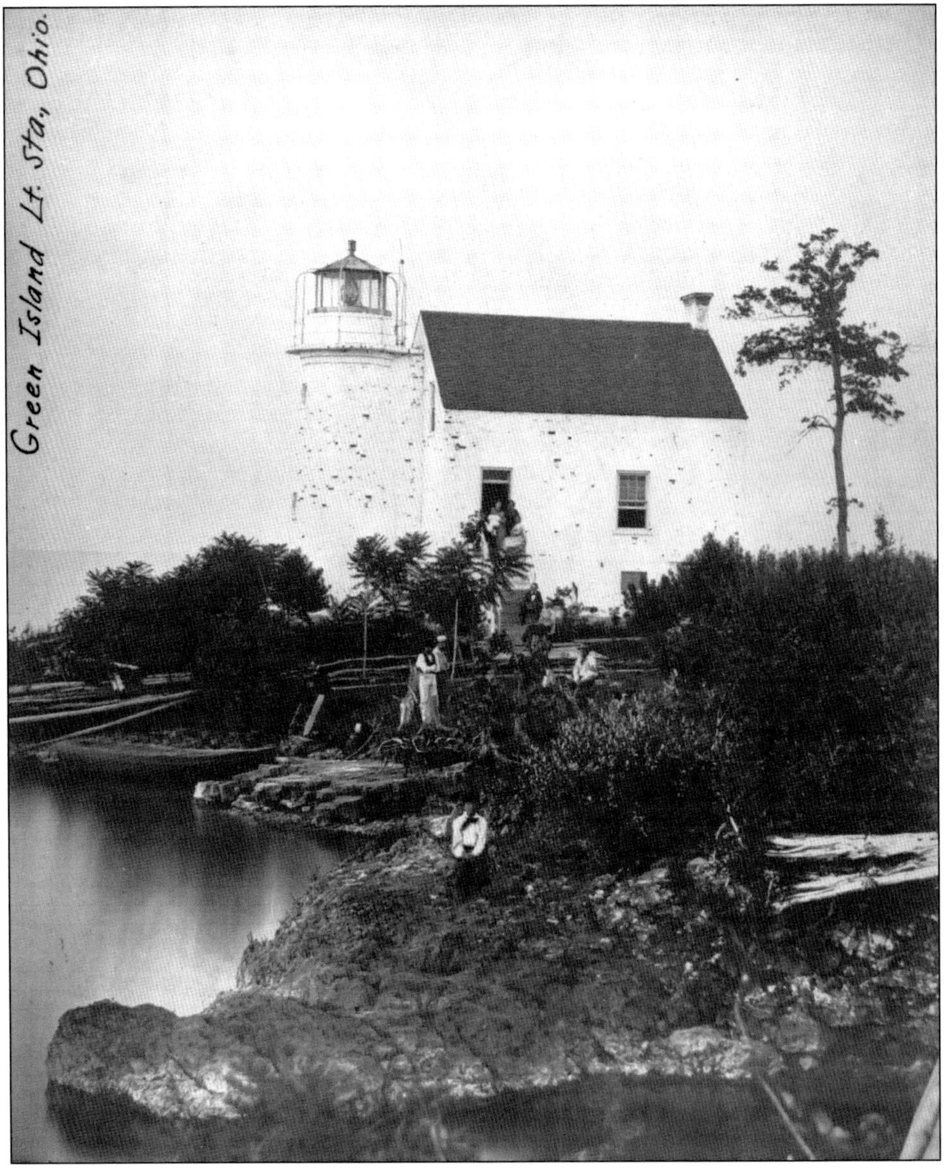

Green Island Lighthouse, built in 1855, went up in flames when the lighthouse keeper, Colonel Drake, and his family were about to sit down to a New Year's Eve dinner on December 31, 1863. At a party a mile away on South Bass Island, the Drakes' son Pitt watched in horror as the lighthouse burned. He and his friends were unable to come to the rescue in the blizzard that occurred that day. Could the lighthouse keeper and family find a way to escape the fire and survive on an island with no shelter and below 25 degrees temperatures? The next morning, Pitt Drake and friends reached the island and searched for survivors, but none was found. As they were about to leave, someone checked a tiny outhouse, and there they were. Crammed between two featherbeds were Colonel Drake, his wife, their two daughters—Sarah Drake and Mrs. Gregoier—and their son-in-law Mr. Gregoier. The colonel recalled, "When I discovered we couldn't extinguish the fire, I knew that I had to do something or everyone would perish. So I told Mr. Gregoier to toss the feather beds from an upstairs bedroom window. I told the others to gather the bedding [and] retreat to the outhouse." This photograph of the lighthouse was taken in September 1858. (NARA.)

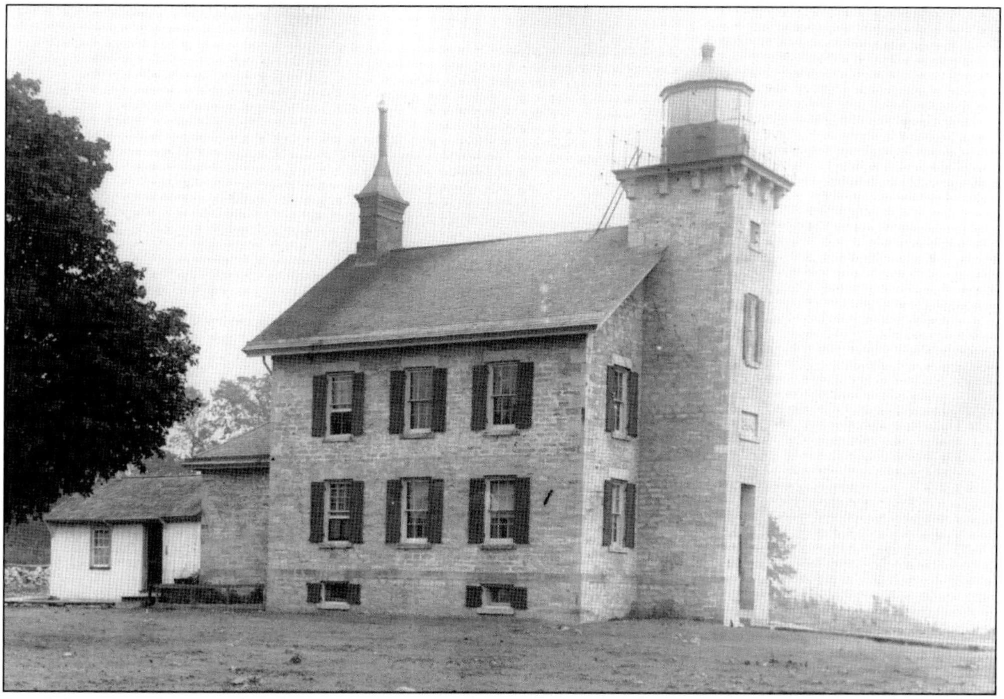

In 1864, after Green Island Lighthouse was destroyed, this two-story stone lighthouse with attached keeper's dwelling was built. In 1820, Green Island was named Strontian Island due to the discovery of a rare mineral, a crystallized celestite, in the side of a cliff. Collectors from all over the world eagerly purchased the strontianite, and the supply was depleted by 1898. The island is managed by the Ohio Department of Natural Resources and is not open to the public. (Both, GLHS.)

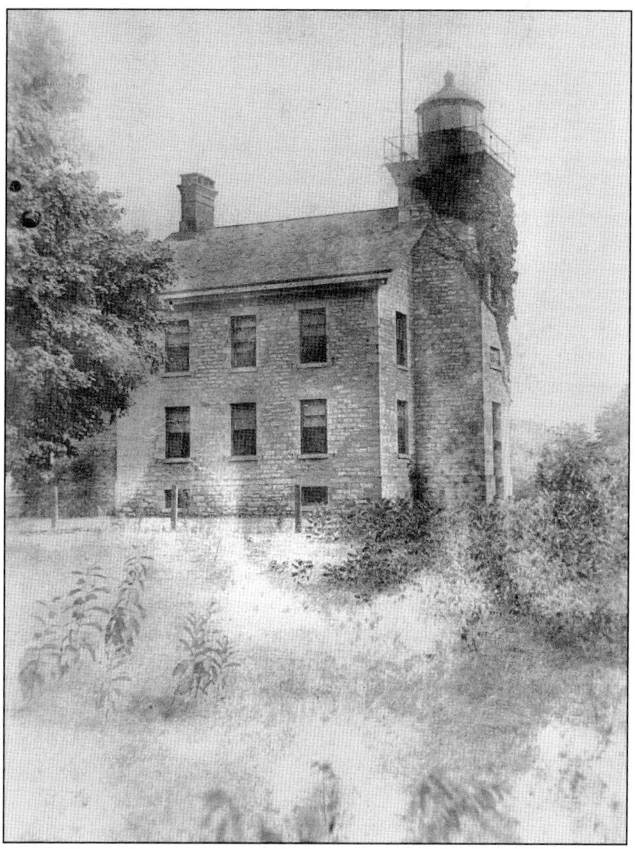

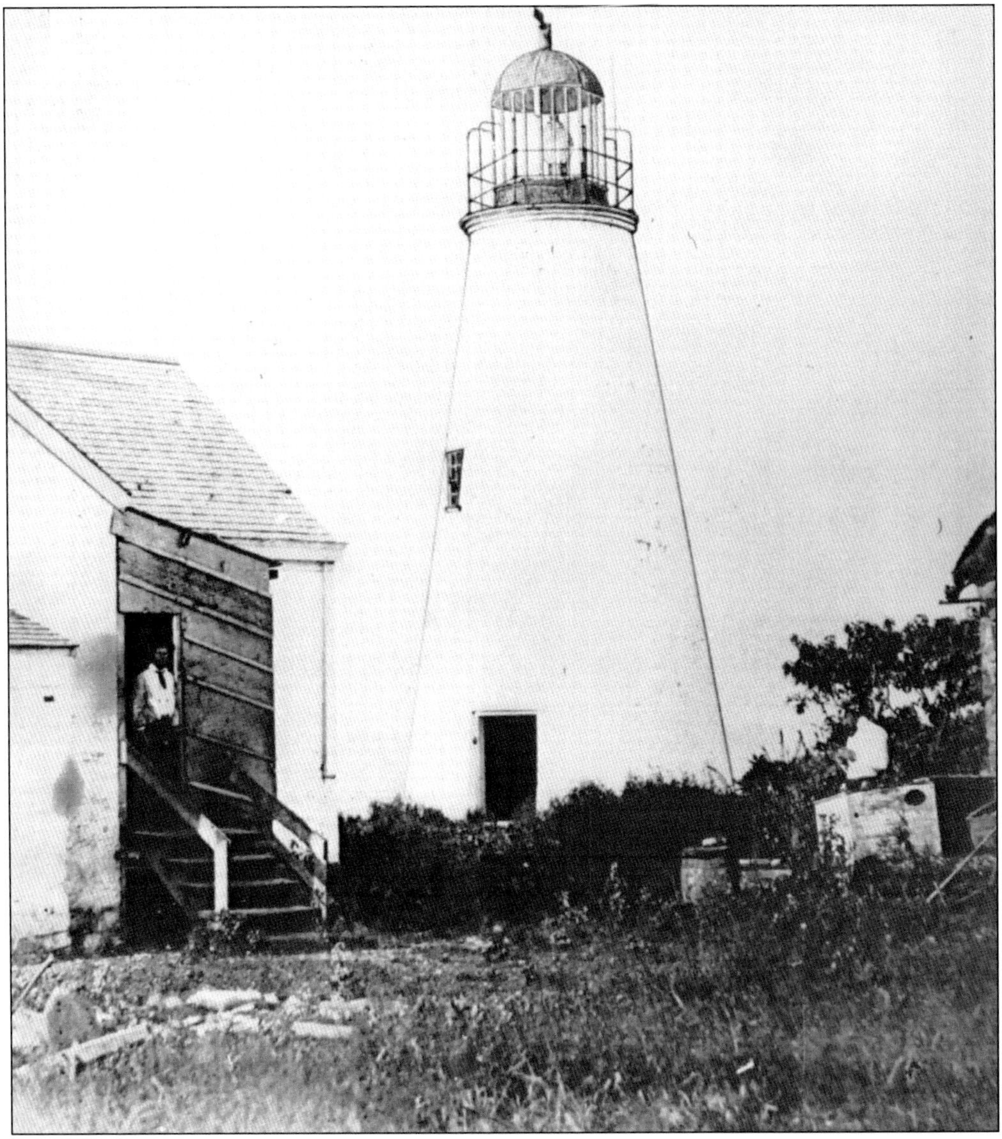

This is a rare picture of the first West Sister Island Lighthouse, built in 1847. After keeper John Edson died in 1868, Harrison Haynes took over the job. Haynes's daughter remembers that her father cultivated the land at West Sister Island and made a specialty of raising turkeys. Shortly before Thanksgiving one year, the family dressed and prepared 75 of the largest turkeys in the West Sister Island flock. The tugboat *Swansen* was to call the next morning to get the turkeys and take them to market. The boat appeared but was stopped by the ice just within sight of those on the island. The daughter recalls that throughout the rest of the winter, the family had turkey as a regular diet. "Morning, noon, and night, it was turkey," she said, and concluded, "I haven't been able to take a bite of turkey since." (GLHS.)

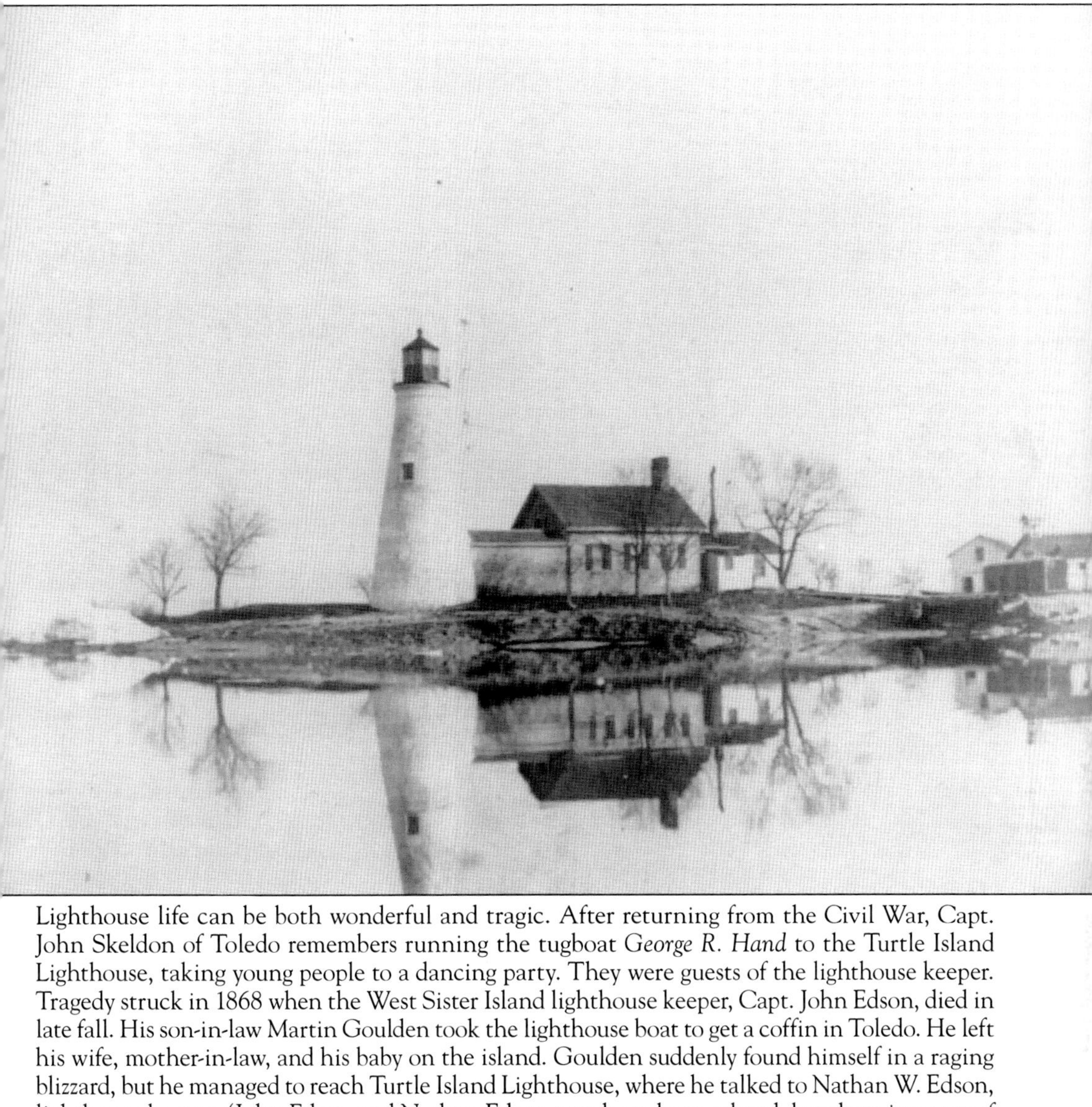

Lighthouse life can be both wonderful and tragic. After returning from the Civil War, Capt. John Skeldon of Toledo remembers running the tugboat *George R. Hand* to the Turtle Island Lighthouse, taking young people to a dancing party. They were guests of the lighthouse keeper. Tragedy struck in 1868 when the West Sister Island lighthouse keeper, Capt. John Edson, died in late fall. His son-in-law Martin Goulden took the lighthouse boat to get a coffin in Toledo. He left his wife, mother-in-law, and his baby on the island. Goulden suddenly found himself in a raging blizzard, but he managed to reach Turtle Island Lighthouse, where he talked to Nathan W. Edson, lighthouse keeper. (John Edson and Nathan Edson may have been related, but there is no proof that they were.) Both men left for Toledo the next day in a small boat. A mile from the Turtle Island Lighthouse, the boat was crushed in the ice, and Goulden and Edson were plunged into the water. They began to walk back to the island but never made it. Mrs. Edson, Mrs. Goulden, and the baby were rescued from West Sister Island in the spring. (GLHS.)

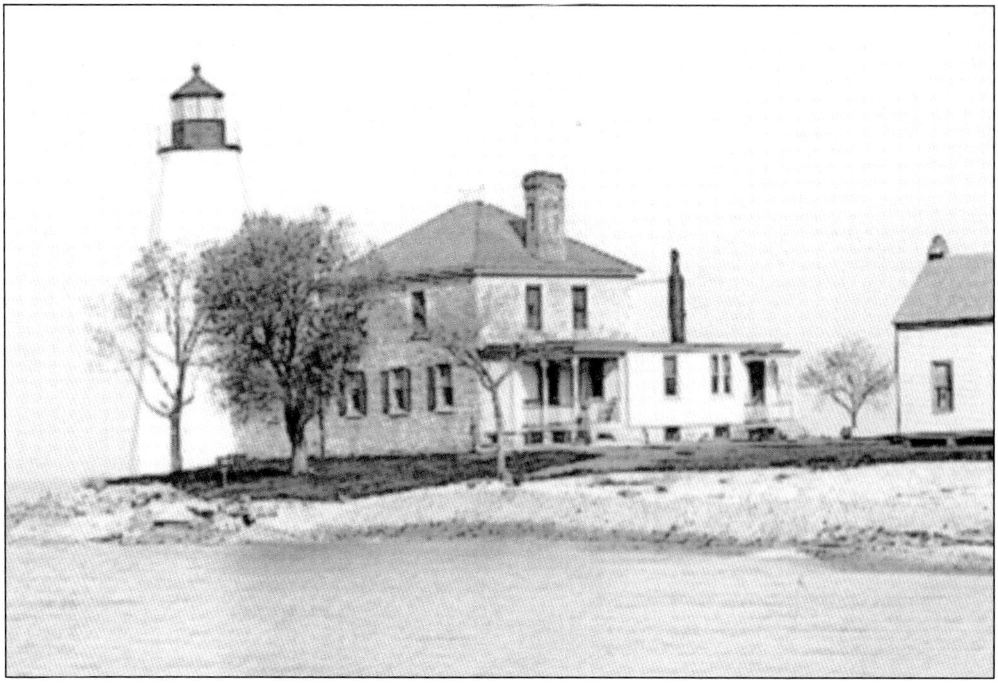

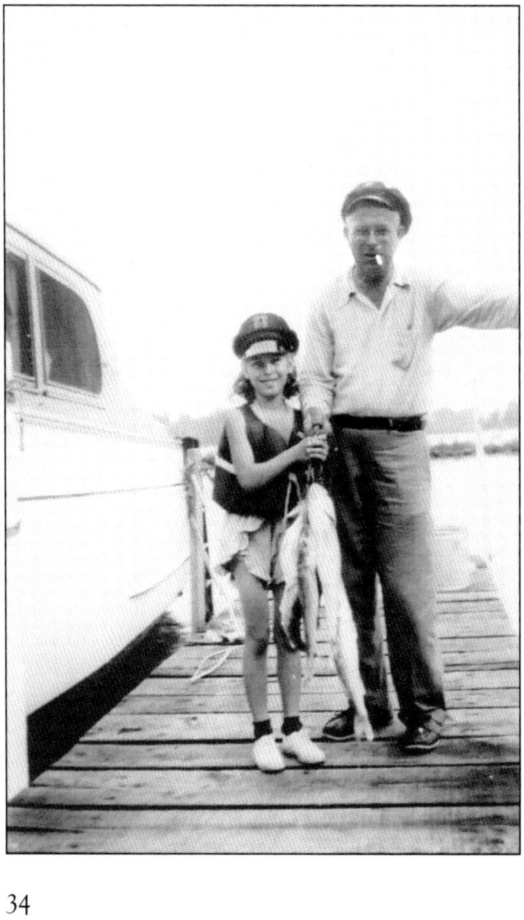

West Sister Island Lighthouse is pictured around 1900. The original birdcage-style lantern used lamps and reflectors. In 1857, a fourth-order Fresnel lens was installed and the house rebuilt, with a passageway to the light added. The beacon was automated in 1937. It was the remotest of all Ohio lighthouses, located eight miles from the mainland on an 85-acre island. The lantern and house were removed, and the island was designated a National Wildlife Preserve in 1938. (USCG.)

A nice string of walleyes was caught near the Lake Erie Islands in this photograph dated 1945. The girl and man are unidentified. Today, fishermen continue to enjoy catching walleye, perch, and bass from Lake Erie. (AC.)

Four

Slightly Sinful Island Lighthouses

Isolated, abandoned, tree-covered Middle Island, just over the border in Canada, appears to be of no importance to anyone today. But during Prohibition, it became so important that a dock and a casino were built next to the 1872 lighthouse. Canadian whiskey became very desirable and difficult to buy during this time, and it did not take long for fishermen and others with boats to realize that money could be made bringing this product to the United States from Middle Island, only seven miles by boat from Put-in-Bay on South Bass Island. It became an ideal place for bootleggers to purchase Canadian whiskey. It was rumored that a boat ferrying whiskey from Middle Island to Put-in-Bay could bring in $10,000 per month.

Most bootleggers were ordinary people, such as the tavern owners on Put-in-Bay who were forced to close during Prohibition or fishermen who wanted to make a little money. When the Depression hit in 1929, most people viewed bootlegging as a way to make a living and keep from going hungry. The savvy people of Put-in-Bay generally knew when the next shipment of whiskey was coming to port. When the liquor arrived, everyone carefully hid it in caves, cisterns, and vineyards before it was shipped to the mainland. Wine was labeled as grape juice before leaving the island so that it would appear legitimate. Shrewd visitors to Put-in-Bay filled their boats with illegal liquor to take back to the mainland and resell. A lot of people were making money.

Money, however, attracts criminals like a light in the dark draws moths. As money was being made on Middle Island, the criminals came. Gangster Joe Roscoe built a seven-bedroom hotel with a casino in its basement. Old-timers say that the hotel was also a brothel. It became a place to party, with music, gambling, and of course, whiskey. Most people who came did not care who owned the Lake Erie Fishing Club, as it was called, or that it had nothing to do with catching fish.

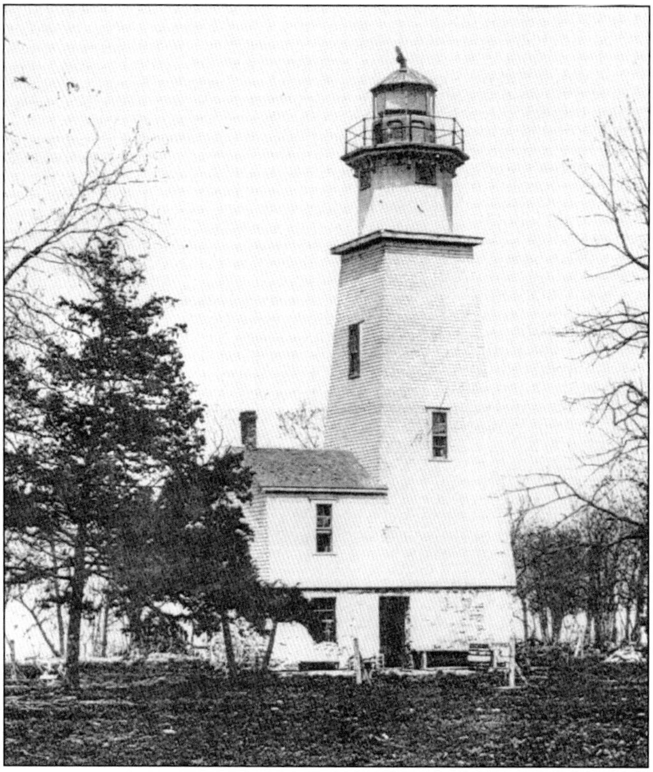

In between Kelleys Island and Middle Island lies the very rocky Gull Reef. It is a good place to catch fish, but dangerous. Gull Reef lies (or hides) just below the surface of the water. Sometimes it is visible, sometimes not, and it is littered with wrecked ships. To deter shipwrecks, a wooden lighthouse was built on Middle Island in 1872. The tower was seven stories high and displayed a fixed red light with a 12-mile visibility. The first keeper was Samuel S. Brown, nephew of abolitionist John Brown of Harper's Ferry fame. The lighthouse was still functional in 1921, although the last keeper, W.K. Wilson, served from 1914 to 1918. In 1958, a fire destroyed the lighthouse, then owned by an American citizen. (AC.)

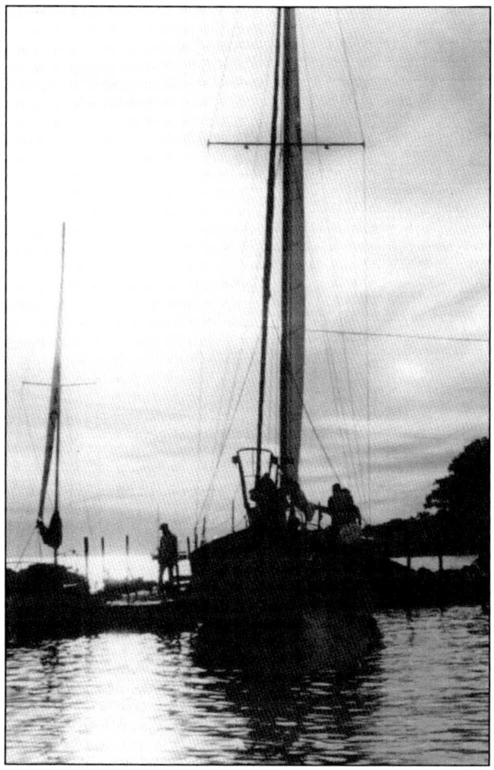

Silhouetted by the setting sun, this sailboat rests easy at the Kelleys Island dock. (AC.)

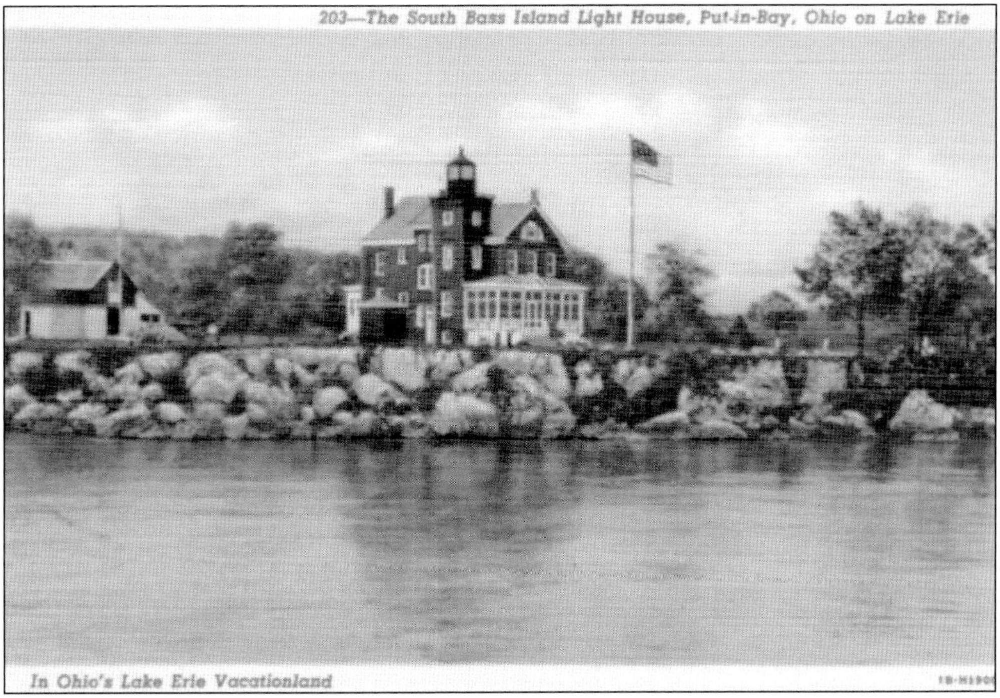

Two South Bass Island Lighthouse inhabitants died falling from the cliffs, one accidentally and one intentionally. On July 10, 1897, Harry H. Riley, the first keeper, moved into the Queen Anne–style lighthouse with his bride. On August 9, 1898, Samuel Anderson was hired as a laborer. Only 22 days later, Anderson committed suicide by jumping from the cliff. Two days after that, Riley, upset over Anderson's death and acting strangely, was placed in an asylum. On April 29, 1925, Charles B. Duggan, keeper since 1908, accidentally fell 80 feet from the cliff and died. (AC.)

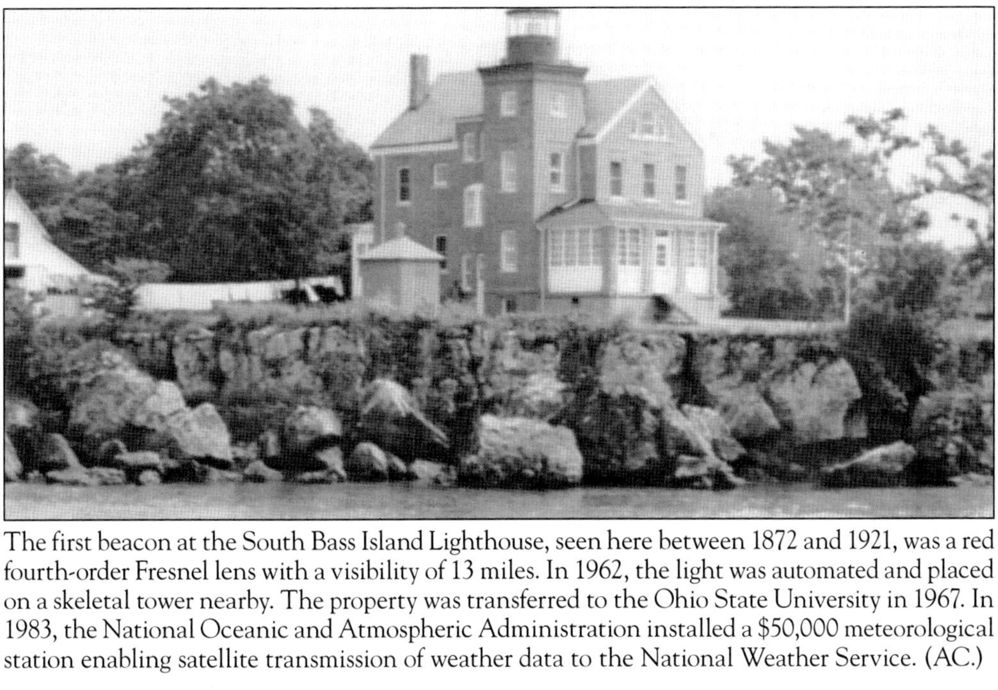

The first beacon at the South Bass Island Lighthouse, seen here between 1872 and 1921, was a red fourth-order Fresnel lens with a visibility of 13 miles. In 1962, the light was automated and placed on a skeletal tower nearby. The property was transferred to the Ohio State University in 1967. In 1983, the National Oceanic and Atmospheric Administration installed a $50,000 meteorological station enabling satellite transmission of weather data to the National Weather Service. (AC.)

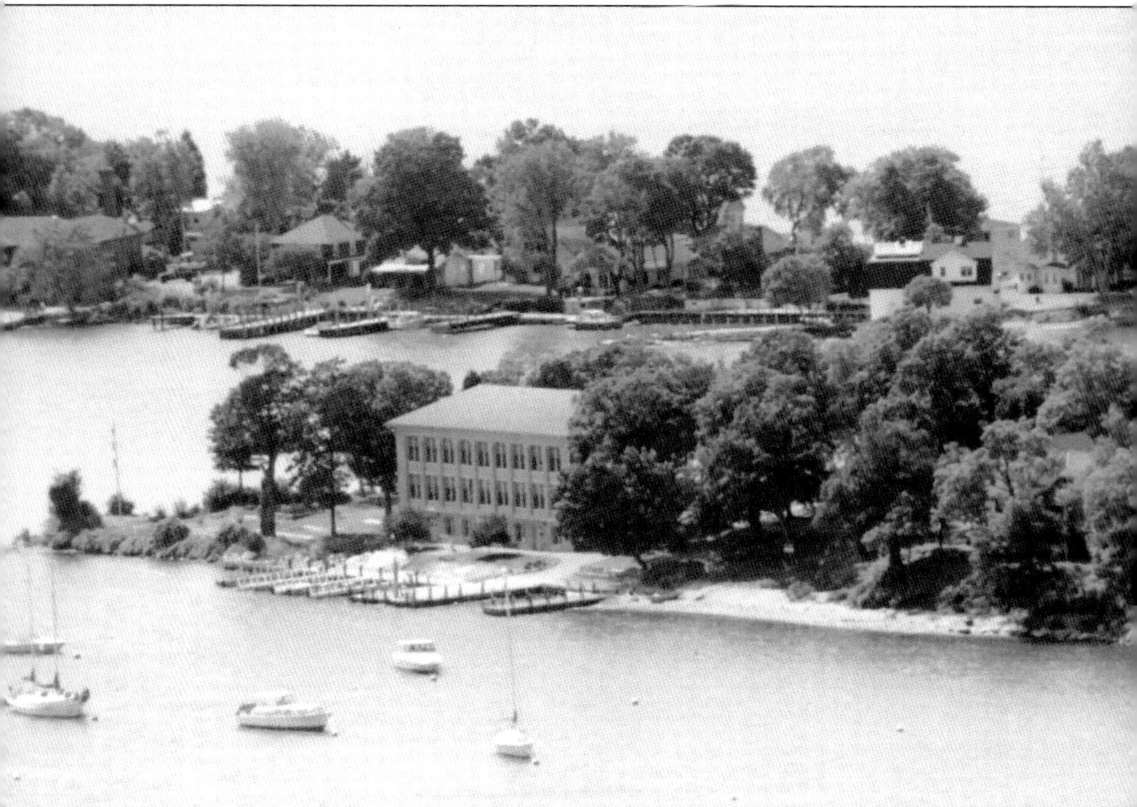

Author Philip Edwards relates a tale from local lore about South Bass Island. It is the story of two people falling in love and of their mysterious disappearance. In 1930, Magi, a pretty young woman working at a hotel on South Bass Island, fell in love with a former commercial fisherman from Leamington, Canada, known as Max Fox. He was a rumrunner—a smuggler of illegal liquor during Prohibition—but was also known for being honest. Everyone on the island liked Max, and his speedboat, the *Midnight Fox*, was the envy of all who saw it. Magi's friends warned her against dallying with this handsome man with the dubious reputation, but she loved him and he loved her. They dated for three months, seeing each other when Max made his deliveries to several local speakeasies at Put-in-Bay. Max knew that sooner or later the Coast Guard would catch him and that his good life would be gone. With the July Fourth weekend approaching, Max and Magi made plans. He was to make one more run to the islands, passing near the Green Island Lighthouse. Magi would meet him in a rowboat near Gibraltar Island and guide him through shallow water into an undeveloped area of the harbor. (AC.)

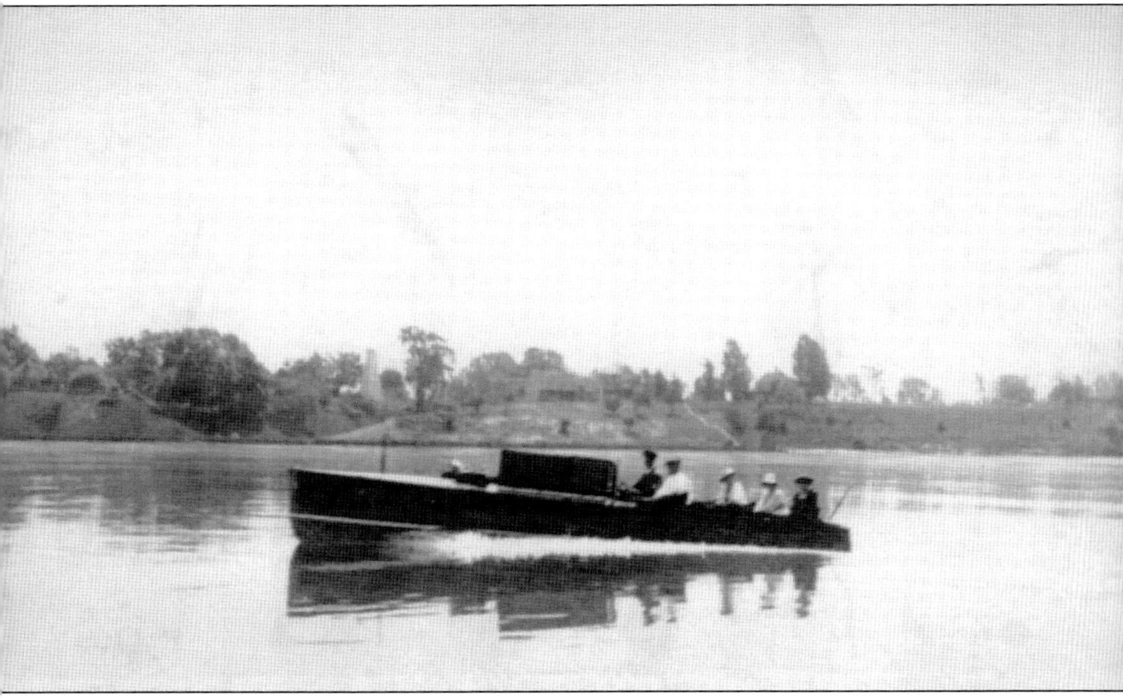

On the night of July 2, Max sped across the lake to meet Magi. All went as planned, and soon the cases of whiskey were unloaded. Max and Magi knew that in a few minutes they would begin their new life together. As their boat left Put-in-Bay, they did not suspect what fate lay before them. There was a sudden bright light and the sound of splintering wood. A Coast Guard ship waiting in ambush fired a steady stream of gunfire at them. Max quickly increased the boat's speed. As the slower Coast Guard boat picked up its pace in pursuit, the men could not locate the *Midnight Fox*. At dawn, the Coast Guard found pieces of wood floating near the ambush area and believed there were no survivors. Max, Magi, and the *Midnight Fox* were never seen again. For over 12 years, friends thought about Max and Magi and their fateful rendezvous. Then in 1942, when World War II news was of interest, a notice appeared in a Leamington newspaper: "To my beloved Captain Max Fox of the Canadian Royal Navy, whose life was lost from a German torpedo in the Atlantic Ocean. Please sleep well, my hero, and may all your nights be filled with my love, Magi." (AC.)

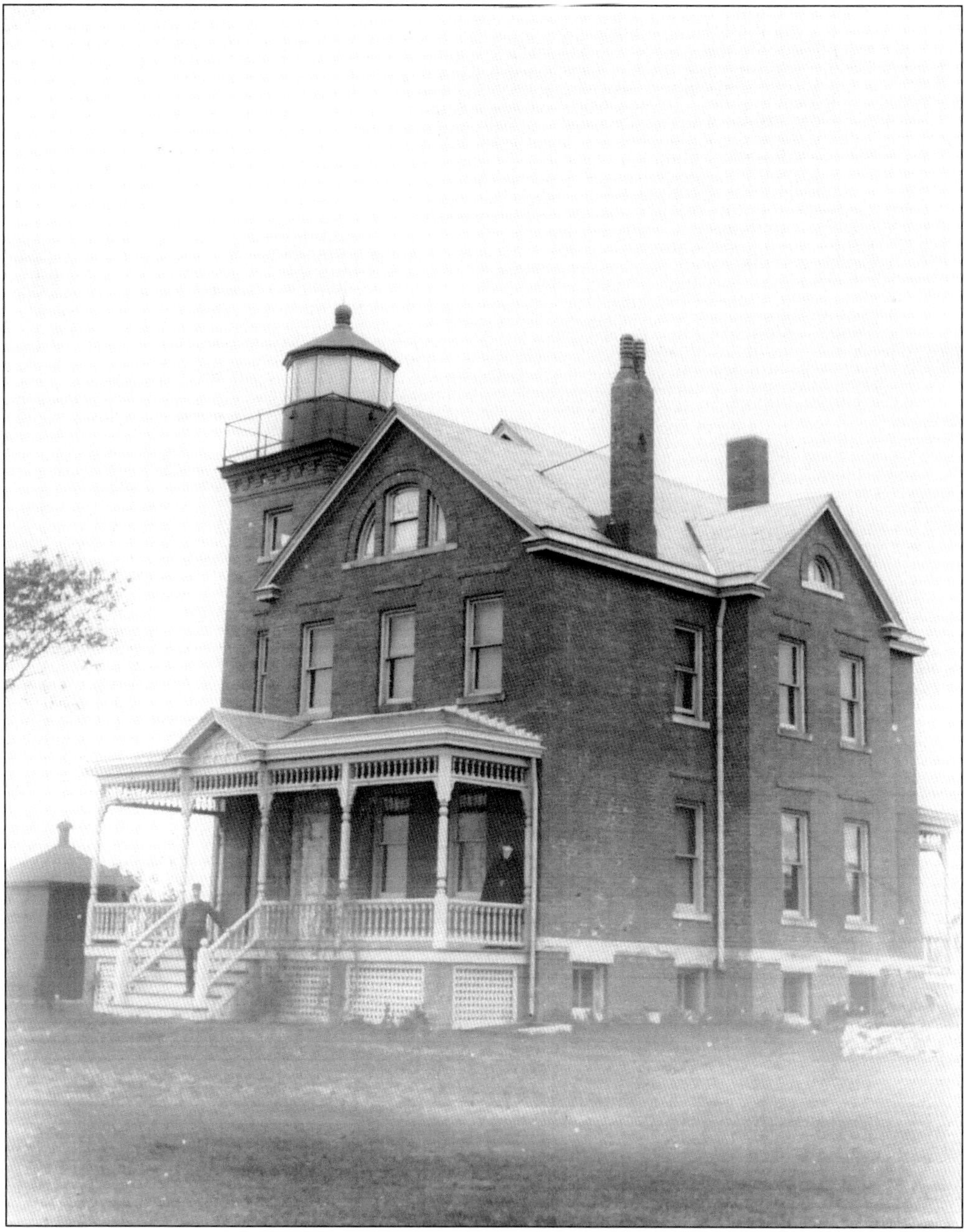

In 1807, Pierpont Edwards purchased South Bass, Middle Bass, Green, Sugar, Ballast, Gibraltar, and Starve Islands for $26,087. After the War of 1812, Edwards's men developed South Bass Island, exporting timber and limestone. On August 22, 1854, the Edwards family sold the land to Jose de Rivera Saint Jurgo for $44,000. He raised grapes and produced fine wines. In 1892, Hotel Victory opened, increasing the island's popularity. On February 15, 1893, the US Lighthouse Board appropriated $3,000 for a lighthouse on the southwest shore of the island. The property was purchased from new owners Mary and Alfred Parker on May 18, 1895. Keeper Col. J. (Orlo) Mason stands on the steps at the South Bass Island Lighthouse in 1904. (GLHS.)

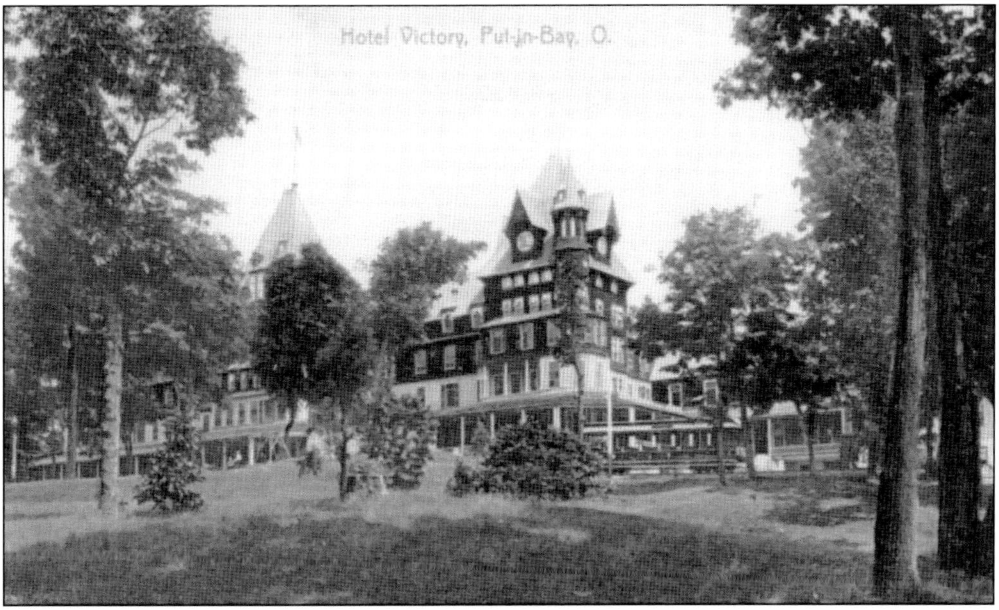

On an evening in August 1919, the grandiose Hotel Victory, near South Bass Island Lighthouse, began burning from faulty wiring. People in Detroit and Sandusky stared wide-eyed toward South Bass Island as massive flames turned the sky orange. With 800 rooms, a 600-foot veranda, a ballroom, and three elegant dining rooms, the hotel was billed as the "Garden Spot of the Great Lakes." Dignitaries had dined in elegance while listening to a 23-piece orchestra. Pres. William Howard Taft had campaigned there. By morning, it was gone, marking the end of an era of grandeur on the island. (AC.)

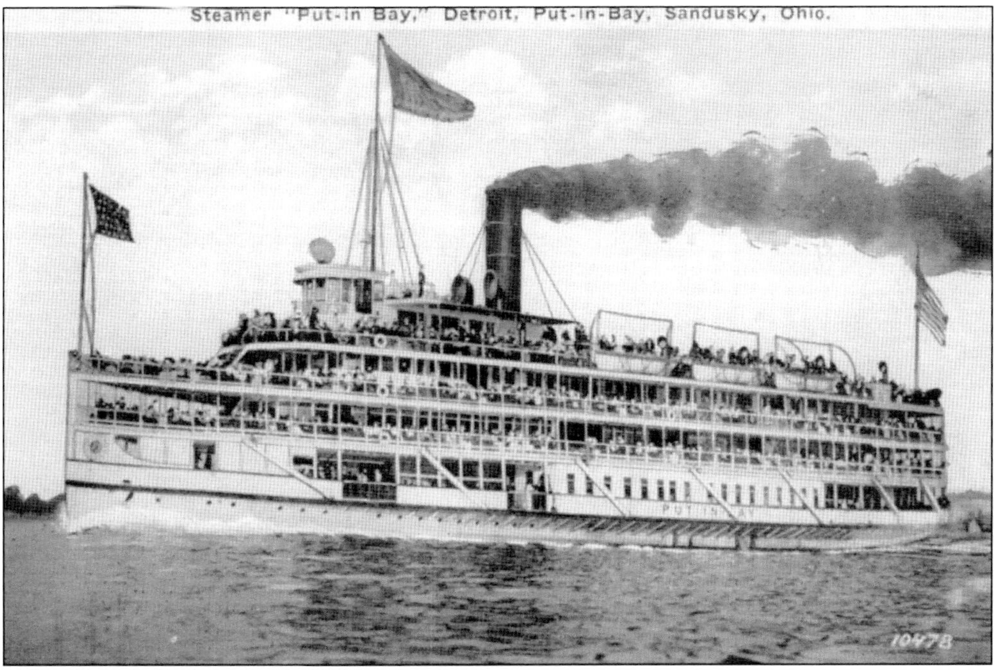

Billed as one of the finest excursion steamers on the Great Lakes, the *Put-in-Bay* ran round-trip from Detroit to Put-in-Bay to Sandusky. (AC.)

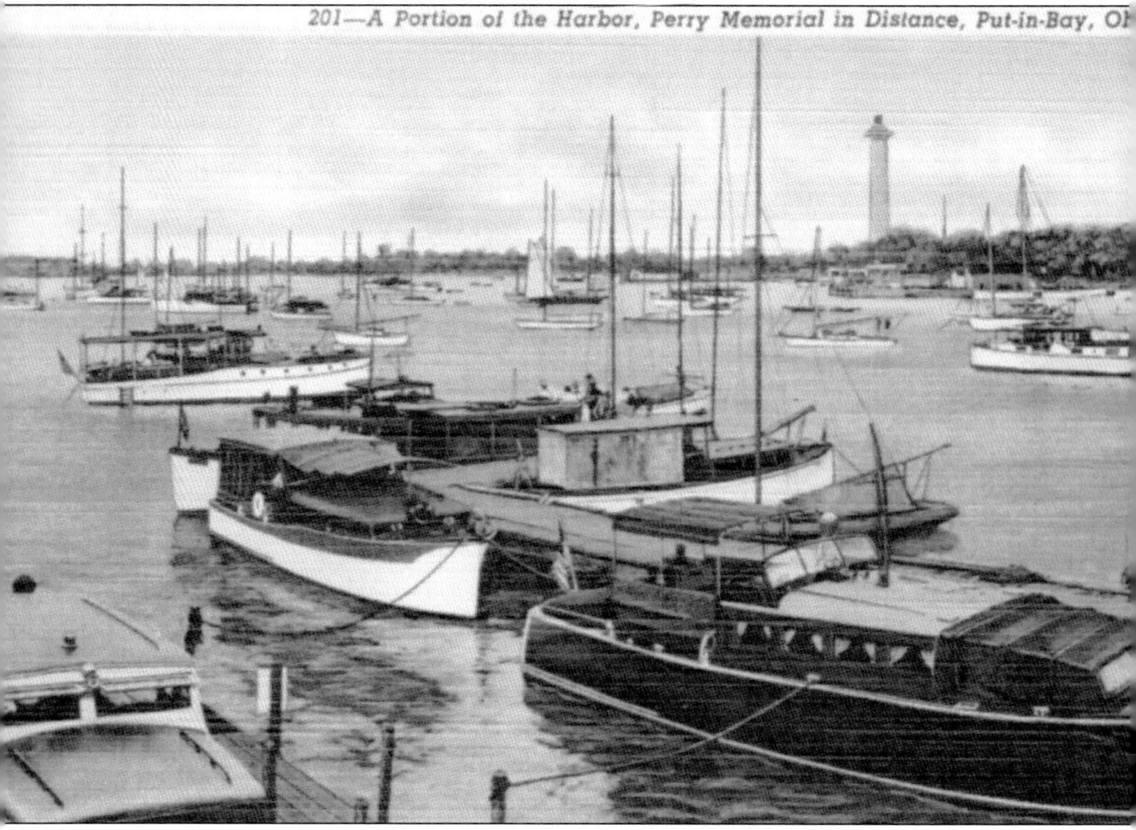

During the War of 1812, Commodore Oliver Hazard Perry had an idea; if successful, the outcome would allow the United States to take control of the Great Lakes from the British. It all began in early fall 1813 when Commodore Perry moved his headquarters from Erie, Pennsylvania, to Put-in-Bay on South Bass Island. When the British ships were seen 10 to 12 miles northwest of Put-in-Bay on September 10, the Americans sailed their vessels to meet them, with Perry on the flagship *Lawrence*. The wind was brisk and the sun shining as the forces began fighting at noon. Cannonballs bombarded the *Lawrence* as Captain Barclay of the British ship *Detroit* concentrated on destroying it. The carnage was terrible. Perry watched his soldiers die, but his stoic face reflected a determination to win. He raised a flag that read, "Don't give up the ship" in order to rally the crew. Though the *Lawrence* was disabled, Perry managed to secure a strategic victory. The Americans were not supposed to win but did, and it changed the course of history. (AC.)

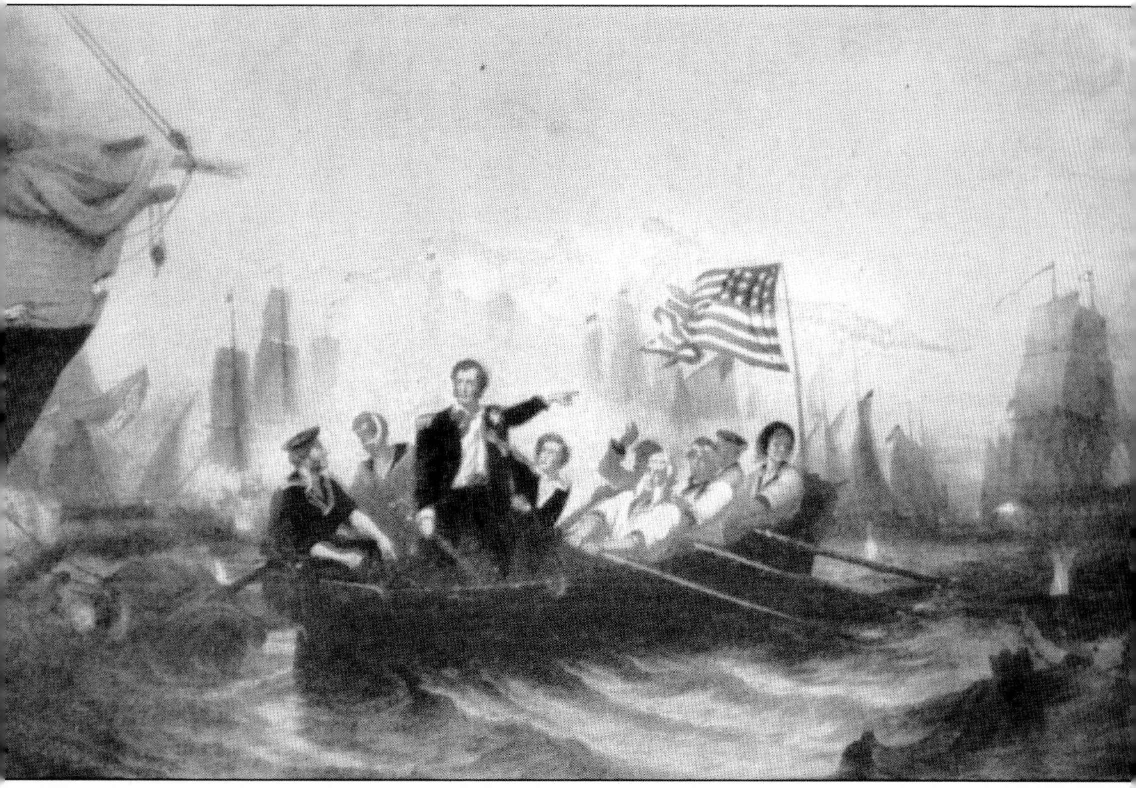

When his ship was destroyed and the battle lost, Perry did something unexpected and unusual. He ordered a cutter boat, and he and his men rowed under heavy cannon fire to the *Niagara*, a ship with no damage. Perry took command and sailed toward the enemy. In maneuvers, the bows and riggings of two British ships, the *Queen Charlotte* and the *Detroit*, accidentally became entangled. Commodore Perry brought the *Niagara* between the two ships, firing cannonballs from both sides. Within 15 minutes, a white flag was raised on the *Queen Charlotte*, followed soon after with a white flag from the *Detroit*. It was 3:00 p.m. Commodore Perry sent General Harrison a note: "We have met the enemy and they are ours. Two ships, two brigs, one schooner, and one sloop." Winning this important battle changed the course of the war and secured American shipping through the Great Lakes. (AC.)

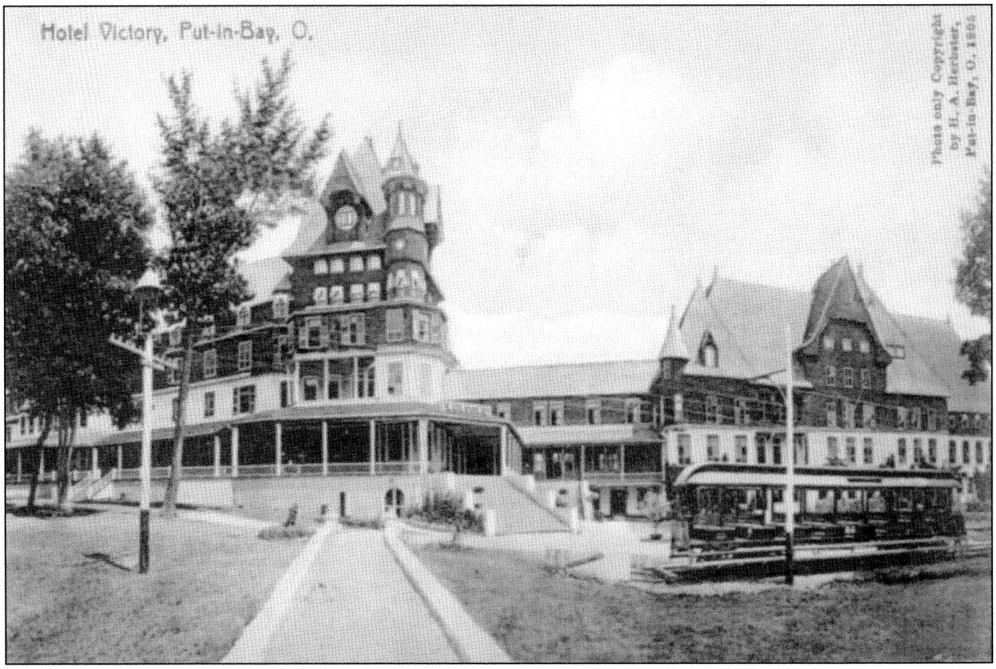

Hotel Victory was a marvel of extravagance. The main lobby had a seating capacity of 1,000 people, and an orchestra played music night and day. The parlors of the Victory showed various styles of elegant furniture. The great ballroom with electric lights was the scene of social dancing and parties. (AC.)

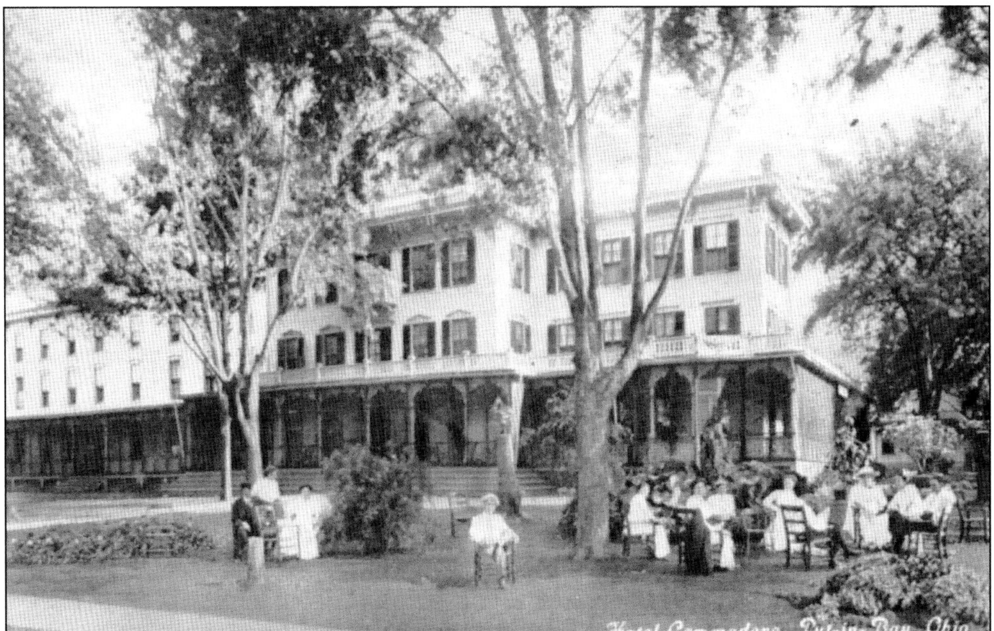

Hotel Commodore faced the Put-in-Bay harbor. The lodging had first-class accommodations, and it was written that tourists found all that they desired in the Hotel Commodore. Formerly the Beebe House, it was remodeled between 1910 and 1912. (AC.)

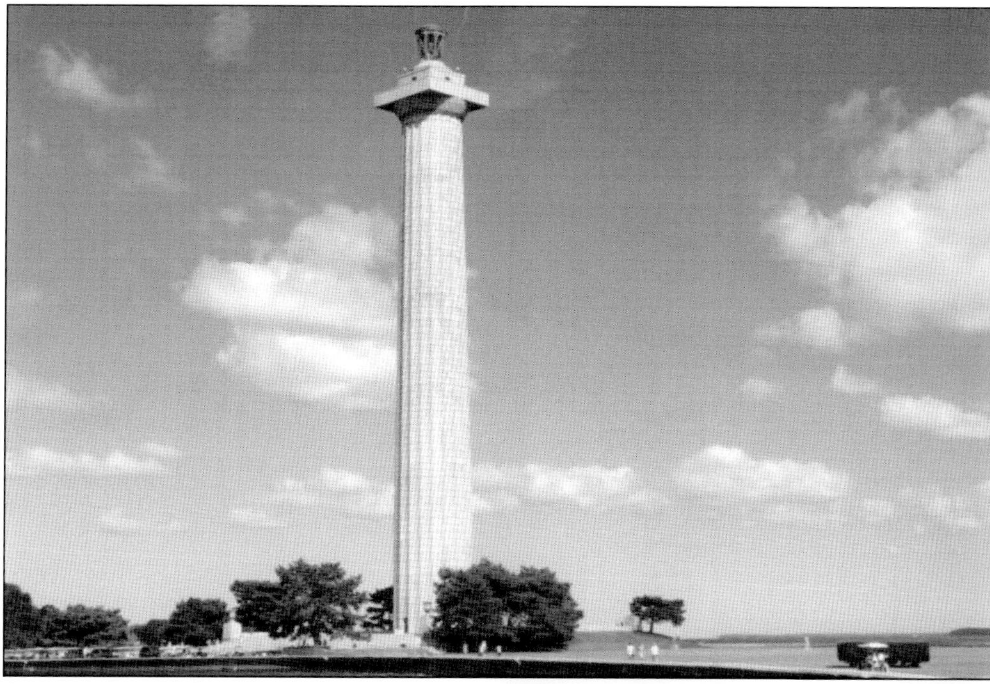

Perry's Victory and International Peace Memorial was constructed between 1912 and 1915 to commemorate the American victory in the September 10, 1813, Battle of Lake Erie. An elevator takes visitors to the top for a spectacular view of South Bass Island and the surrounding islands. On a clear day, Pelee Island in Canada can be seen. The pink granite tower rises 352 feet and supports an 11-ton bronze urn. With pictures and figures, a museum exhibit explains the battle that ensured American access to the Great Lakes. (AC.)

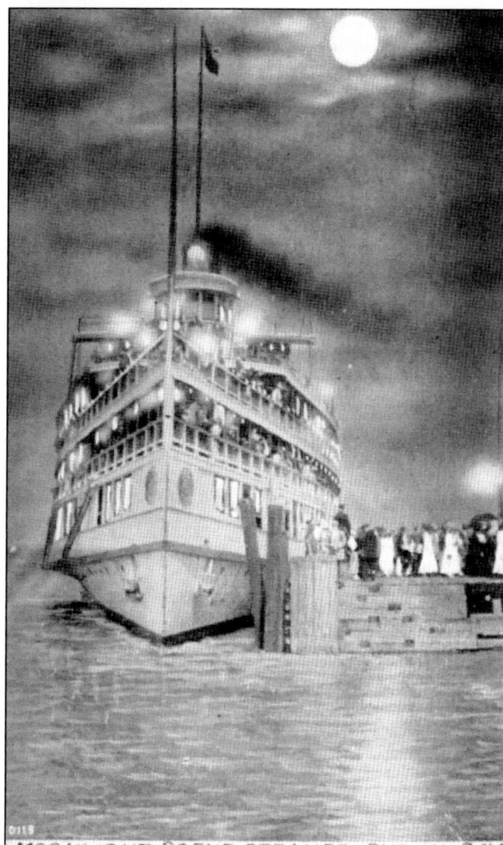

This moonlight scene shows passengers disembarking from the steamer *Put-in-Bay* around 1915. (AC.)

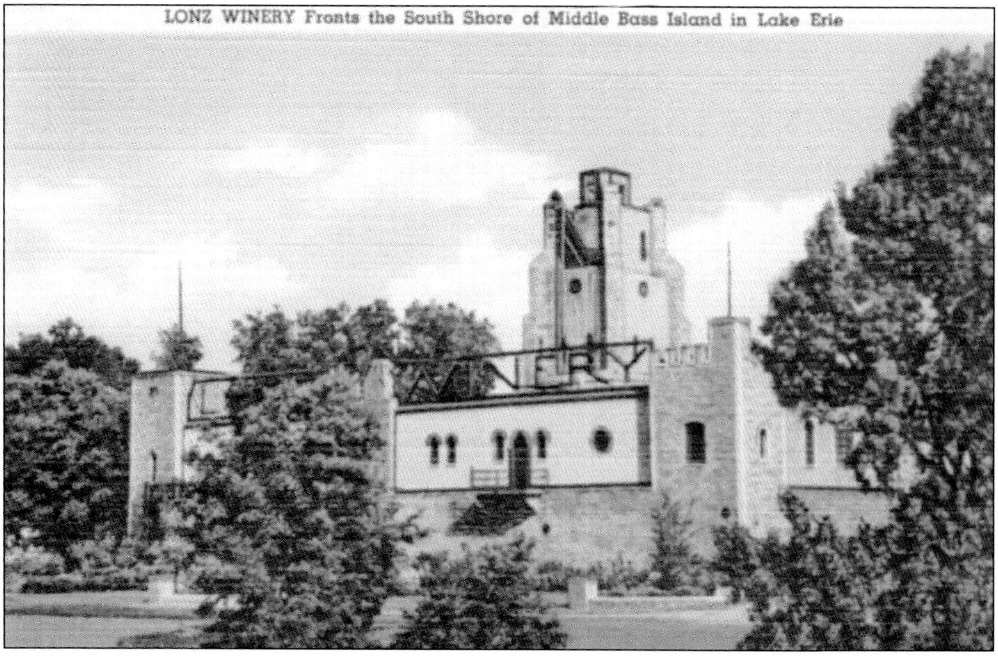

The Lonz Winery is across the small harbor from Put-in-Bay on Middle Bass Island. This unique winery and historical landmark was a party place for many years until tragedy struck several years ago. People were laughing, having fun, and sipping wine on a beautiful summer day when a room on the second floor, made with cement flooring, collapsed onto the wine tasters on the first floor. Many people were injured, and the winery was closed. (AC.)

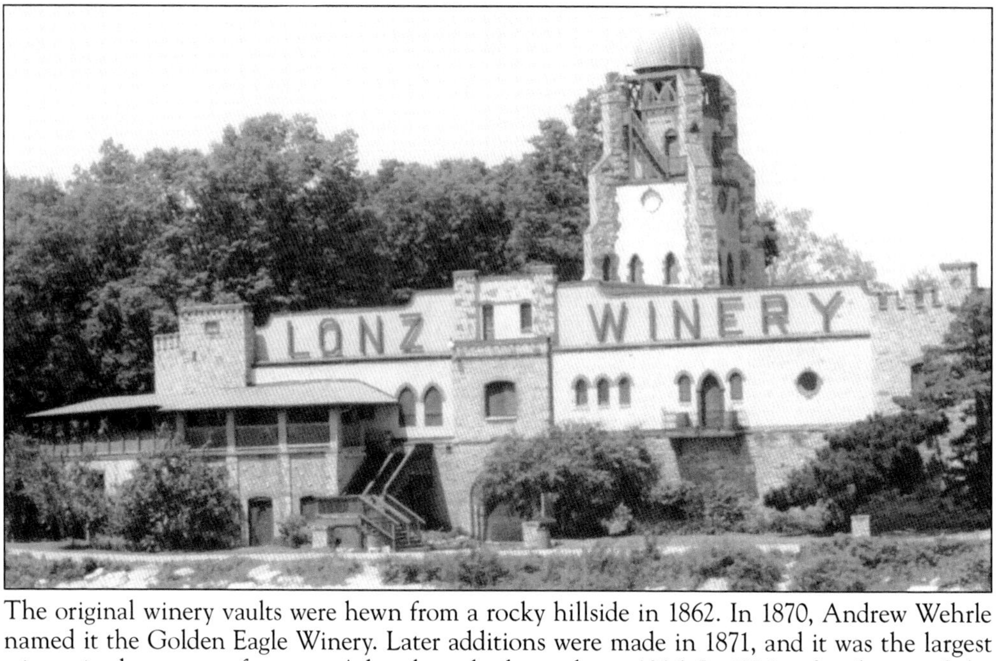

The original winery vaults were hewn from a rocky hillside in 1862. In 1870, Andrew Wehrle named it the Golden Eagle Winery. Later additions were made in 1871, and it was the largest winery in the country for years. A hotel was built nearby in 1906. In 1923, a fire destroyed the upper structure of the winery. In 1934, George F. Lonz designed the stone structure built by Henry Blocker on top of the 1870 wine cellar. The winery is pictured in 1995. (AC.)

Five

From Ugly Duckling to Beautiful Swan

George Washington, Alexander Hamilton, and John Hancock are said to have all visited the Portland Head Lighthouse in Maine and to have been inspired with visions for a free and better country. Henry Wadsworth Longfellow visited the Maine lighthouse and wrote the poem "The Lighthouse." Ohio lighthouses inspire people, too. The following was written by Philip Edwards of Marblehead, Ohio:

> In 1974, the Marblehead Lighthouse was in the process of being resurfaced and repainted. During this restoration, one of the men working on the inside wall found a small, old leather pouch tucked behind a loose stone. Inside the pouch were two very old handwritten notes. I purchased these notes over a decade ago. The parts of the first note that are legible are reproduced below.
>
> "My Lonely Keep—Remembering that unusual day we first met, I was once again filled with the joy of life and all it has to offer. Thy whimsical ways and lively style, rekindled the far reaches of my heart. A feeling I thought I had forever lost. Each day I am drawn to the entrance of the lane leading to the Light. Fighting temptation, God, Himself, only knows of my melancholy ritual. You have become an emotional part of my life, but until thee commits, I can only dance with your spirit in my mind. Let us not leave our remaining time drift past us.
>
> I shall derive much pleasure if our souls could share the warm moonlit summer nights and the cold dark nights of winter. I hope that this is not a romance I have created in my mind? If I shall not hear from you again, my memories of our encounters at the Light will forever live in my heart. A frightening event was to be our strange destiny. What would keep most people apart, has brought us together. Knowing we must forever conceal the secret we share about . . ."
>
> I'm sorry to say that at this point years of moisture merged with the ink. I have read the notes over and over many times. Each time, I am swept back to that light and a timeless moment. What could it be that keeps the mystery of the notes alive after all these years?

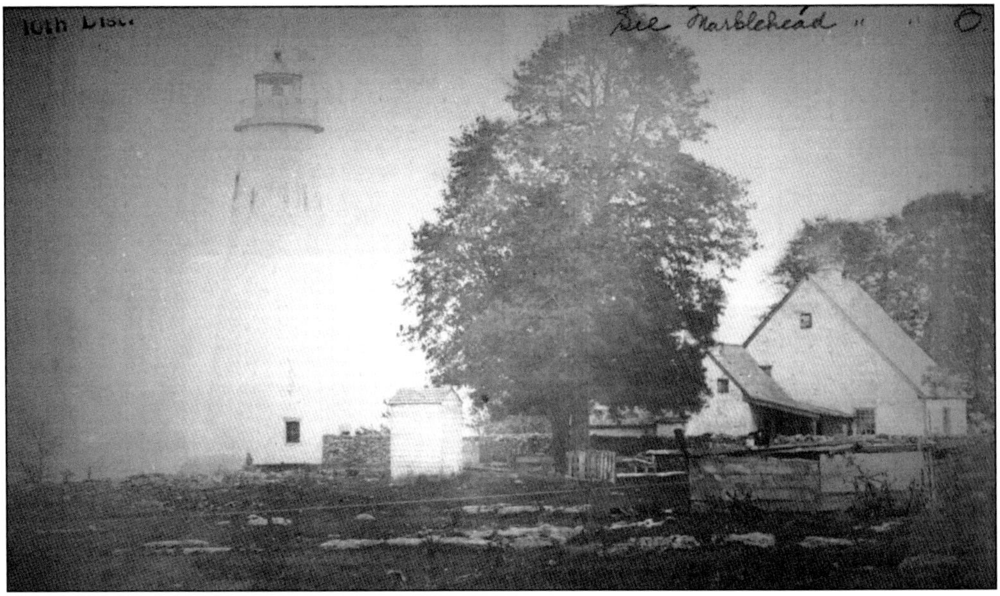

In this rare October 1859 photograph are the first keeper's house, built in 1821, and Marblehead Lighthouse. Beginning June 24, 1822, Benejah Wolcott was the lighthouse keeper. Wolcott kept two homes. During the summer, he and his wife lived here, and in the winter, they lived nearby in a house Wolcott built on his farm on Bayshore Drive. This residence was constructed of native limestone with a separate kitchen and outhouse. Stephen Wolverton subcontracted its construction to William Kelly, a stonemason, who built the lighthouse at the same time. (NARA.)

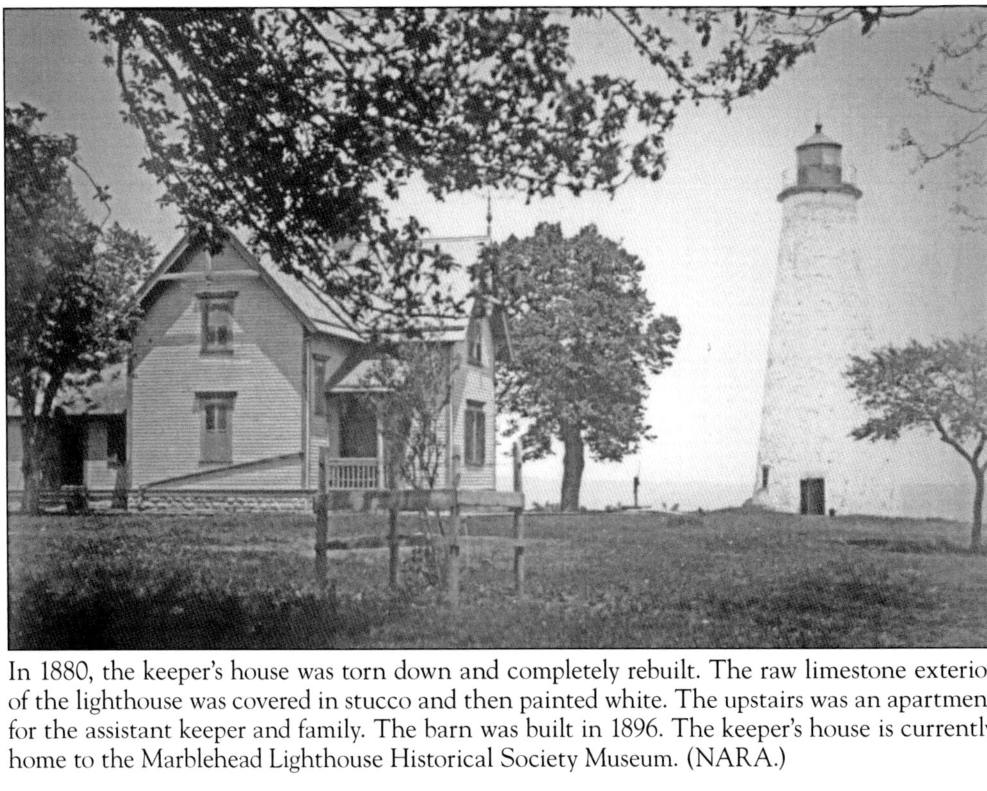

In 1880, the keeper's house was torn down and completely rebuilt. The raw limestone exterior of the lighthouse was covered in stucco and then painted white. The upstairs was an apartment for the assistant keeper and family. The barn was built in 1896. The keeper's house is currently home to the Marblehead Lighthouse Historical Society Museum. (NARA.)

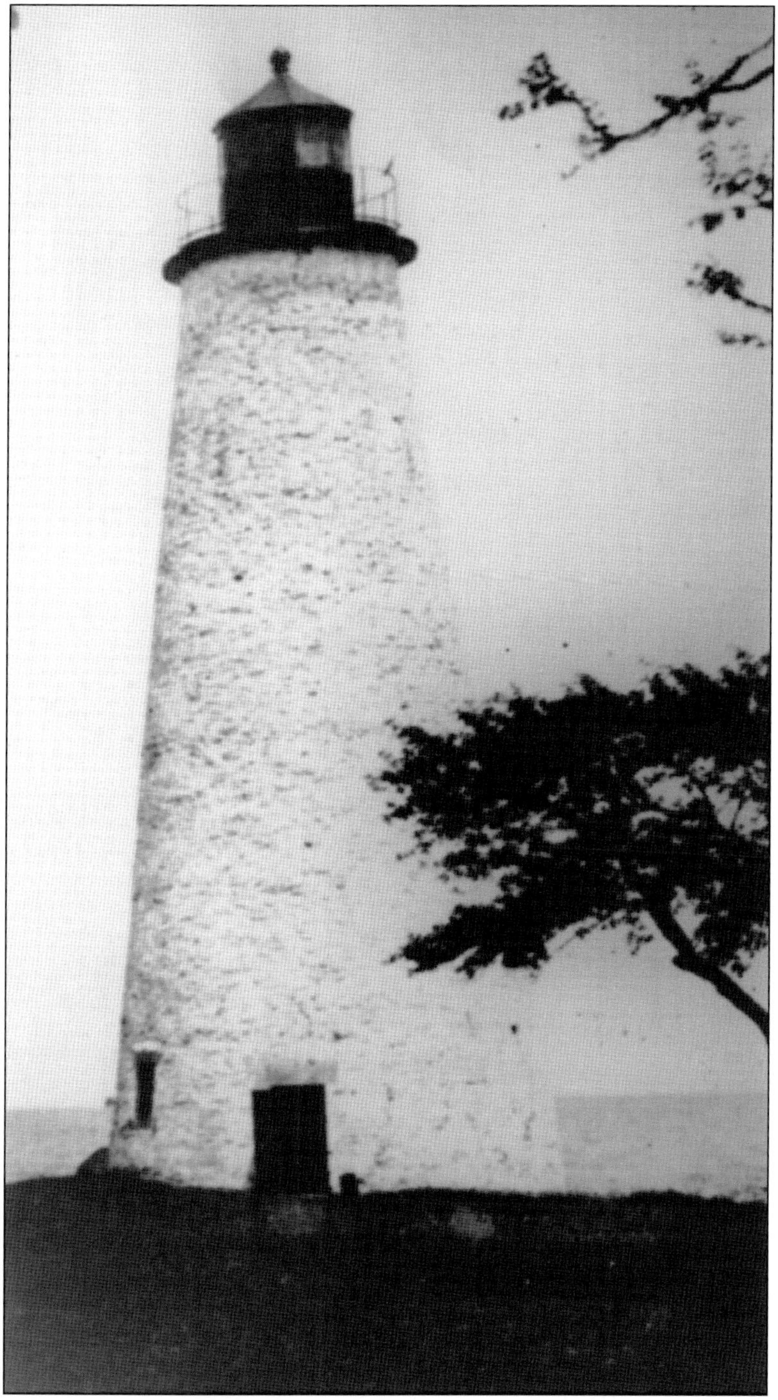

This is the oldest known printable photograph of Marblehead Lighthouse, called the Sandusky Bay Light until 1870. The lighthouse was built in 11 weeks, from September to November 1821, by William Kelly, his crew, and his 13-year-old son, John Reid Kelly. The 50-foot structure had a base diameter of 25 feet and a top diameter of 12 feet. The walls were five feet thick at the bottom, tapering to two feet at the top. The native limestone was left unpainted. (GLHS.)

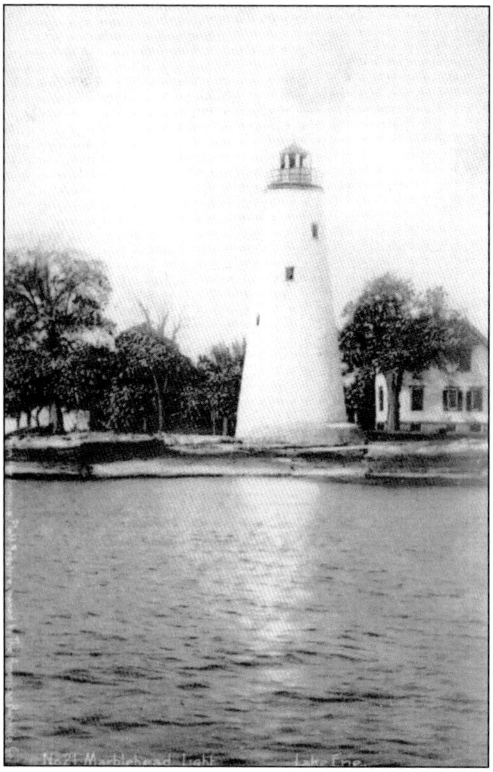

This c. 1885 Marblehead Lighthouse photograph was taken after the replacement keeper's house was built in 1880 but before 1897, when 15 additional feet were added to the top and the windows were embellished. In 1821, this white beacon consisted of 13 Argand lamps fueled by whale oil with a reflector behind each lamp. Whale oil was expensive by 1858, so a fourth-order Fresnel lens was installed that required only one lamp. (AC.)

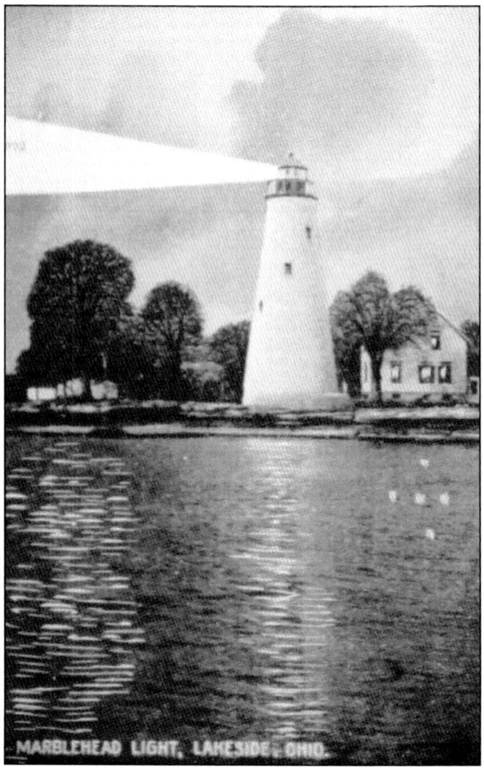

Marblehead Lighthouse is shown by moonlight in this c. 1885 image. In 1930, the white light was changed to red. In 1969, the red light was changed once again, this time to green. (AC.)

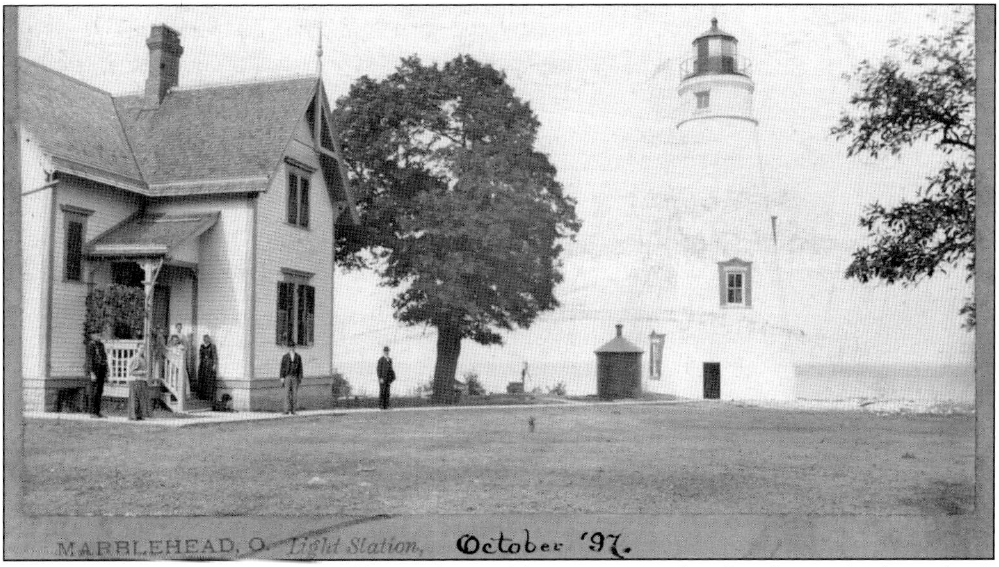

The transformation from ugly duckling to beautiful swan occurred in October 1897 when a brick watch room at the top of the lighthouse was built, adding 15 feet to the top of the tower, and attractive window embellishments were added that beautified the lighthouse. These changes helped make Marblehead Lighthouse the stunning structure seen today. A larger lantern from a decommissioned lighthouse in Erie, Pennsylvania, replaced the old one. Johanna McGee (pictured, but unidentified) replaced her late husband, George McGee, as lighthouse keeper upon his death in 1896. (USCG.)

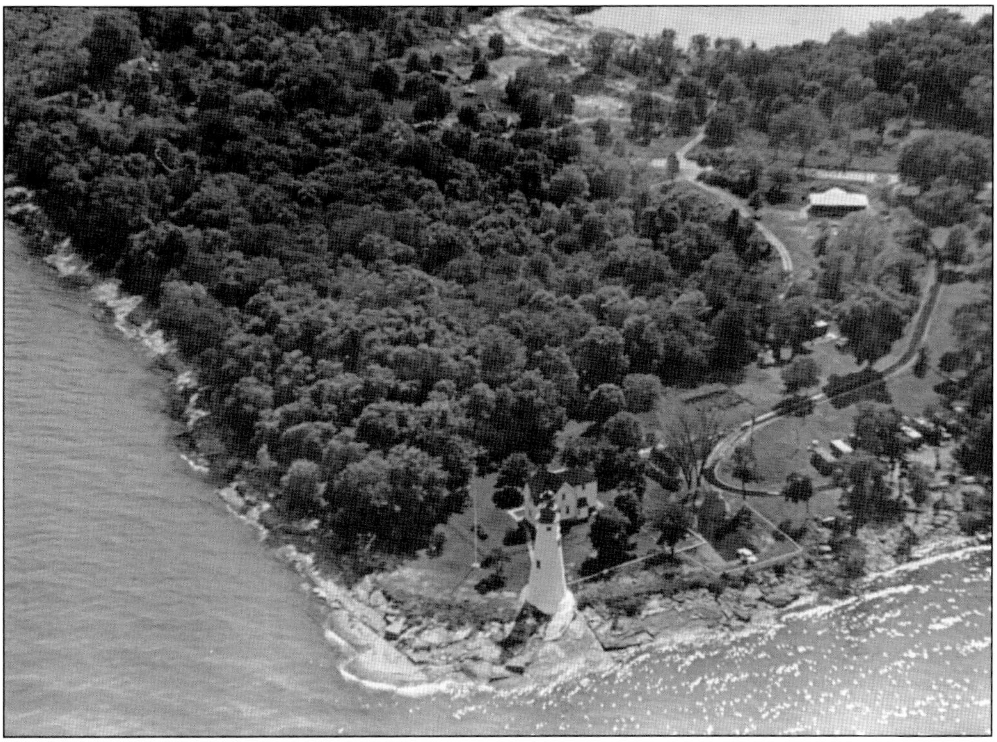

In this aerial view is the land surrounding the Marblehead Lighthouse. (SL.)

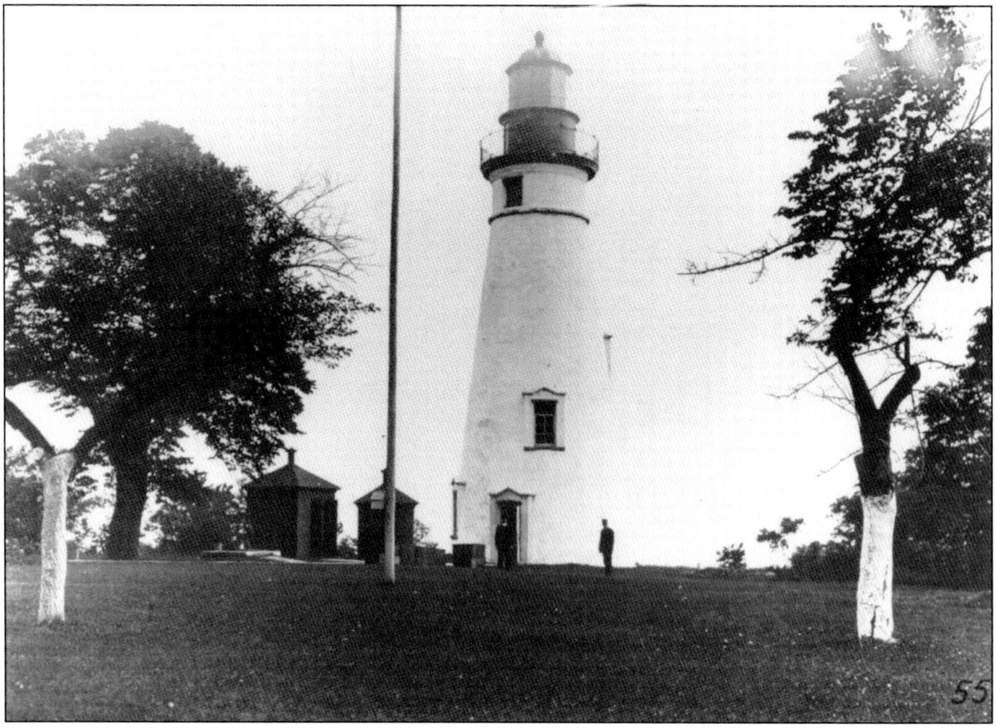

Charles (Cap) Hunter, keeper since 1903, is standing in front of Marblehead Lighthouse in this June 1911 picture. Cap Hunter loved to entertain visitors to the lighthouse, telling them stories about the lighthouse and the sinking of the *Consuelo* (1875) and the *Empire* (1857). (USCG.)

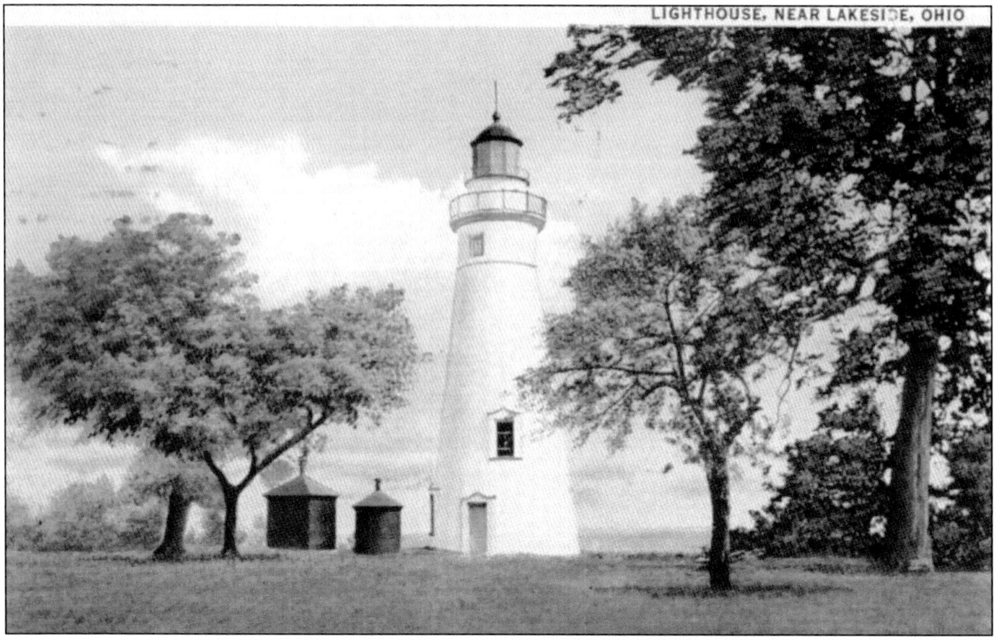

Between 1888 and 1891, a detached round oil container was built. It held flammable kerosene and mineral oil. Between 1905 and 1906, a square iron oil storage house was added with a 540-gallon capacity. (AC.)

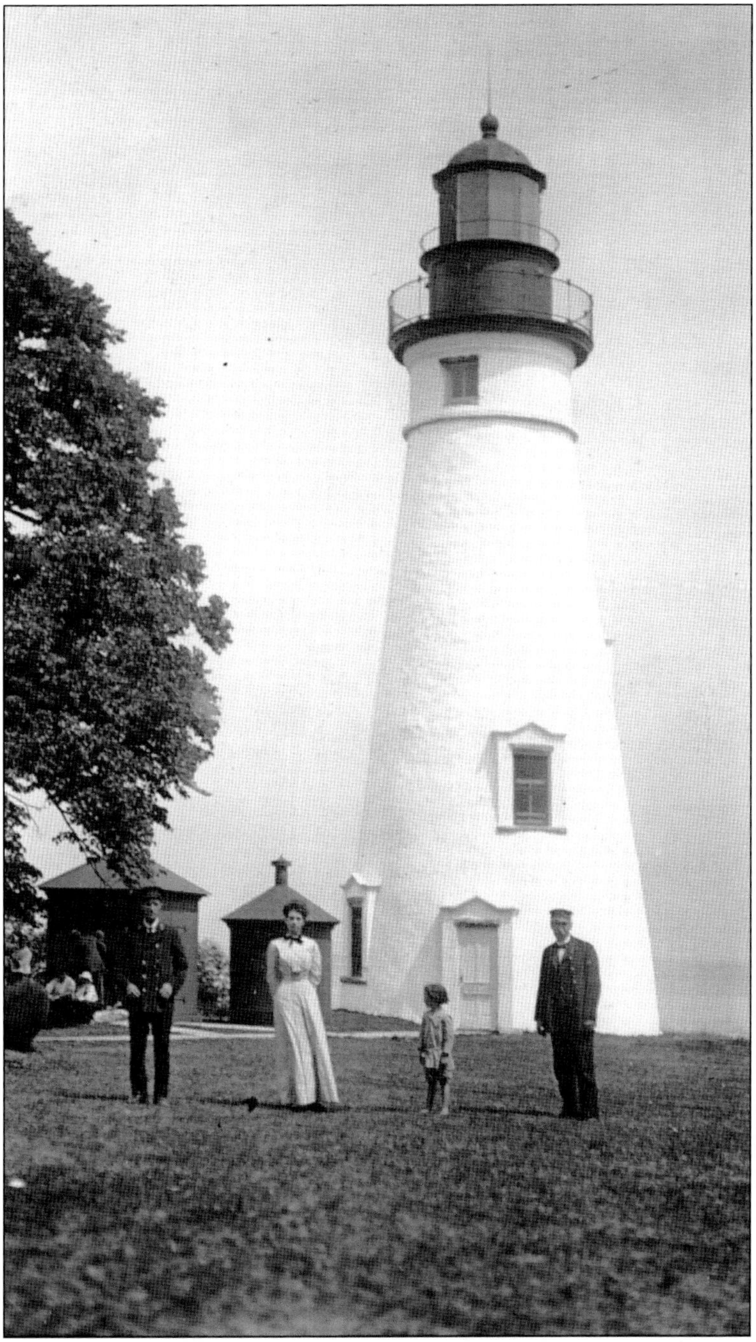

Cap Hunter (far right) was previously the keeper of the Buffalo Lighthouse. He retired as the Marblehead keeper in 1933. The assistant keeper, Edward Herman (far left), replaced Hunter and served until 1943, when the lighthouse duties were transferred to the Coast Guard. Cap Hunter loved to spin stories about the lighthouse. Perhaps he was about to entertain the visitors sitting in front of the square oil-storage building in this c. 1923 image. Hunter remarked that his job became much easier with the installation of electricity in 1923. The candlepower increased from 42,000 to 350,000 and visibility increased to 16 miles. (SL.)

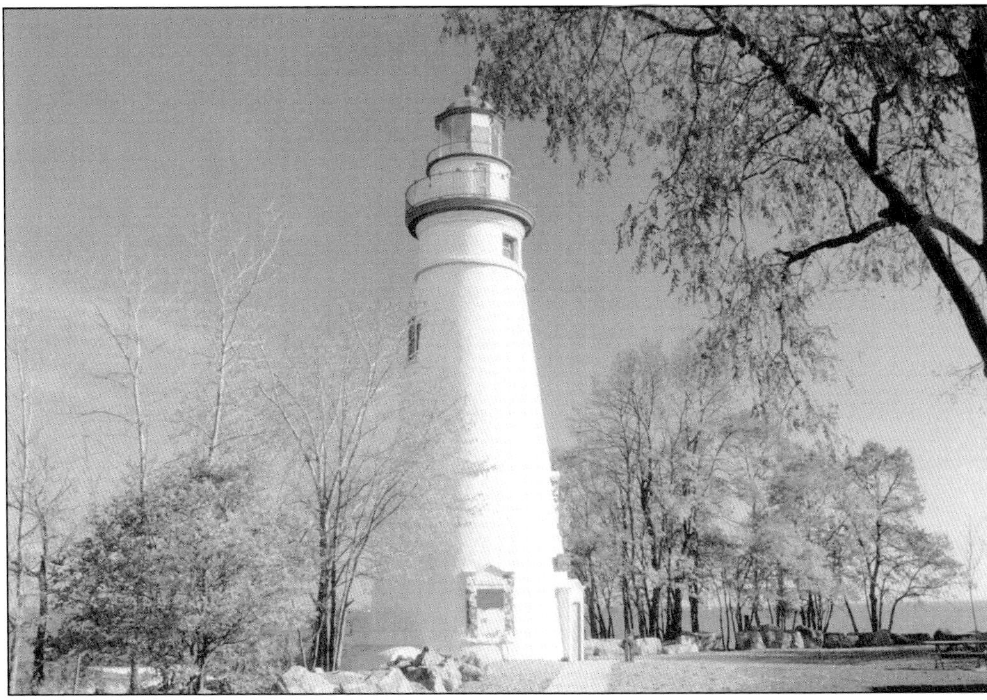

In 1857, the barge *Empire* was traveling from Toledo to Tonawanda, New York, when it wrecked near Marblehead Lighthouse. Lighthouse keeper Jared B. Keyes saw the disaster and wanted to save the sailors. He contacted eight volunteers, including his son Robert and his son-in-law William Clemons. A strong sea was running, and when the men attempted to launch the boat, they were thrown back onto the beach with a broken oar. Retrieving more oars, they launched the lifeboat again in a different area and were able to reach the *Empire*, saving the lives of the captain and sailor. The Marblehead Lighthouse is shown here in 1990. (AC.)

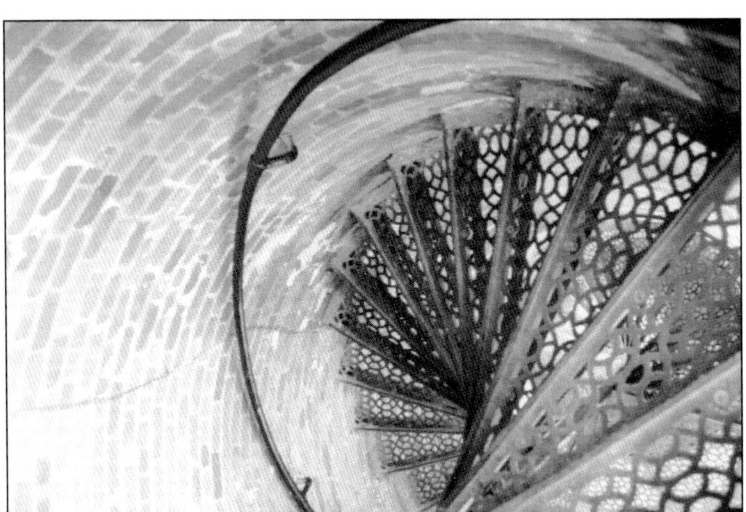

In August 1945, a temporary watch room was constructed on the lake side of the tower at the lower lantern-deck level to better protect boaters. In 1949, a permanent watch room was constructed in the same location. The room was removed in December 1956. This stairway leads to the lantern room at the top. (AC.)

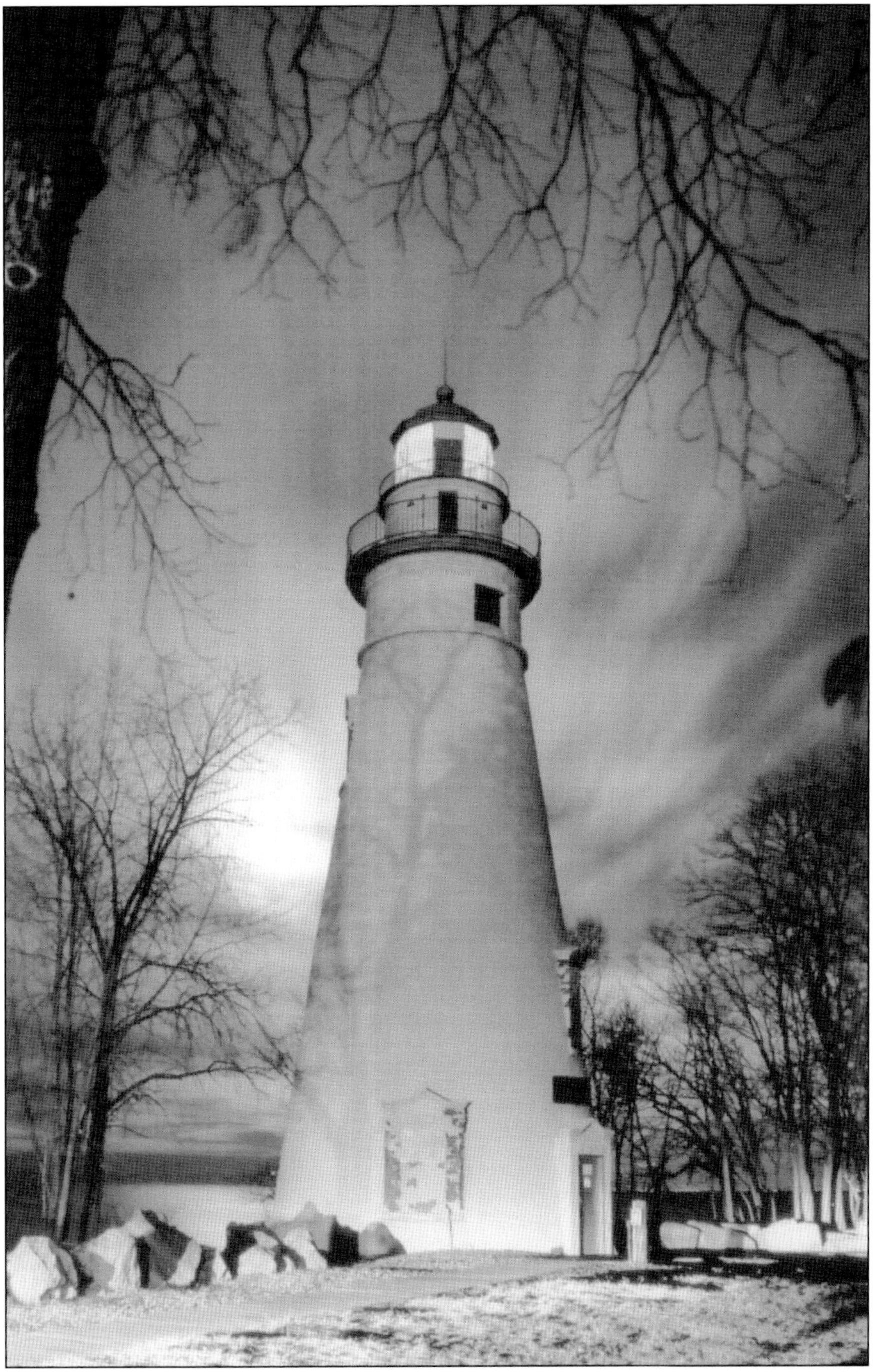

The notorious 40-foot *Vietta*, an old wooden boat with splitting seams that leaked like a sieve, ran liquor during Prohibition. Against everyone's advice, the captain and crew left Canada for the Marblehead Lighthouse (pictured) and Sandusky Bay with a boatload of liquor. It was midnight, and the boat was slow. When close to the lighthouse, the Coast Guard overtook and seized the *Vietta* and began to tow it. This was an important capture, and everyone onboard the Coast Guard boat was elated that they had apprehended such an important rumrunner. (AC.)

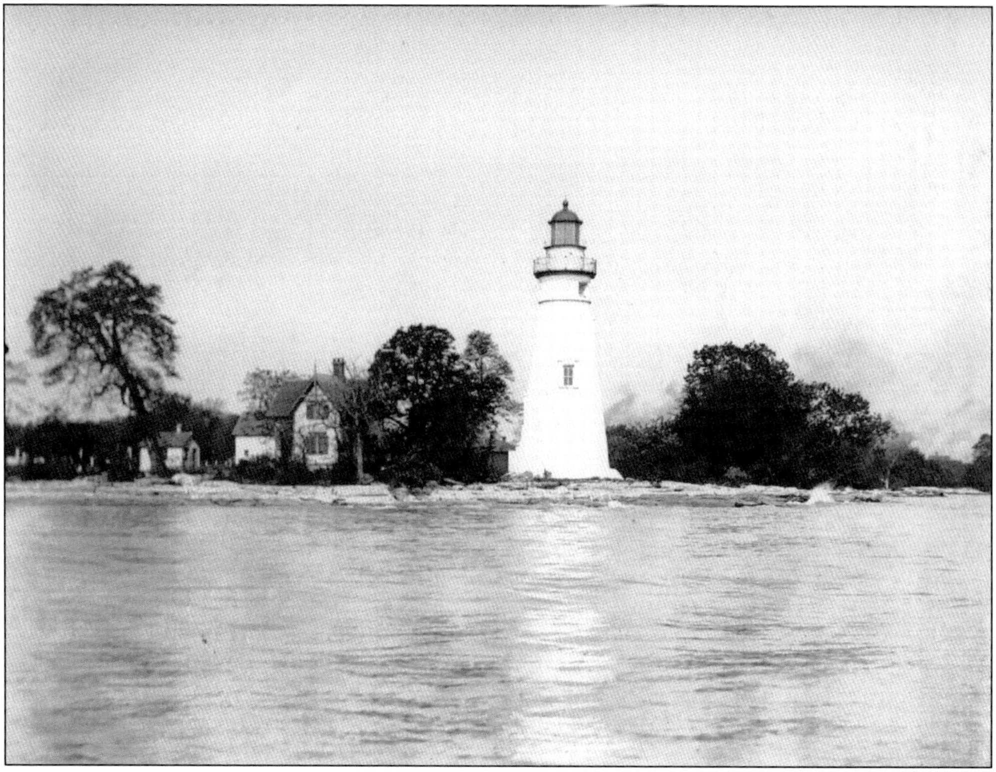

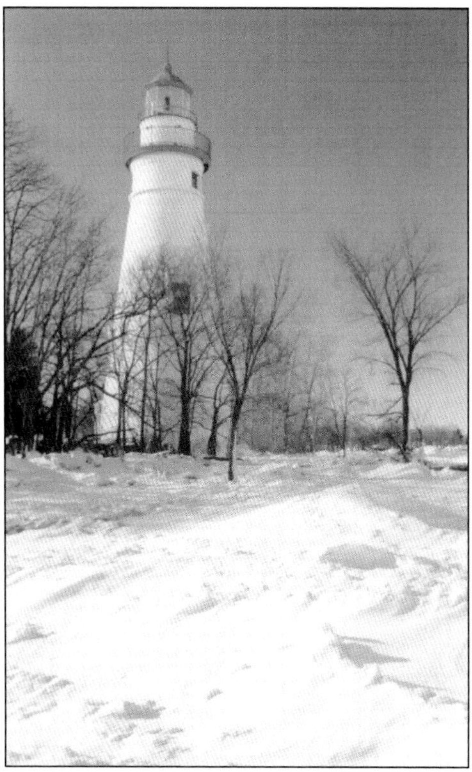

In their haste to bring the *Vietta* to Sandusky to show off their prize, the Coast Guard men forgot to take any liquor or other evidence onto their own boat. They also failed to notice that the boat was sinking. Before they could reach Sandusky, the *Vietta* suddenly sank not far from Marblehead Lighthouse (pictured). The two men from Canada were caught red-handed, but since the Coast Guard had no evidence, they could not be convicted. Back in Canada, the captain of the *Vietta*, Mike, commented, "I knew what was going to happen as soon as they took me in tow, but do you suppose I was going to tell those guys my boat was leaking?" (SL.)

Marblehead Lighthouse is pictured surrounded with snow. (AC.)

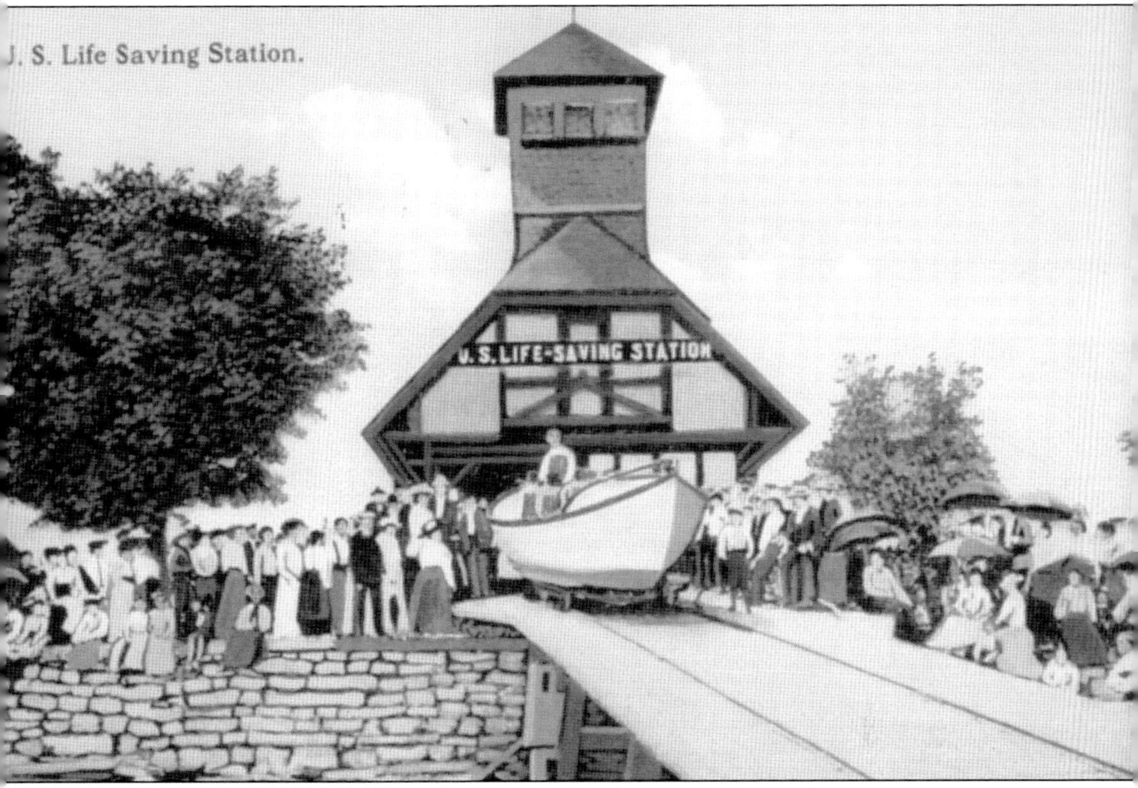

On May 1, 1875, as howling winds rattled windows and noisy raindrops splattered against glass, Lucien Clemons did what he always did when it stormed—look at the lake for boats caught in the gale. He spotted a schooner, the *Consuelo*, struggling and watched it roll over in the heavy seas. He wanted to rescue those onboard, so he contacted his brothers, Hubbard and A.J. The three men decided to take their skiff to the wreckage site to attempt to save any survivors. An hour later, they hauled a sailor and a mate onboard, but then they had difficulty rowing back to shore. People from Kelleys Island also saw the schooner capsize. Eager to help, the captain of the tugboat *Winslow* sailed his vessel from Kelleys Island immediately. After finding no other survivors, the tugboat captain tossed a line to Clemons and began towing his boat to safety. Pictured is the Marblehead Life-Saving Station, built in 1876. Lucien Clemons became the first life-saving keeper here. (AC.)

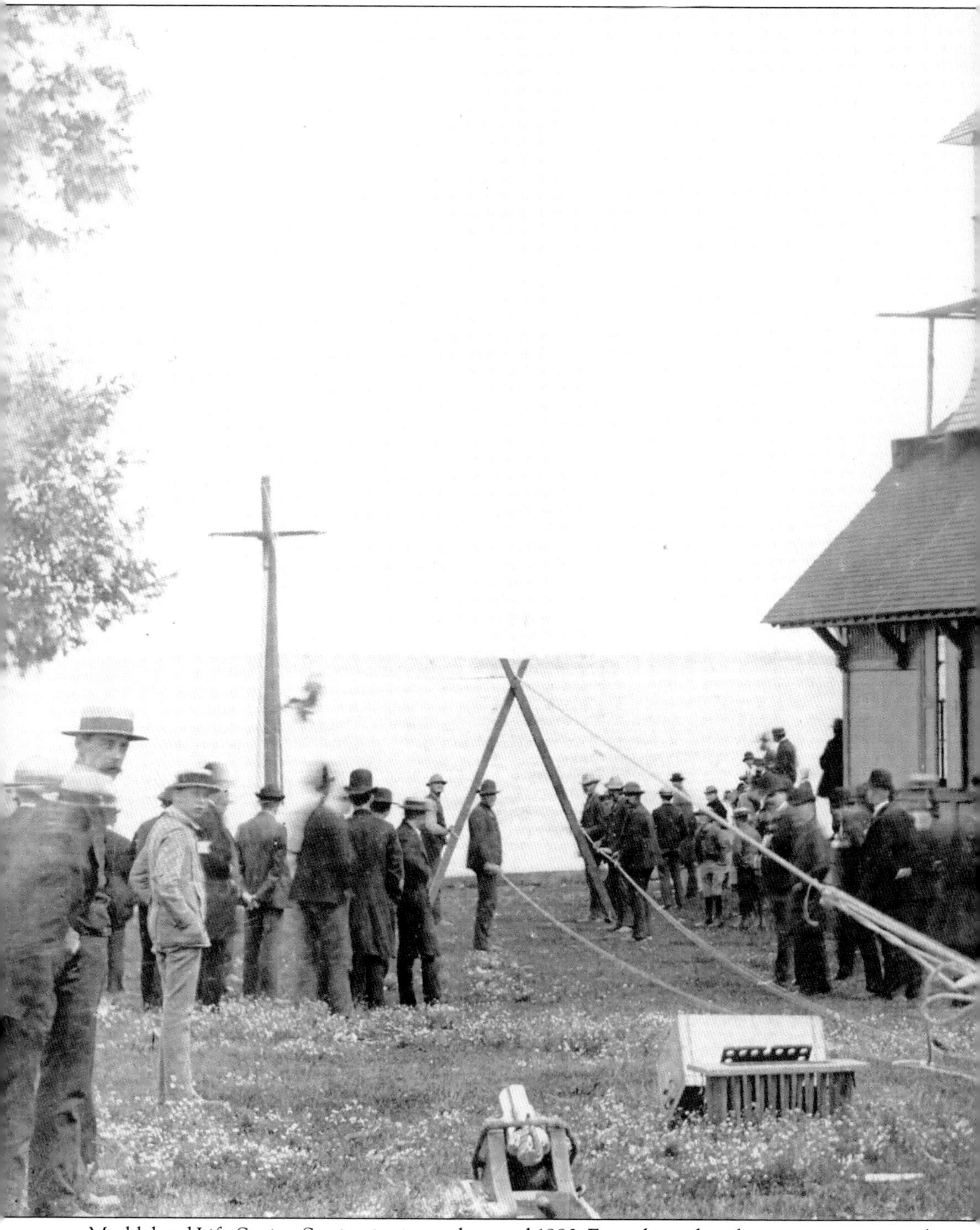

Marblehead Life-Saving Station is pictured around 1880. For risking their lives to save two people on the wrecked *Consuelo,* the three brothers, Lucien, Hubbard, and A.J. Clemons, received the Gold Lifesaving Medal from the Life-Saving Service for "extreme heroic action." In 1876, Lucien Clemons became the first Life-Saving Keeper, serving until 1897. The Marblehead Station was

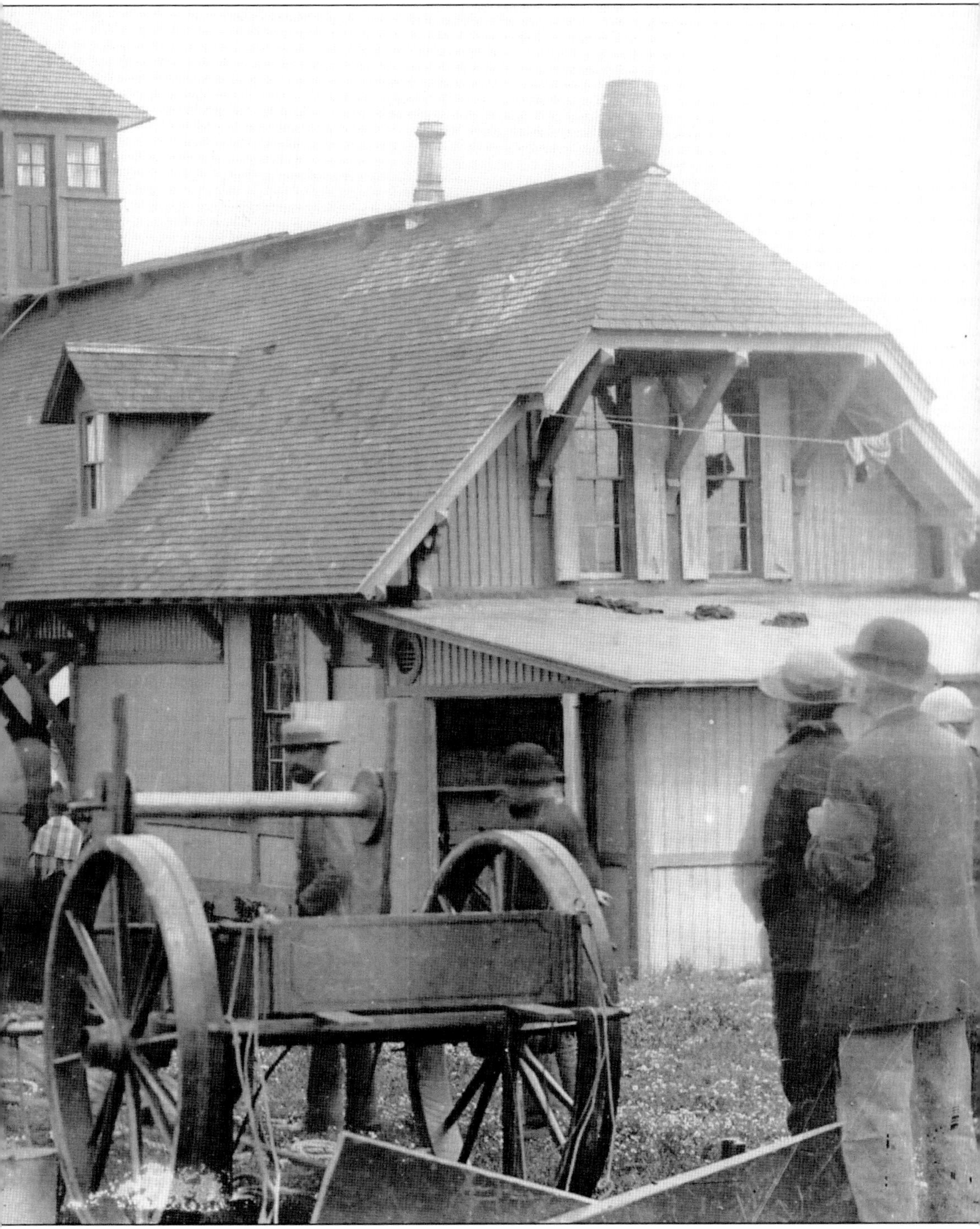

moved toward the lake 15 feet and an 80-foot pier was added in 1878 for launching the lifeboat. The watchtower was added to the boathouse around 1880. Notice the Lyle gun in the grass in the bottom left-hand section of this photograph. Other new lifesaving stations in 1876 were at Fairport and Cleveland, Ohio, and at Presque Isle, Pennsylvania. (GLHS.)

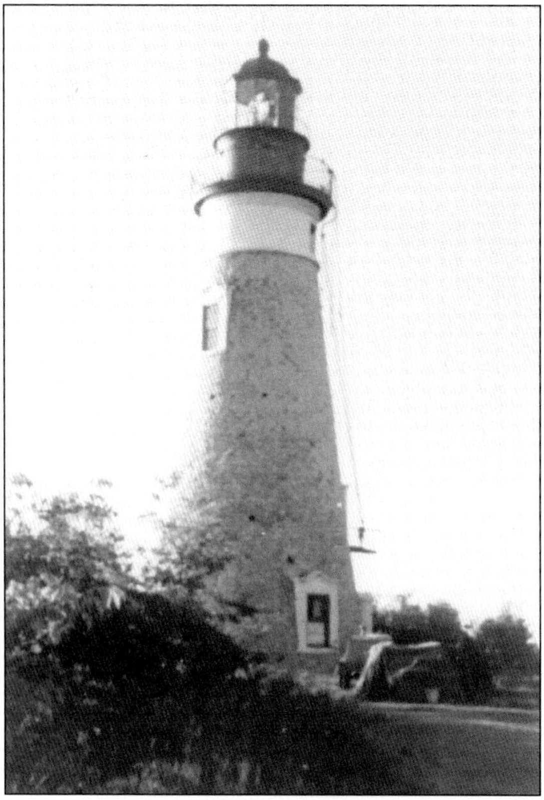

The Marblehead Lighthouse, photographed in 1974, is about to receive granite surfacing after being skinned, repainted, and readied for a sealing coat. Damage from a bad flood left the structure in need of repairs. (GLHS.)

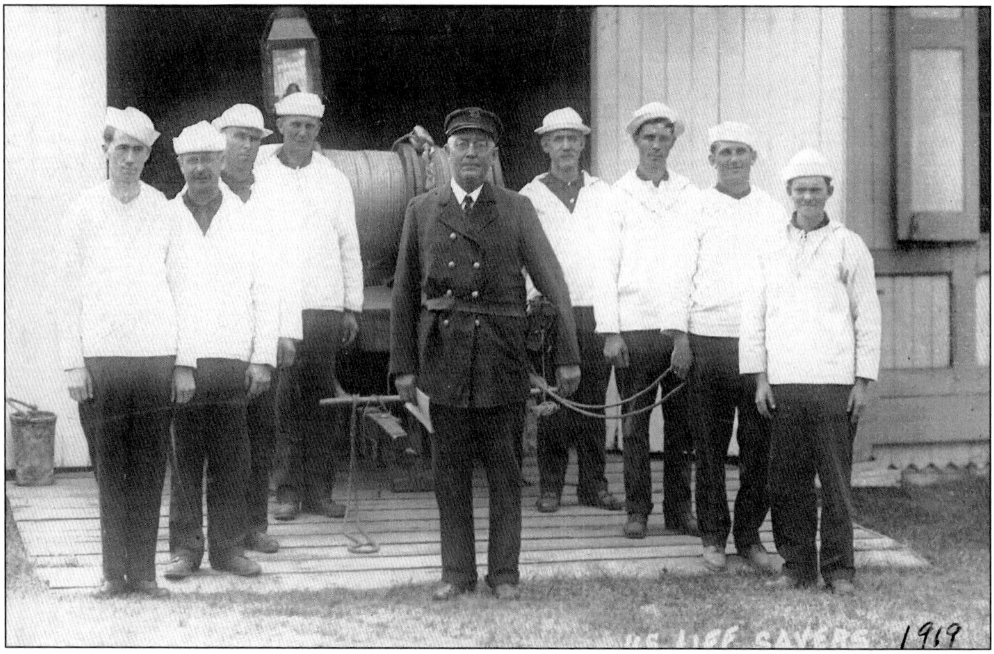

The Marblehead Life-Saving crew is captured in this photograph from around 1914. The photograph includes, from left to right, Gilbert Clemons, John Gallagher, Jim Gordon, Ernest Hass, keeper Dan Griesser, Dan Mulcahy, Paul Farmer, Ray Morton, and Jerry Tracy. (SL.)

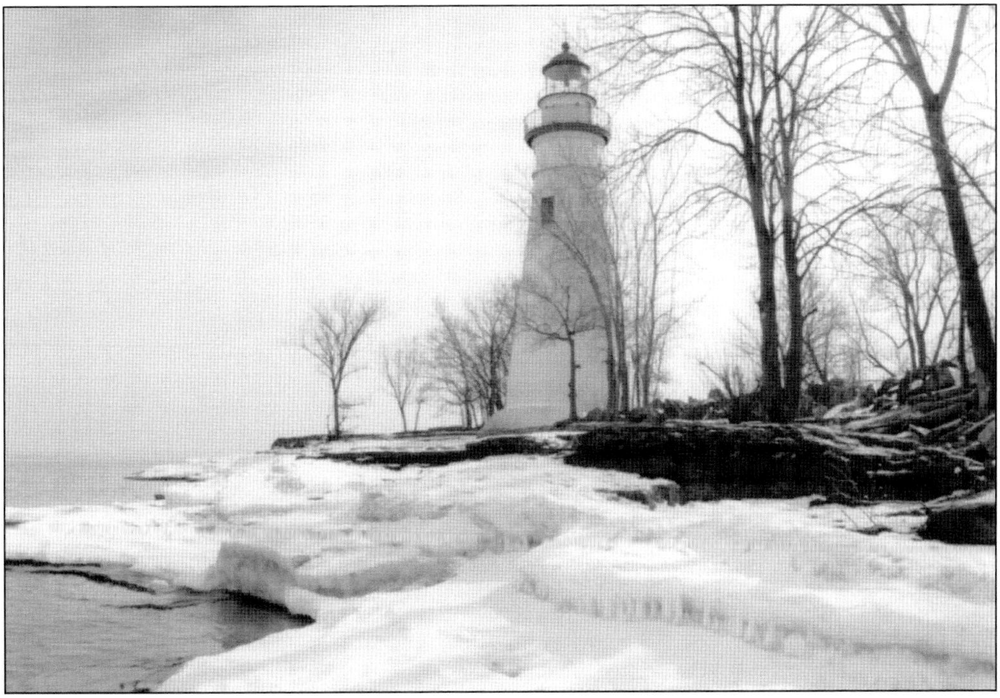

A reflection of the lighthouse appears on the calm surface of Lake Erie. Over the years, the Marblehead Lighthouse keepers and their years of service were Benejah Wolcott, 1822–1832; Rachel Wolcott, 1832–1834; Jeremiah Van Benschoten, 1834–1841; Roderick Williston, 1841–1843; Charles Drake, 1843–1849; Lodowick Brown, 1849–1853; Jared Keyes, 1853–1858; W. Dayton, 1859–1861; Thomas Dyer, 1861–1865; Russell Douglas, 1865–1872; Thomas Keyes, 1872–1873; George McGee, 1873–1896; Johanna McGee, 1896–1903; Charles Hunter, 1903–1933; and Edward Herman, 1933–1943. (AC.)

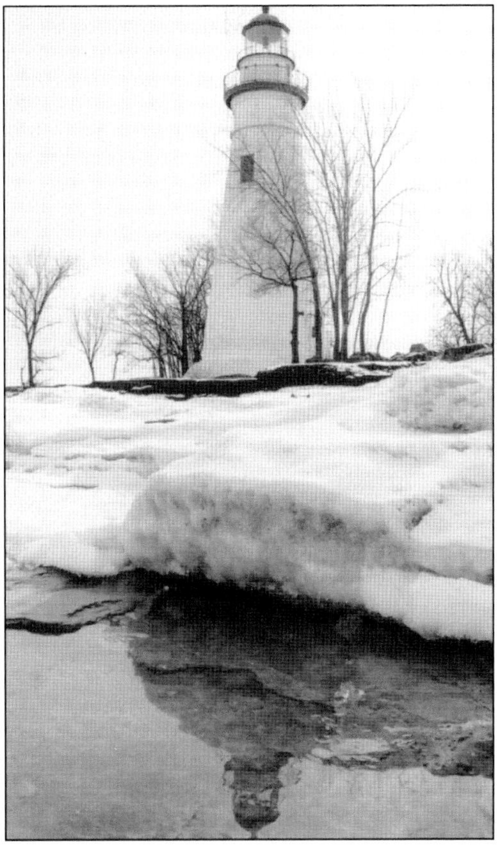

Snow covers the frozen lakeshore near the Marblehead Lighthouse. Lighthouses are often considered romantic, and many couples have been married at this lighthouse. (AC.)

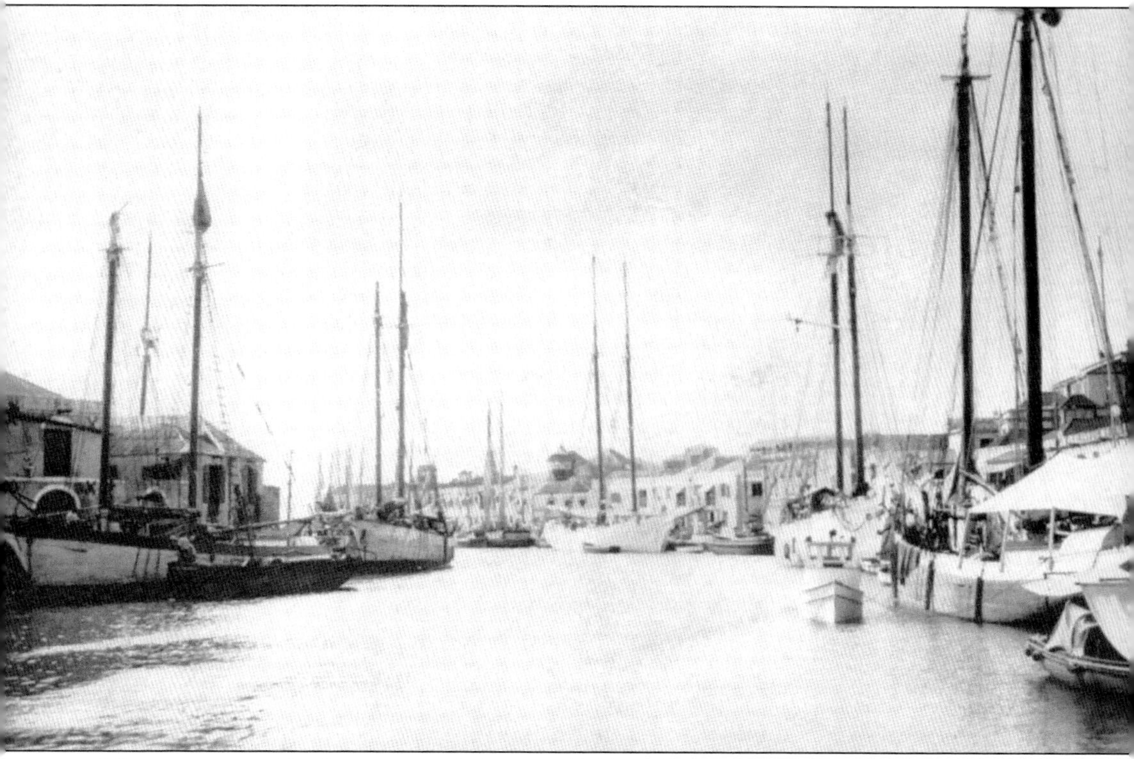

This is a typical harbor scene of the late 1800s, when schooners carried freight on Lake Erie. (AC.)

Six

Lighthouses at Famous Cedar Point

The first Cedar Point Lighthouse, built in 1839, was replaced on August 6, 1862, by a stone structure that was 10 feet higher than the original. The main lighthouse and range lights guided ships from Cleveland, Detroit, and Put-in-Bay to popular Cedar Point and Sandusky.

The Cedar Point Range Light was a mystery. With no lantern room to house a beacon, how could it cast a light? Through a chance discovery, a duplicate lighthouse was discovered in Toledo. Capt. George Stoddard lived in the Toledo Range Lighthouse and operated the light from 1868 to 1905. It became known as the Stoddard Range Light. Some accounts called it a half-a-house because of the manner in which the roof slants. Articles written about and photographs taken of this unusual Toledo lighthouse revealed the secret location of its illumination. An article states, "Along the top of the second floor at the rear is a series of 21 windows." It continues, "Old-timers remember that various colored lights were shone from the upper windows over the bay." The mystery of the Cedar Point light was solved.

Louis Zistel's advertisement in the *Sandusky Daily Register* on July 16, 1870, reads, "For Cedar Point—The new steamer *Young Reindeer* will make a trip to the Cedar Point Beer Garden from the foot of Columbus Avenue every evening."

As if anticipating events to come, the July 29, 1867, *Sandusky Register* comments that "somebody should erect a bathhouse on the lake side of Cedar Point, about a quarter of a mile from the lighthouse."

Bathhouses were established. James West placed an ad in 1878 letting the beachgoing public know that the renting of bathing suits and bathhouses was reduced to 10¢ each. In 1882, people were warned against bathing in the nude by Cedar Point bathhouse owners.

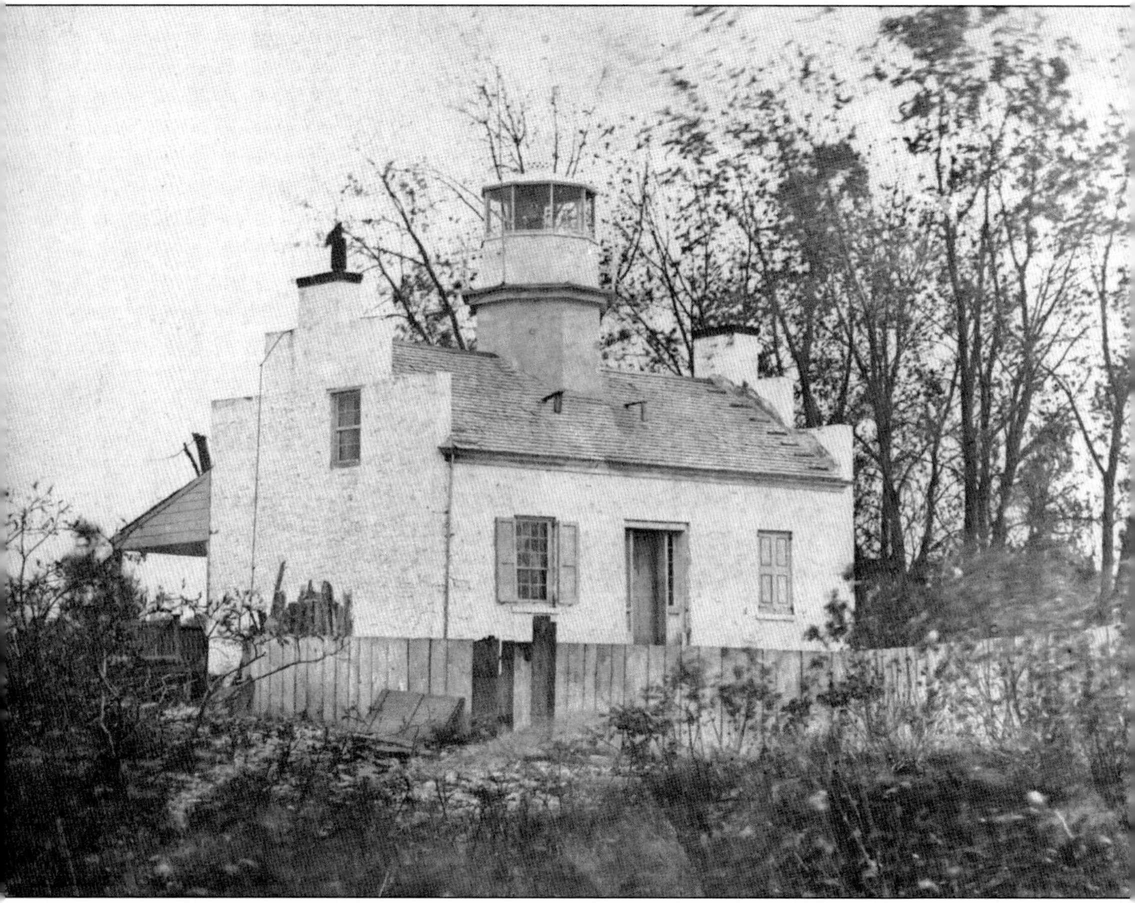

Taken in October 1859, this is a rare photograph of the first Cedar Point Lighthouse built in 1839. Congress appropriated $2,500 for a beacon light near the entrance to Sandusky Bay on May 16, 1837, and another $3,000 on August 4, 1838, according to the *Cleveland Herald.* In 1849, range lights were added to line up with the main lighthouse. These lights were replaced in 1851 and 1853. One range light was square with an 18-inch-by-24-inch glass and a 12-inch reflector. The light held one quart of oil and was raised and lowered by pulleys. The August 6, 1862, *Sandusky Daily Commercial Register* reports that "work on the new lighthouse is nearly completed and this stone structure will be 10 feet higher than the old light." (NARA.)

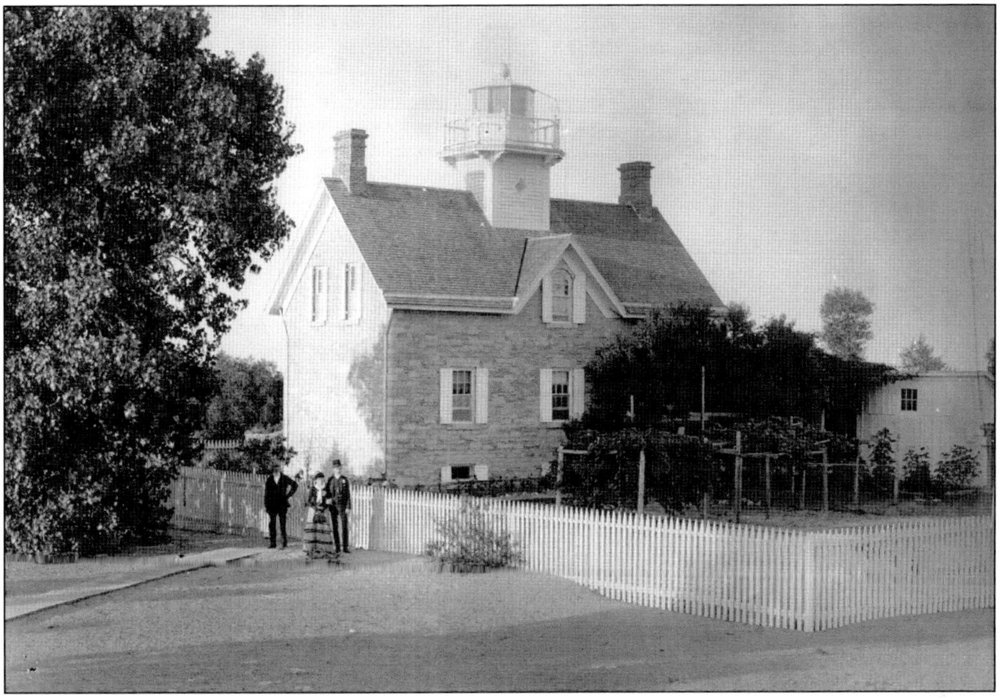

The dome of the old Cedar Point Lighthouse was removed and attached to the new structure. The lighthouse was discontinued in 1904 and the lantern room removed. Daniel Finn was the last lighthouse keeper, serving from 1901 to 1904. After 1904, Frank Ritter, lighthouse keeper of the Sandusky Range Lights, maintained the building and other range lights in the area. The Cedar Point Amusement Park purchased the old Sandusky Bay Coast Guard Station on October 28, 1987, for $425,000, restored the lighthouse, and allowed public access in 2001. (SL.)

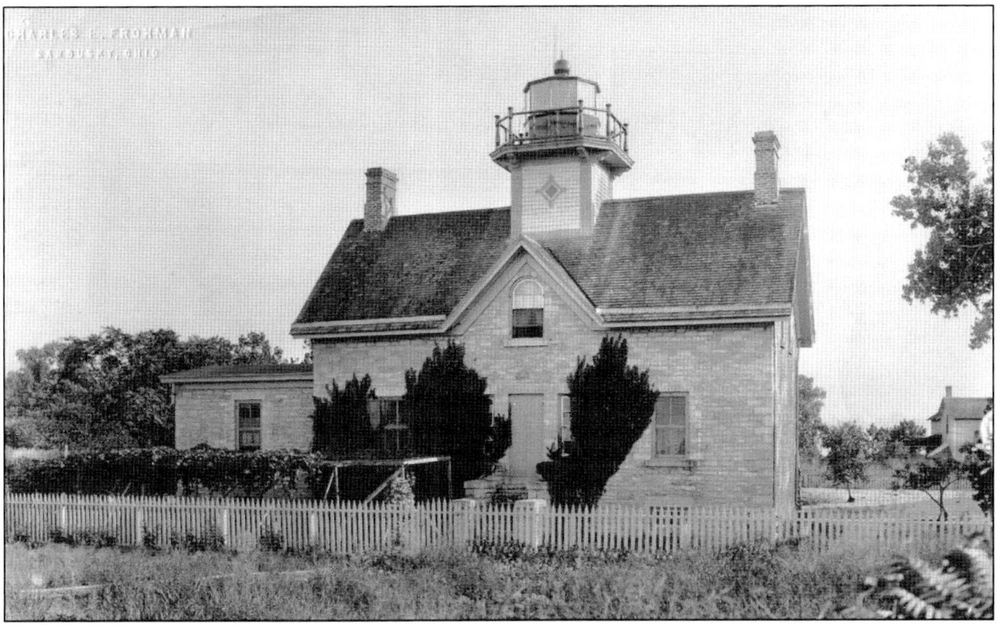

Cedar Point Lighthouse stands vigil. (GLHS.)

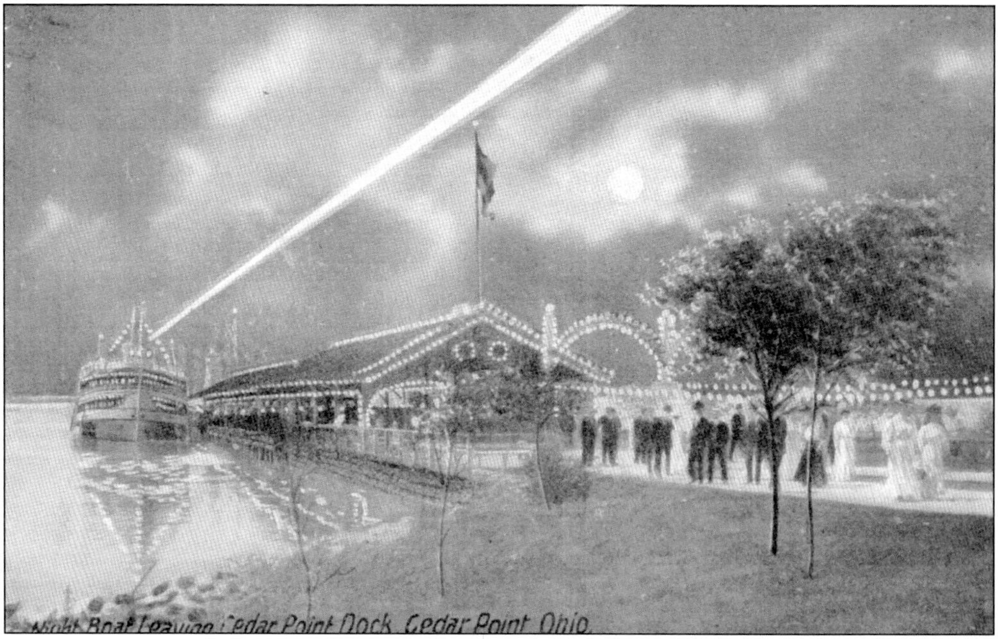

An unidentified boat leaves the Cedar Point dock by moonlight in 1913. (AC.)

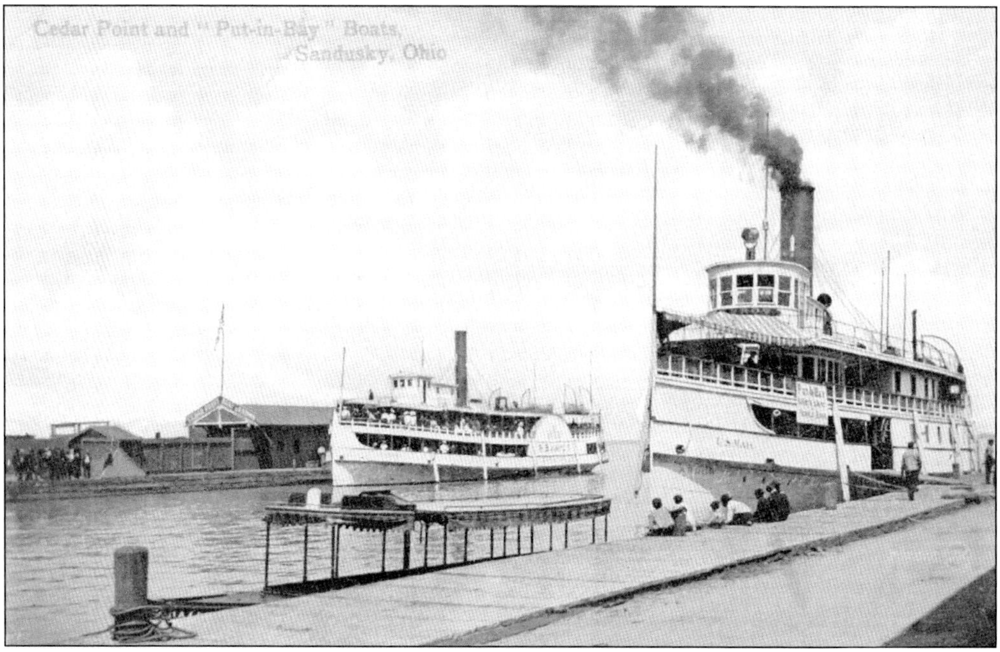

On their way to Cedar Point Park, the *R.B. Hayes* (left) and *Put-in-Bay* stop at the Cedar Point dock in Sandusky. (AC.)

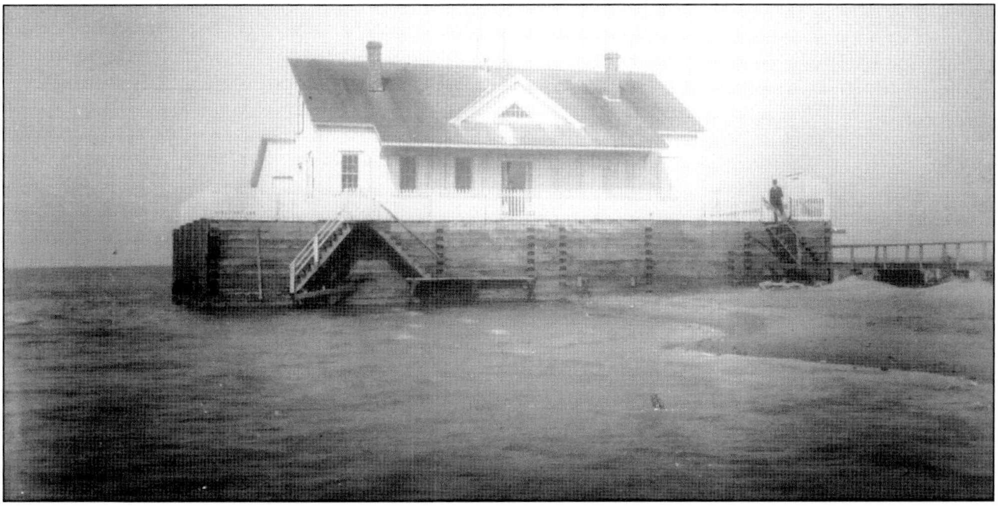

"Flames lick up the old lighthouse on Cedar Point," reads a newspaper headline from July 4, 1910. The old Cedar Point Range Lighthouse, near the *Eastland* boat dock and the jetty extending into the lake, was totally destroyed by fire. People who had no intention of going to Cedar Point on Monday evening were attracted by the flames and visited the area. Fishermen who kept their nets within the building sustained the only material losses. This light aligned with the main Cedar Point Light, and both were used before a straight channel was dredged around 1900. This photograph was taken around 1885. (NARA.)

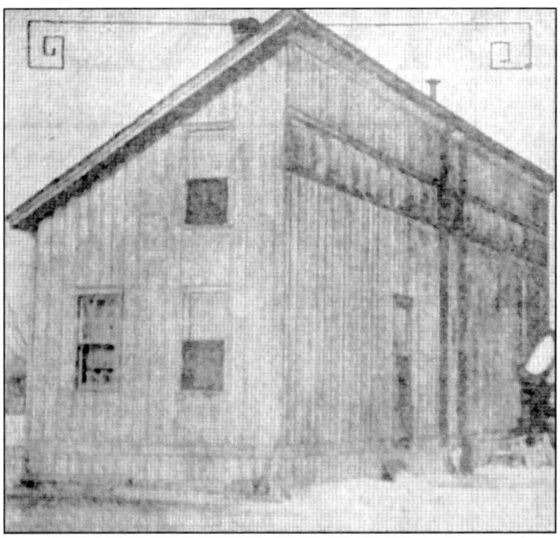

This unusual Toledo Range Lighthouse, known as the Stoddard Range Light, was pictured in the *Toledo Times* on March 13, 1923, and in the *Toledo Blade* on both February 8, 1929, and September 1, 1953. The windows on the second floor were used to display the beacon. This "half-a-house" is identical to the Cedar Point Range Light. Both lights were built in 1867 to 1868. (There is more information on this one in chapter one.) (TL.)

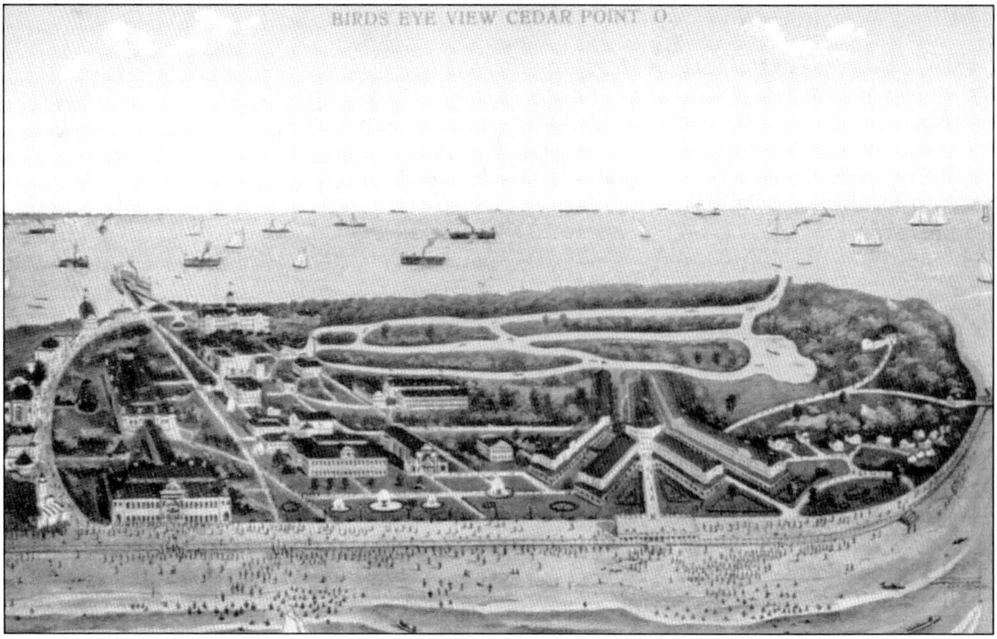

Cedar Point has been a popular destination since the late 1800s. These views show the early development of the peninsula. The Cedar Point Lighthouse is located in the upper left-hand part of the property. It is visible next to the *Eastland* boat dock in the image above. (Both, AC.)

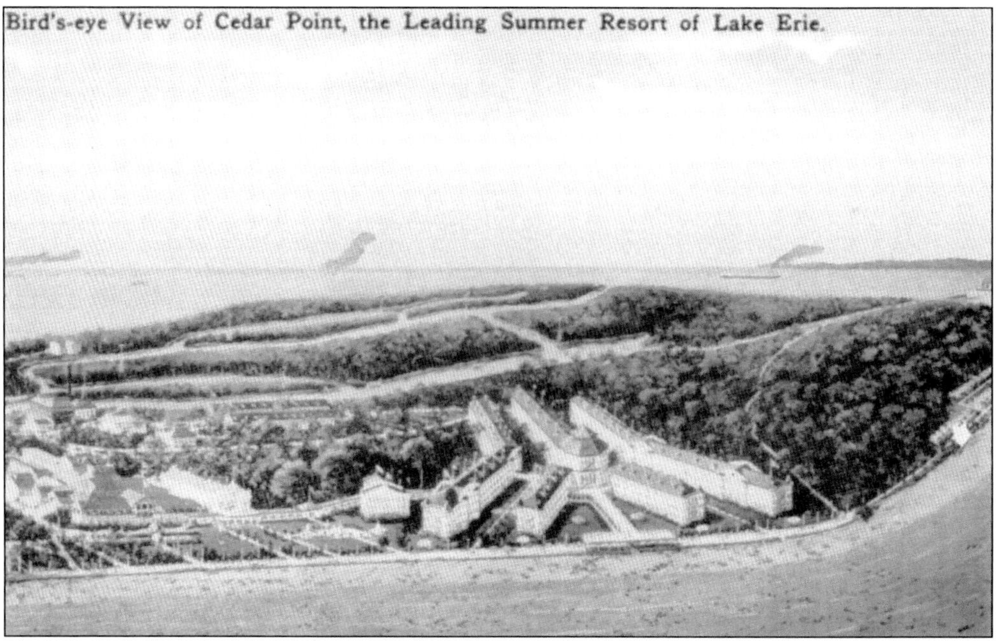

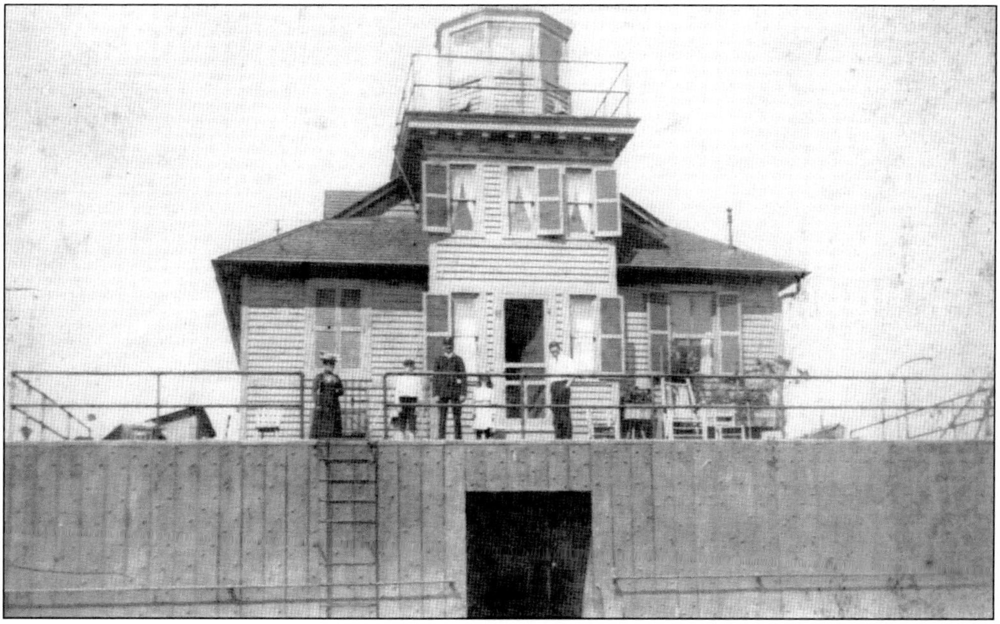

Water from 10 to 25 feet deep surrounded the Sandusky Bay Front Range Channel Lighthouse (pictured), but that did not prevent Frank J. Ritter and his wife from raising a boy and girl at the lighthouse. From 1896 to 1903, the family lived at the lighthouse from March 1 until December 20 each year. For Frank Ritter, taking the kids to school meant rowing them in his boat to Sandusky on Monday and picking them up on Friday. The children stayed with their grandparents during the school week. (SL.)

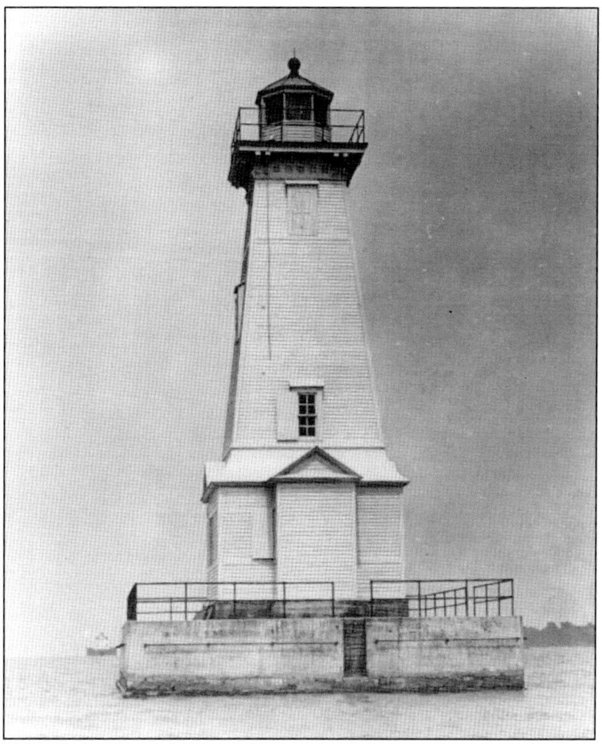

Frank J. Ritter first took charge of the range light at Johnson's Island in Sandusky Bay. Then he transferred to Cedar Point where he served for 37 years, retiring in 1929. He rowed or sailed his boat to outer and inner range lights, beacon lights, and other lights every day, filling them with coal oil and trimming the wicks. Electricity made the job easier. The Sandusky Bay Rear Range Channel Light was built in 1896, the beacon rising 250 feet to line up with the Sandusky Bay Front Range Channel Lighthouse, which was occupied by Ritter and family. (SL.)

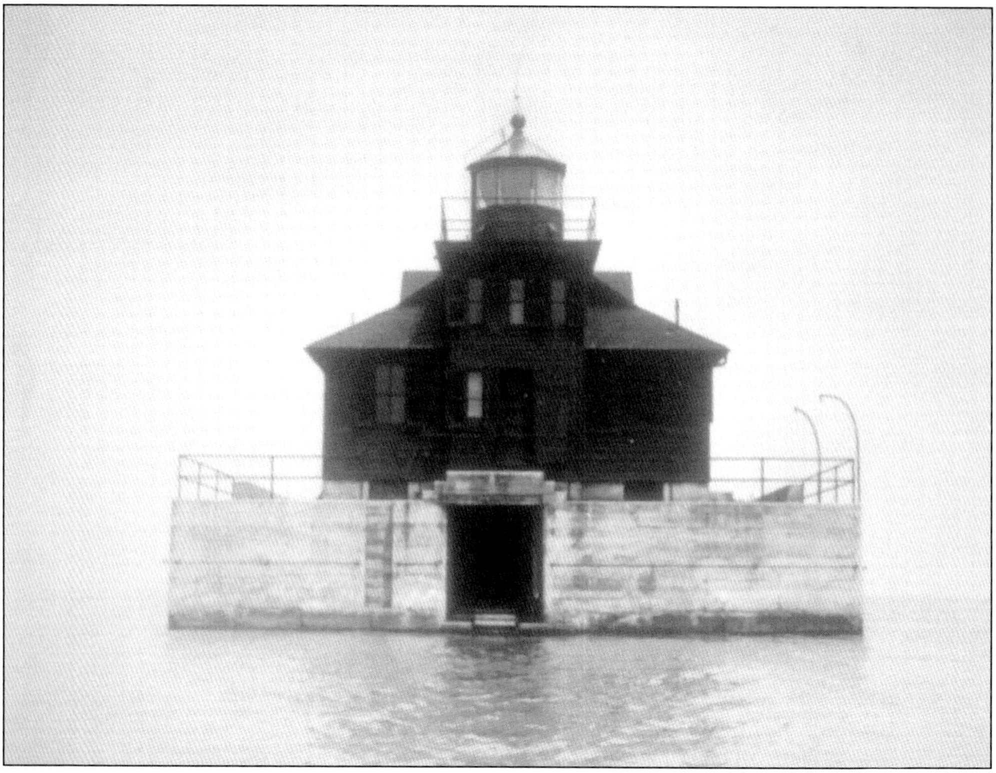

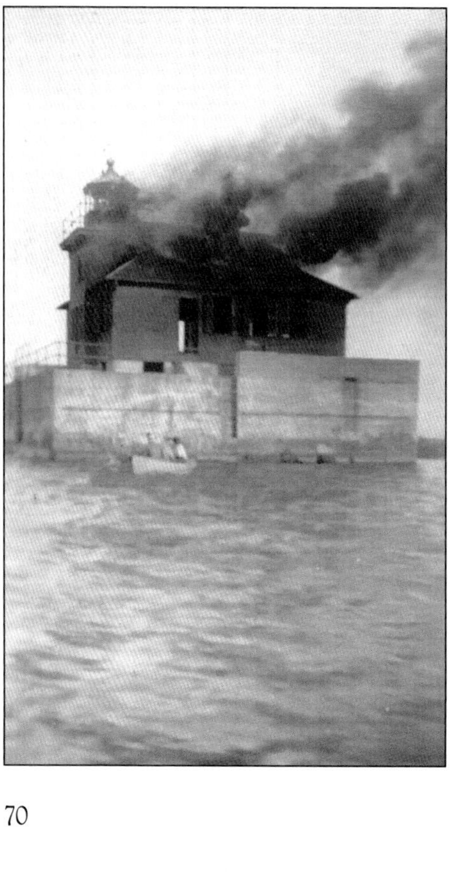

Secrets in the construction of the 1895 Sandusky Bay Front Range Channel Lighthouse reveal a different era with different standards. An article from 1895 reports how well water will come from Sandusky Bay and not too far distant a sewage pipe will descend into the bay. (NARA.)

The Sandusky Bay Front Range Channel Lighthouse burns in 1926. A pole with an electric light replaced it. (SL.)

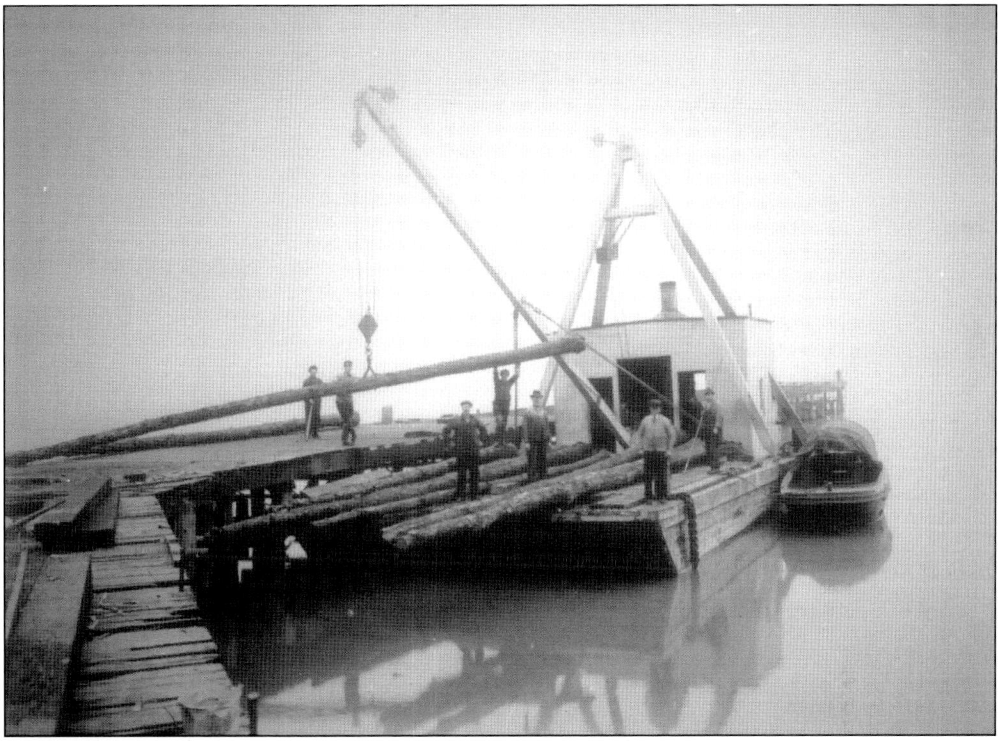

The Cedar Point Depot and wharf on Sandusky Bay are pictured in 1904. (NARA.)

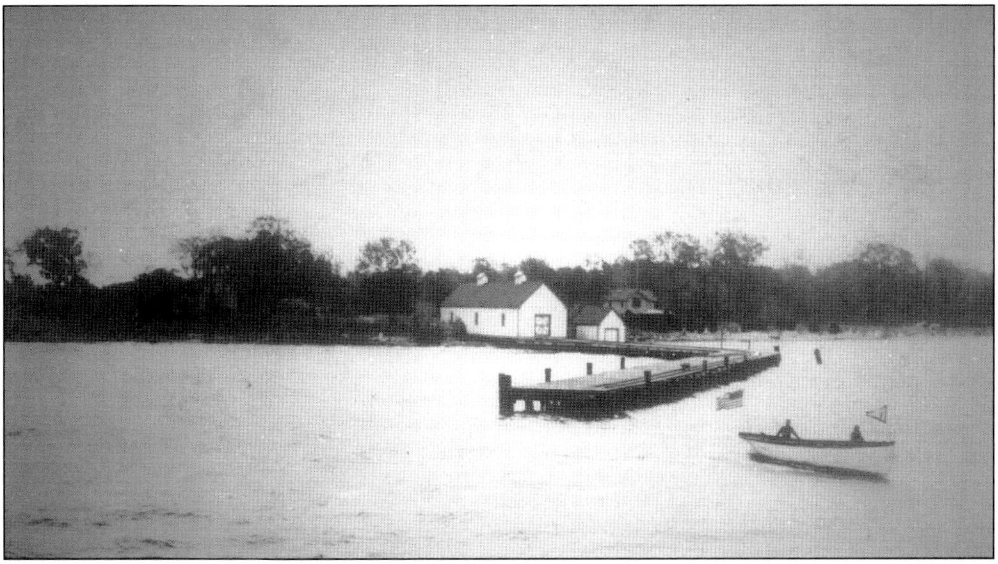

A lighthouse keeper, possibly Frank J. Ritter, is rowing the boat from the depot. Ritter saved many lives over the years. For example, two vessels were caught in a storm near the east end of Kelleys Island en route from Cleveland to Detroit. The ships began to sink, and the occupants were sending distress flares. Ritter saw the flares, lowered his lifeboat from the Front Range Lighthouse, and rowed to the Marblehead Life-Saving Station to notify the lifesavers, who hurried to the scene behind Kelleys Island and rescued 35 men and one woman. There were no telephones at that time. (NARA.)

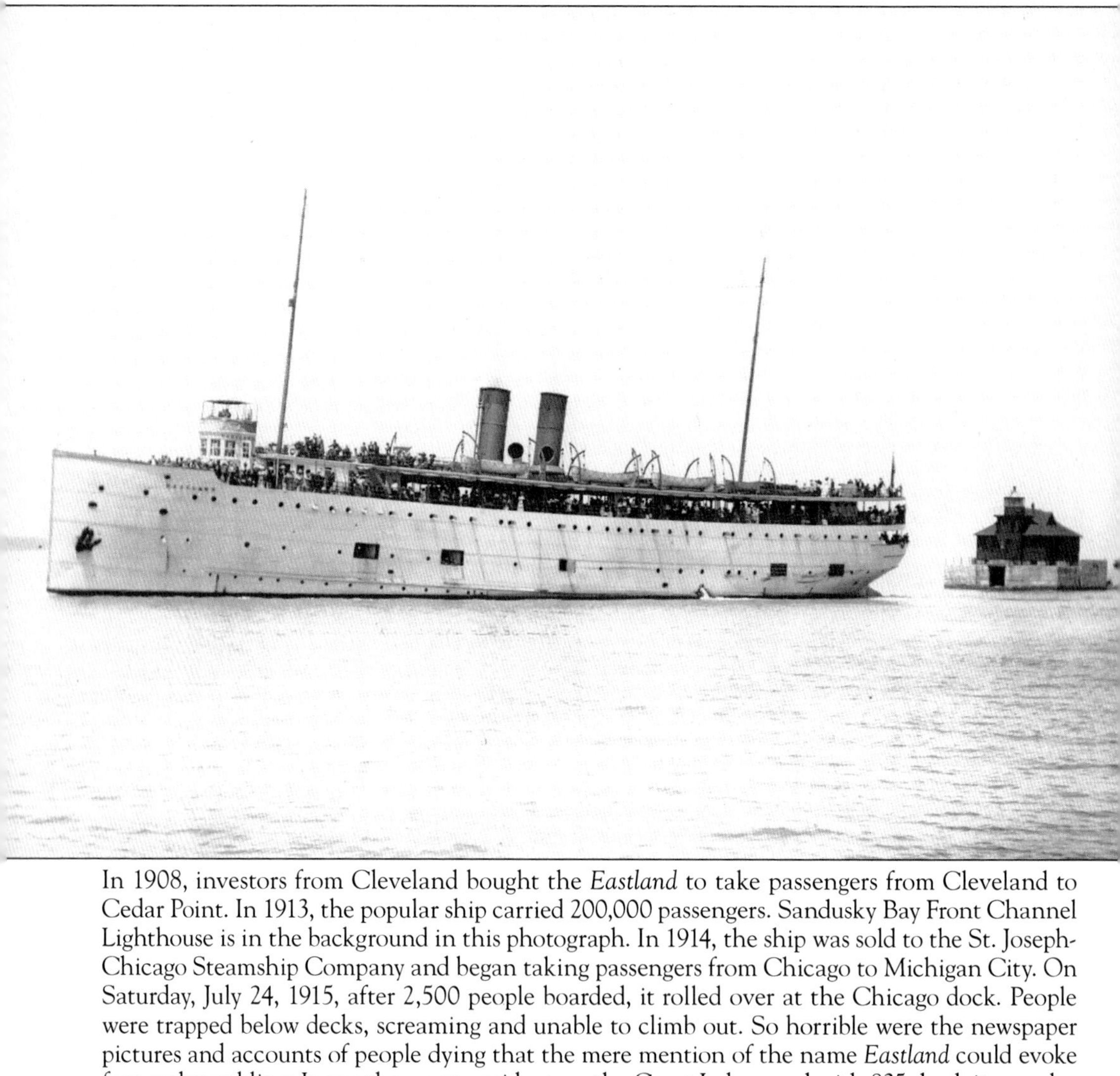

In 1908, investors from Cleveland bought the *Eastland* to take passengers from Cleveland to Cedar Point. In 1913, the popular ship carried 200,000 passengers. Sandusky Bay Front Channel Lighthouse is in the background in this photograph. In 1914, the ship was sold to the St. Joseph-Chicago Steamship Company and began taking passengers from Chicago to Michigan City. On Saturday, July 24, 1915, after 2,500 people boarded, it rolled over at the Chicago dock. People were trapped below decks, screaming and unable to climb out. So horrible were the newspaper pictures and accounts of people dying that the mere mention of the name *Eastland* could evoke fear and trembling. It was the worst accident on the Great Lakes, and with 835 dead, it was also the largest loss of life. (SL.)

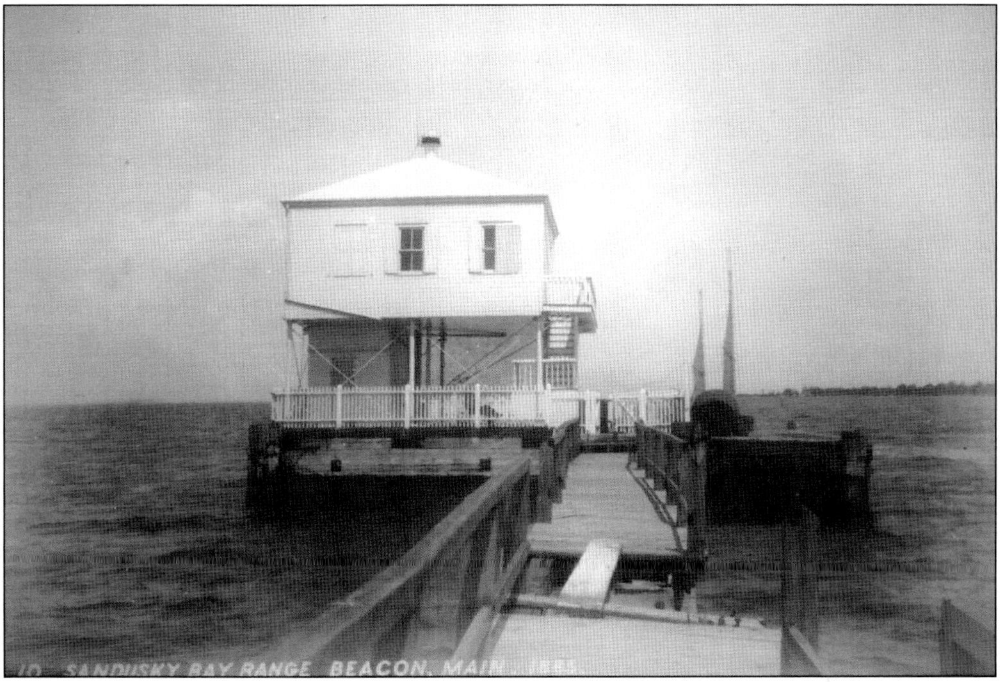

Pictured above is the Sandusky Bay Main Range Beacon in 1885. The catwalk looks a bit tricky with its single wooden plank. The Sandusky Bay West Range Beacon is in the photograph below. (Both, NARA.)

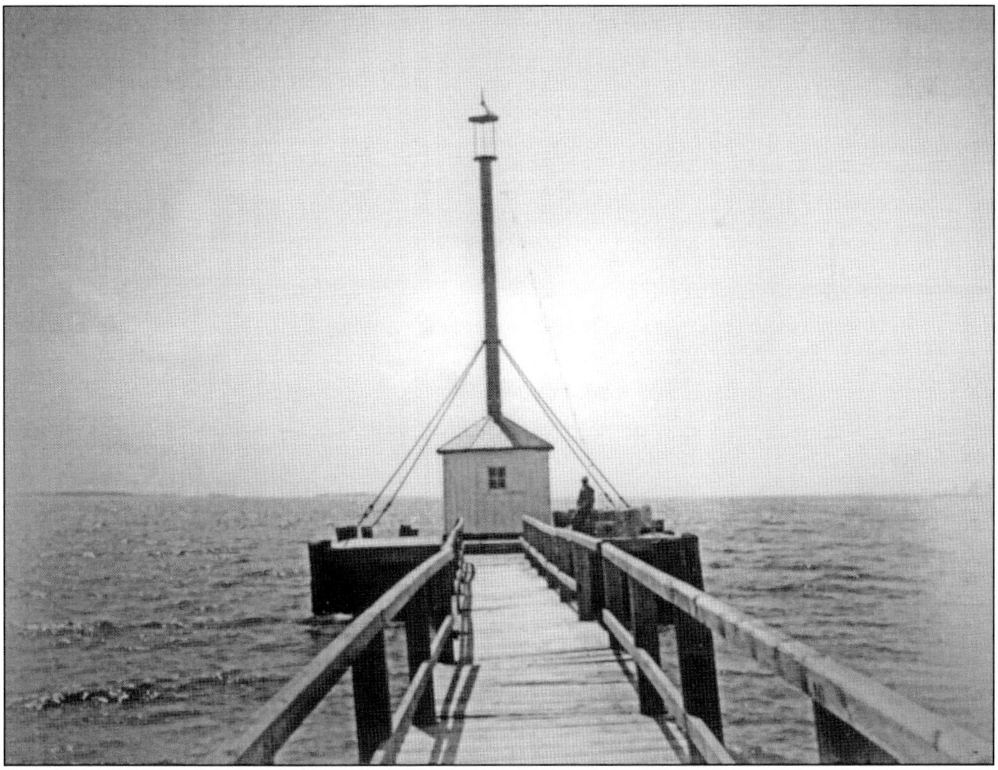

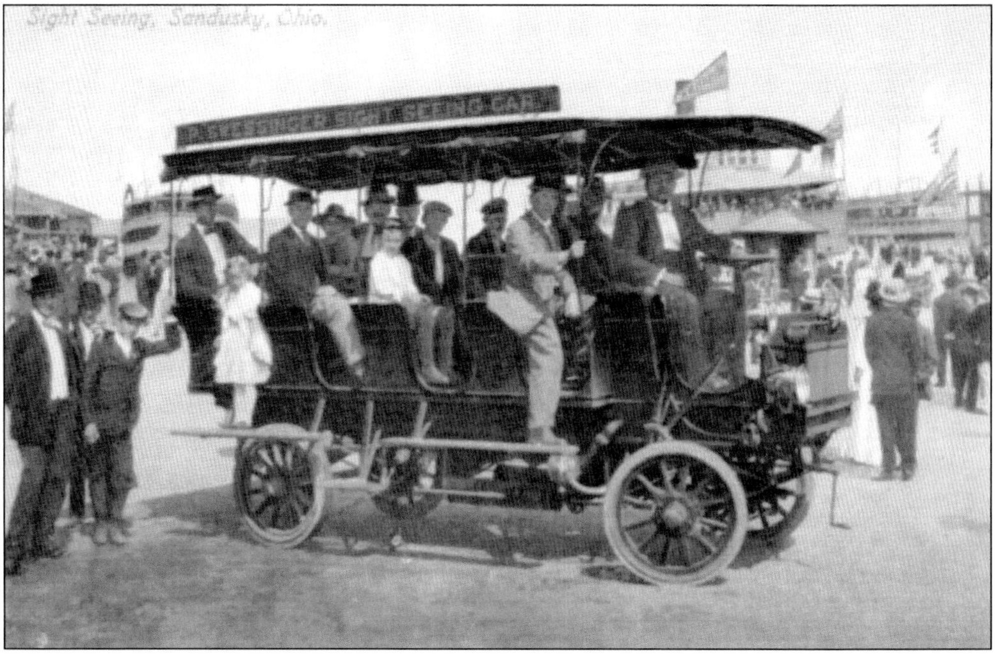

In 1911, a sightseeing bus at Sandusky takes people to the Cedar Point boats. (AC.)

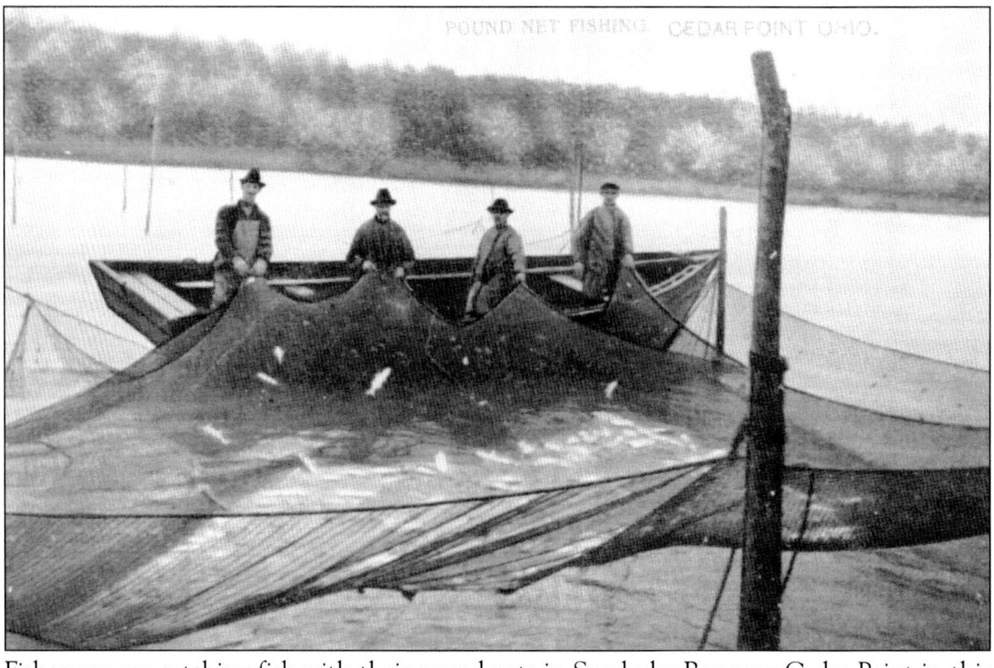

Fishermen are catching fish with their pound nets in Sandusky Bay near Cedar Point in this photograph from 1908. This type of fishing is now illegal. (AC.)

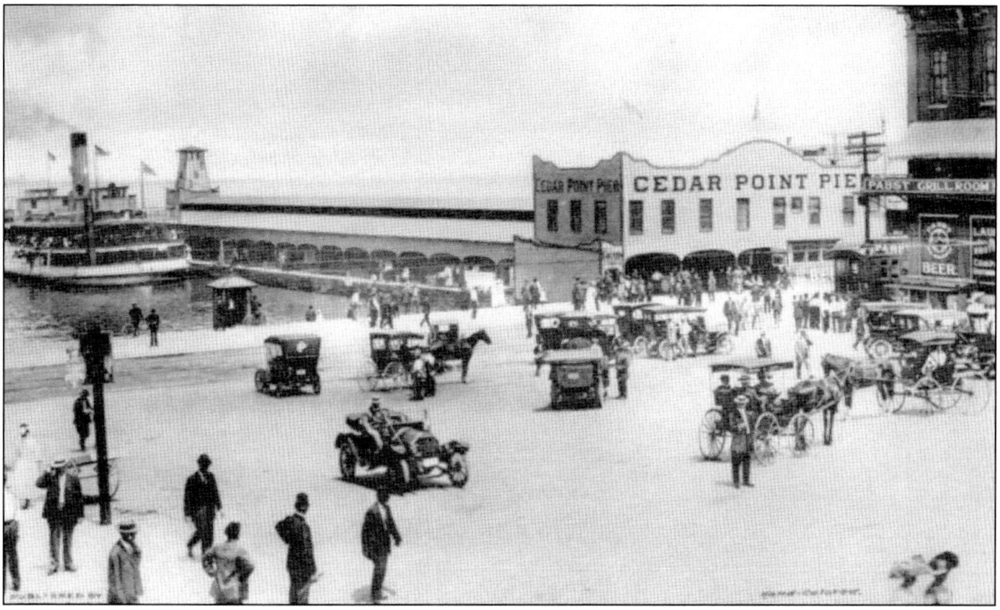

The reservations manager at the Breakers Hotel at Cedar Point was on the G.A. *Boeckling* for its 4:30 p.m. trip to Sandusky on June 28, 1924. While waiting on the boat and wondering why it was not leaving on time, he watched the sky grow dark and felt the wind increase. A whirling funnel cloud passed to the south. Then, he says, the captain came aboard, started the engines, and the boat left. When they approached Sandusky, they saw the effects of the tornado. The Cedar Point building pictured, the old yacht club next to it, and other stone buildings on the street were gone. A boat was sunk at the pier, its upper deck showing. The tornado missed Cedar Point Park, but it destroyed several homes on the causeway. (AC.)

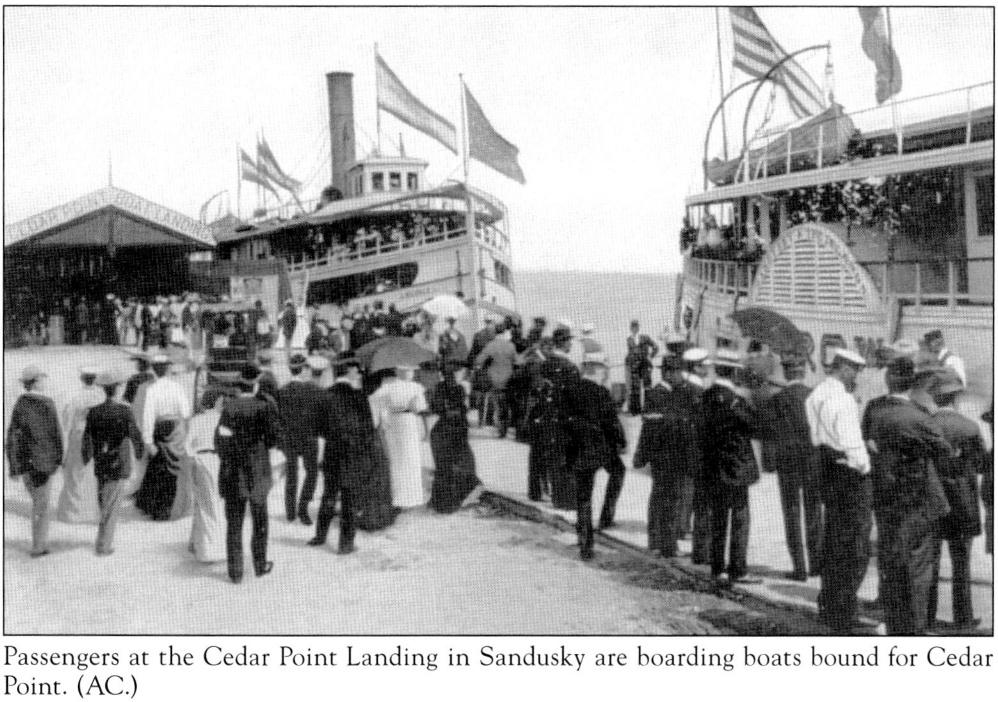

Passengers at the Cedar Point Landing in Sandusky are boarding boats bound for Cedar Point. (AC.)

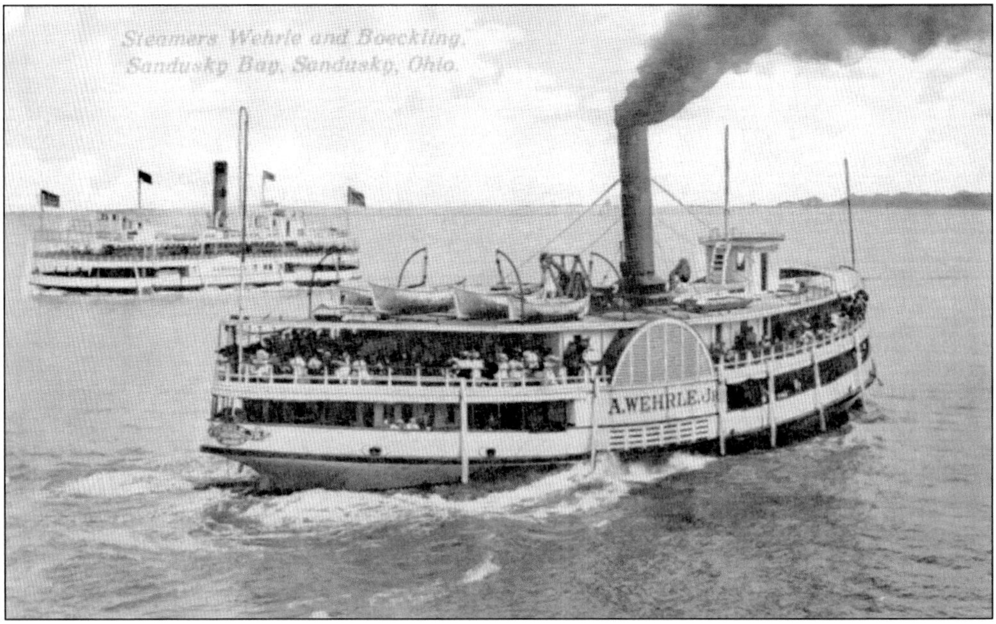

A memory-maker, the G.A. *Boeckling* steamship (background) was a double-ended ferry, meaning that it could be operated from either end and need not be turned around before heading back to the other shore. The center floor on the lower deck was cut away to reveal the shiny pistons of the engine, a feature that fascinated both children and adults alike. Memories of these silver, pulsating rods and pistons could last a lifetime. It ran from June 27, 1909, until 1952. The *A. Wehrle, Jr.*, bound for Cedar Point, is in the foreground. (AC.)

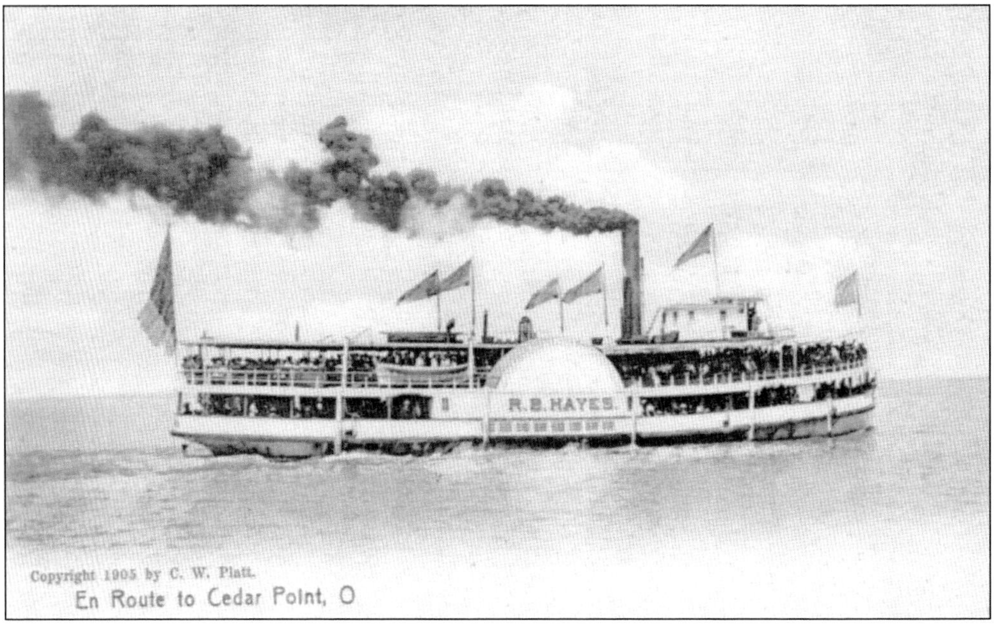

The *R.B. Hayes* was one of the first steamboats to take passengers from Sandusky to Cedar Point. (AC.)

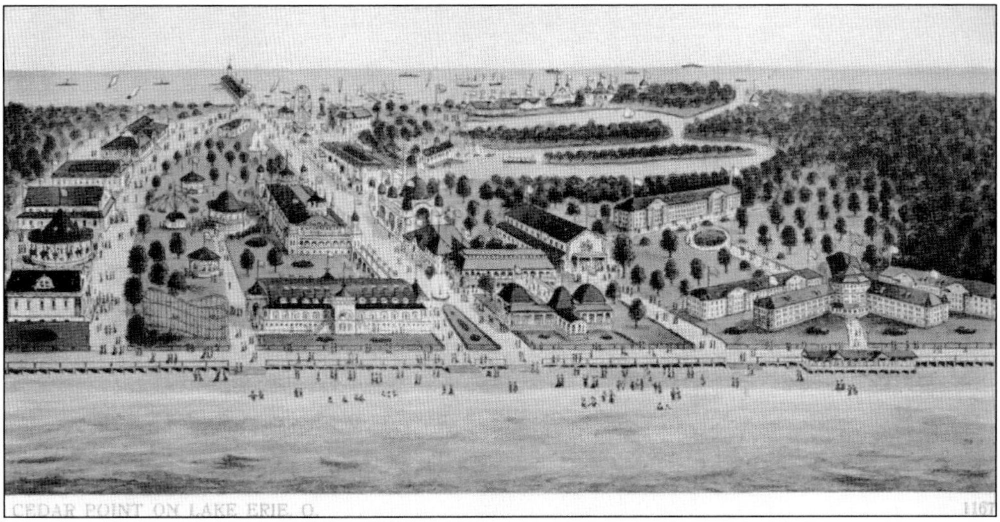

An aerial view of Cedar Point is depicted in this 1906 drawing. (AC.)

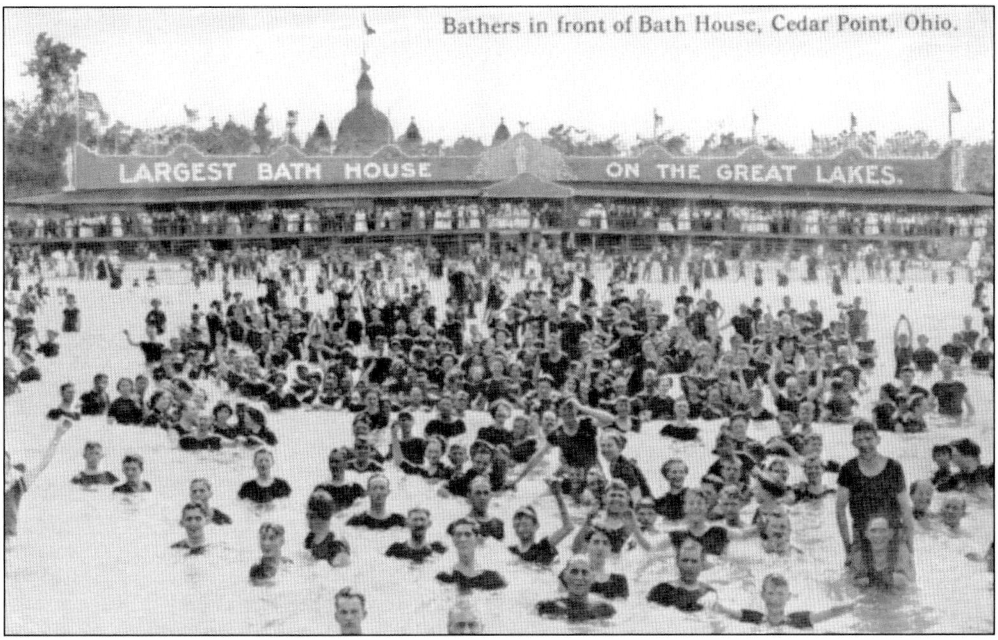

Sightseers and swimmers are pictured in front of a Cedar Point bathhouse in 1905. (AC.)

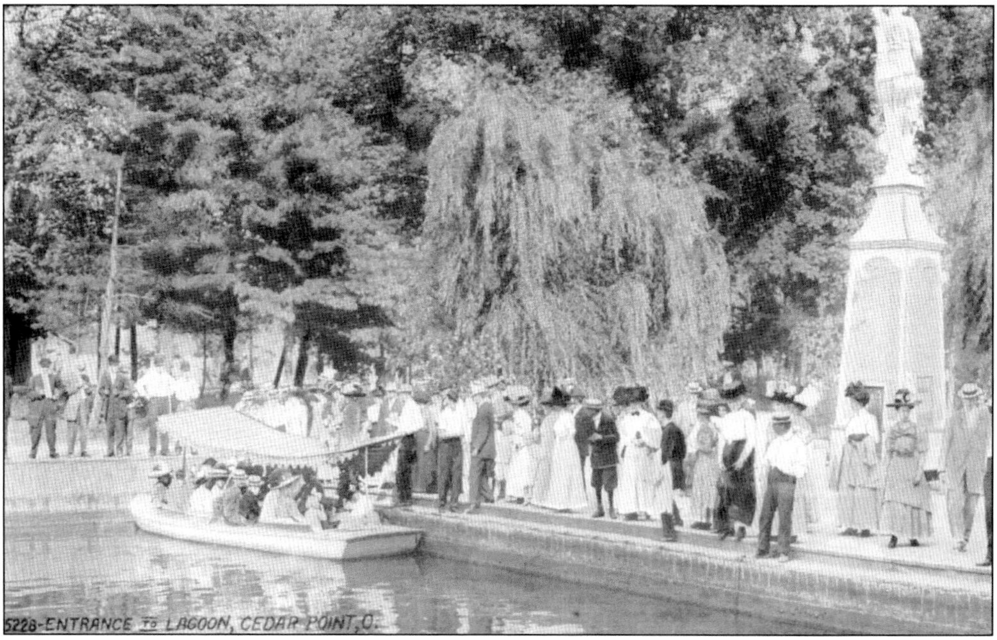

In 1904, the Detroit Dredging Company dug four miles of lagoons. They were 10 feet deep and 60 to 150 feet wide. The effort cost $25,450 and eliminated the mosquito-infested swamps. The company also dredged an opening to the bay near the lighthouse. (AC.)

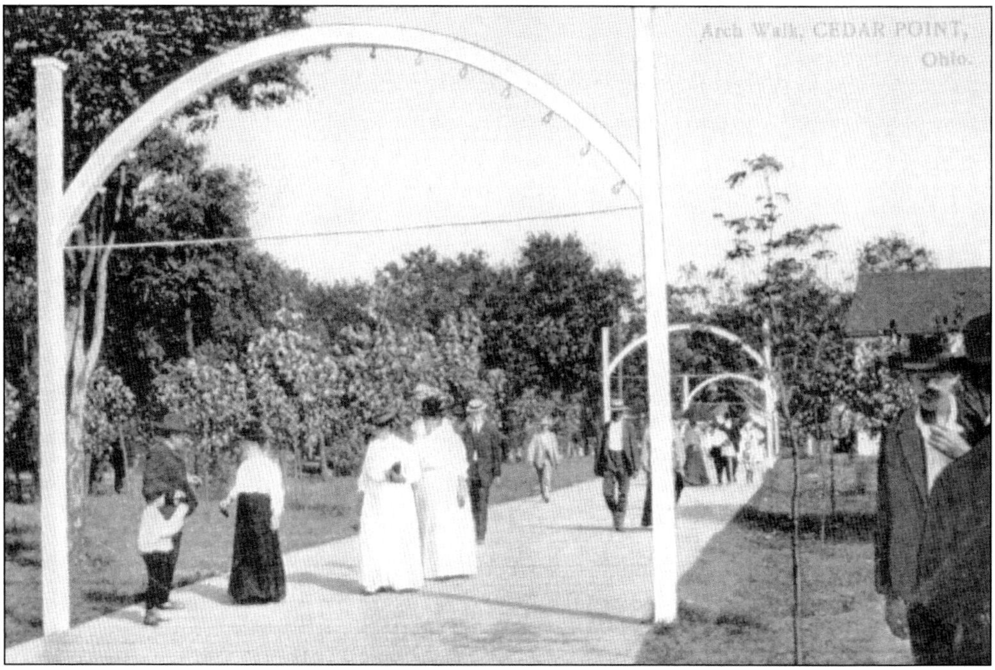

People are out for a walk on the famous arch walk at Cedar Point in this photograph from 1908. (AC.)

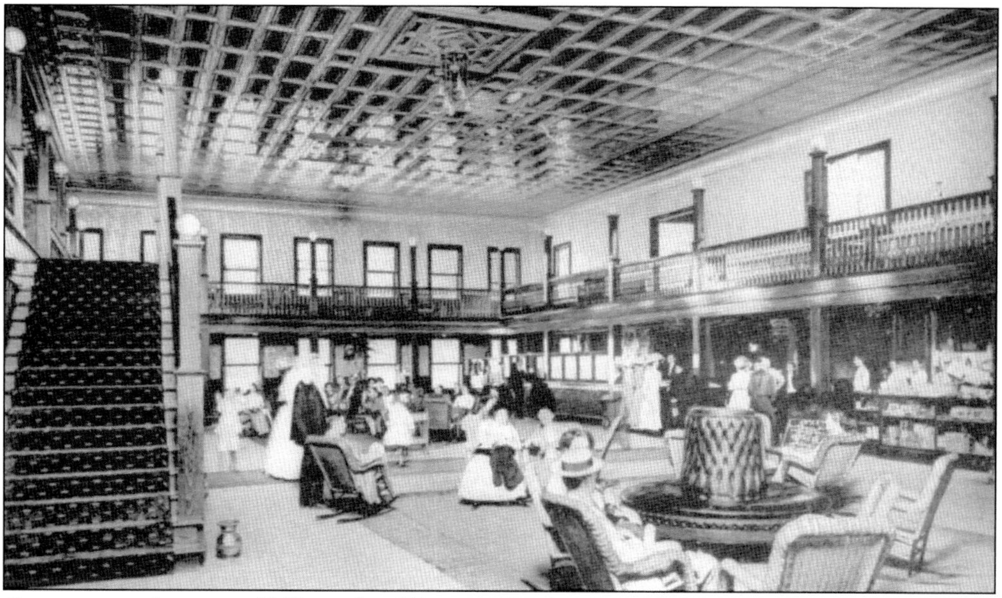

Construction began in 1902 on the 650-room Breakers Hotel, designed by Knox & Elliott of Cleveland. By the 1903 season, tourists were staying at the hotel and enjoying the beach. It was built by John and George Beir of Sandusky. Hotel rates for the Breakers were as follows: a single, per week, was $5 to $7; a double, per week, was $7.50 to $10; the day rates were $1 to $2. Hotel rates at the White House and Bay Shore Hotels were as follows: a single, per week, was $3.50 to $5; a double, per week, was $5 to $7; the day rates were $1 to $1.50. (AC.)

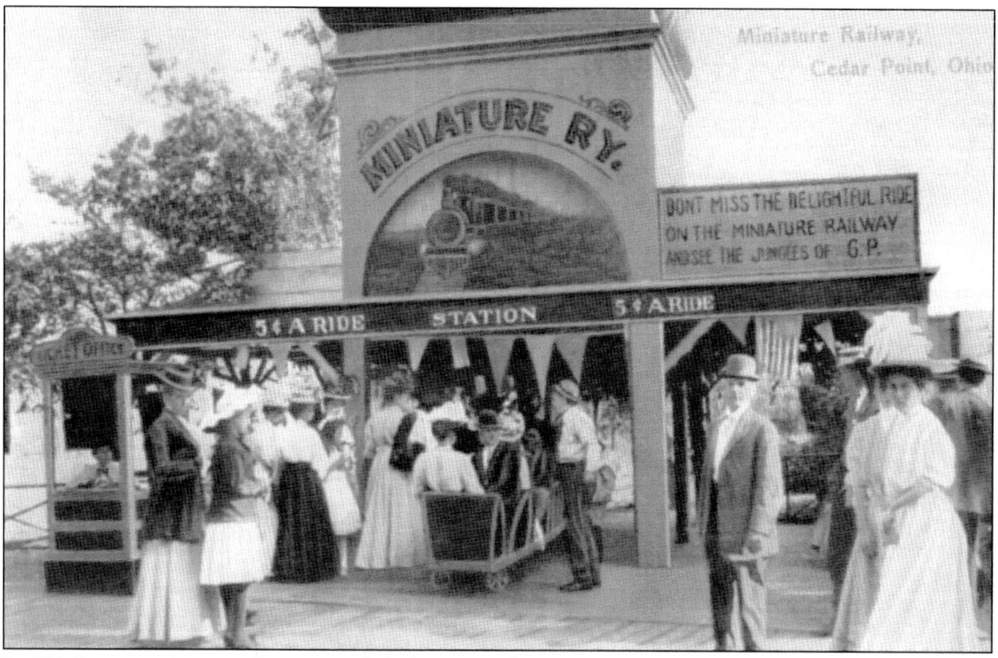

In 1906, a new electric plant provided electricity for Trip to Rockaway, House of Mirth, Chateau Alphonse, Auto Tour, Circle Swing, Electric Theatre, Illustrated Song Exhibition, Figure 8 Roller Toboggan, Miniature Railway (pictured), 12 bowling alleys, Box and Ball game, Penny Arcade, Shooting Gallery, a merry-go-round, and a skating rink, all at Cedar Point. (AC.)

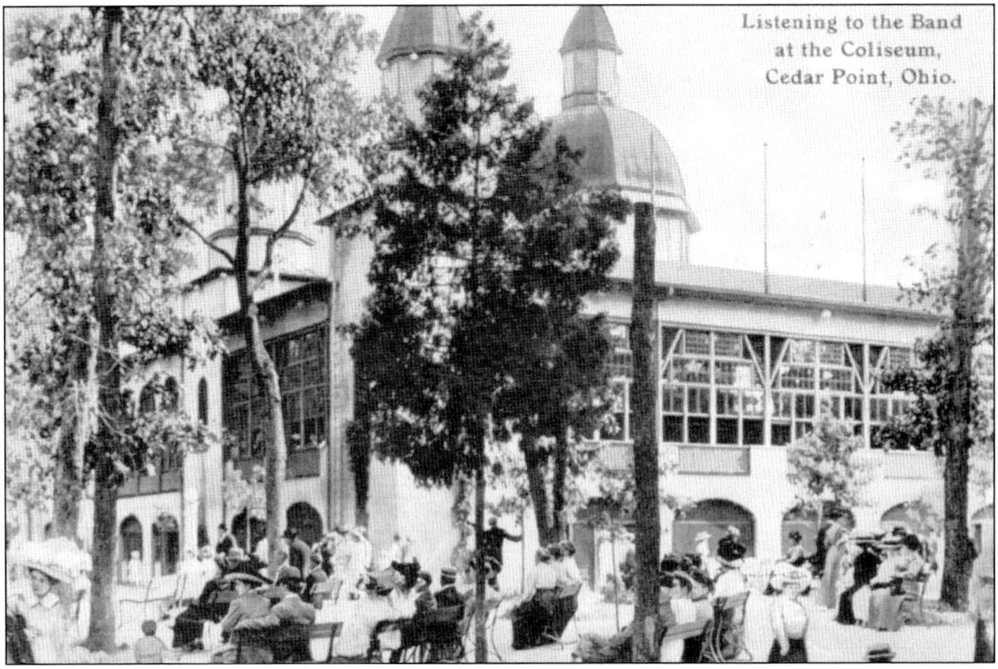

Built in 1905, this mammoth pavilion was known for years as the Coliseum. Pictured in 1911, it was 300 feet by 150 feet, with domes rising 40 feet higher than the Breakers Hotel. It had 90,000 combined square feet of floor space on the two levels. (AC.)

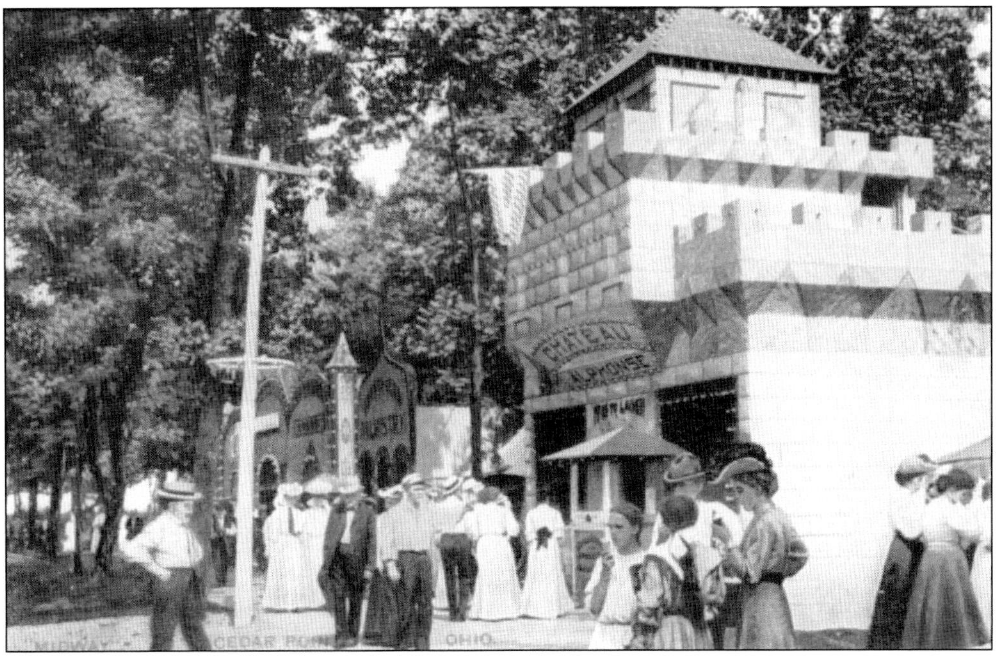

Chateau Alphonse is pictured here in 1915. (AC.)

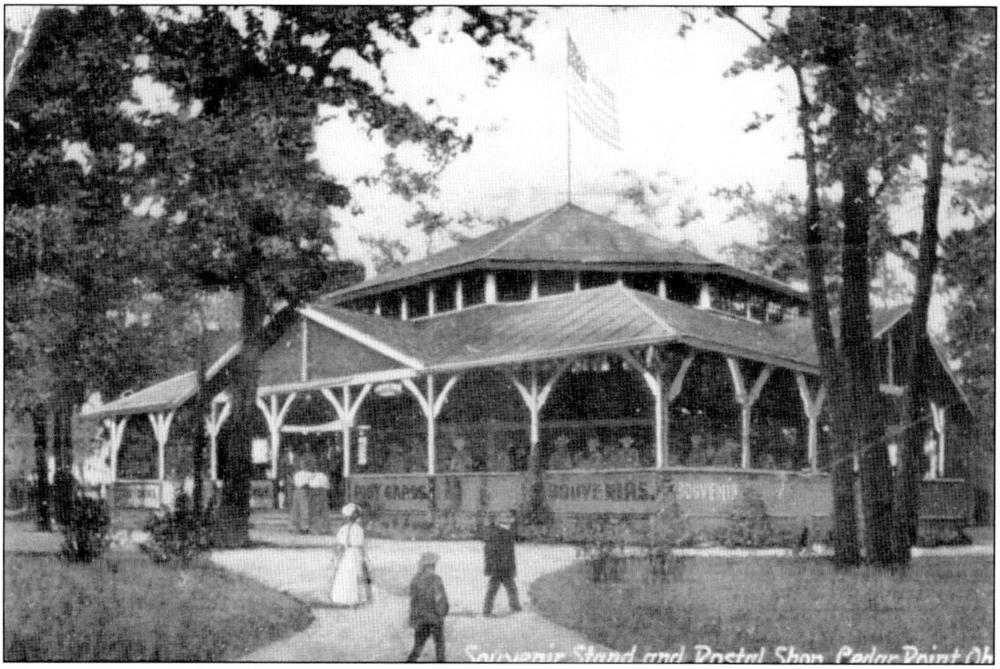

The souvenir stand and postal shop are shown around 1914. (AC.)

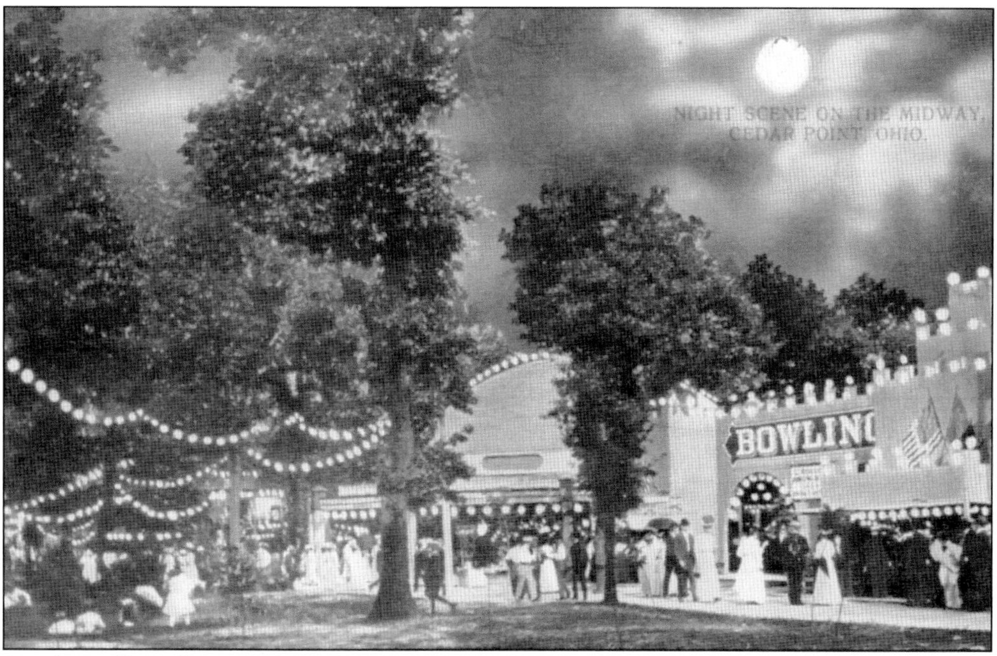

People stroll on the moonlit midway in 1910. (AC.)

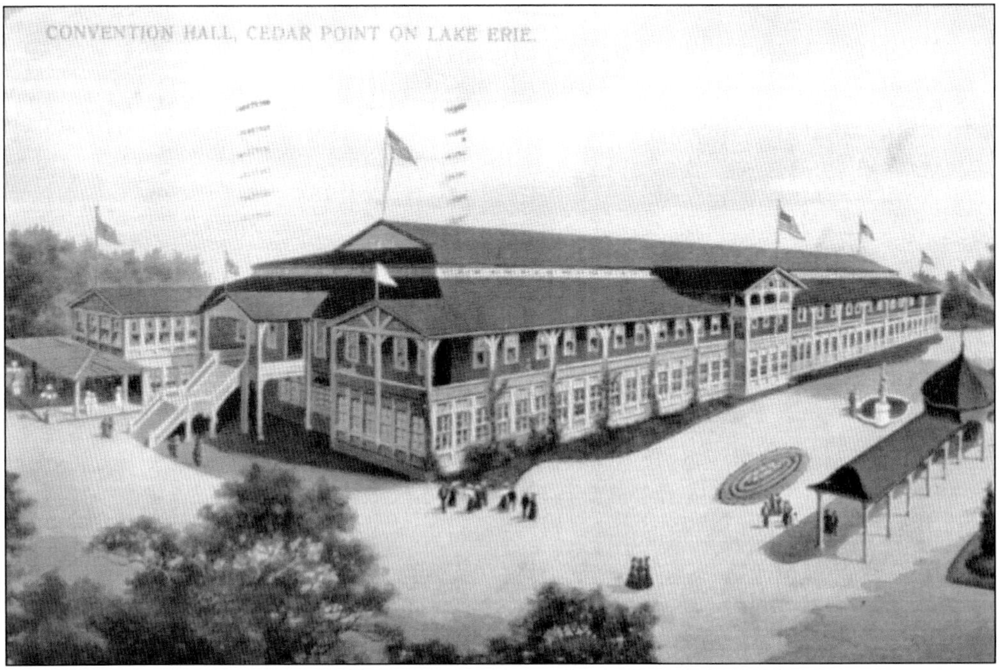

The Cedar Point Convention Hall was impressive in the early 1900s. (AC.)

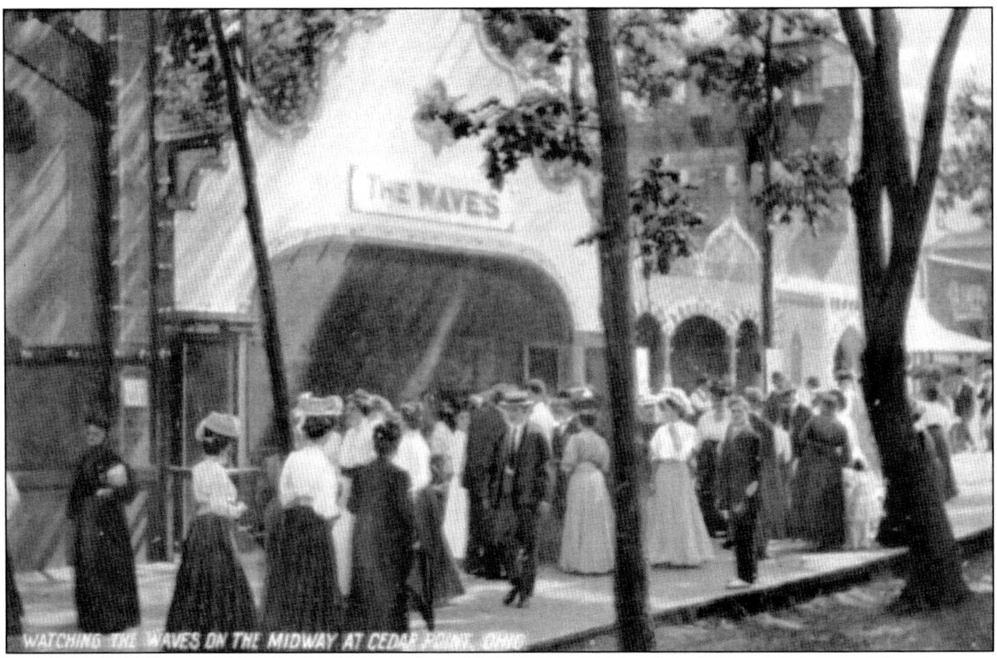

Tourists walk past the Waves, an attraction at Cedar Point in the early 1900s. (AC.)

Seven

MYSTERY OF THE LOST LIGHTHOUSE

At the onset of the Depression in 1929, the 1877 Vermilion Lighthouse began leaning toward the water after a bad Lake Erie ice storm removed its foundation. The Buffalo Corps of Engineers was notified, but only days later, Vermilion residents awoke to discover that their lighthouse was gone. People responsible for the structure said it sank to the bottom of the lake. Locals were devastated that their beautiful lighthouse had disappeared forever, but Vermilion residents never gave up hope that someday they might find their beloved lighthouse.

Olin W. Stevens was the lighthouse keeper at Vermilion prior to 1929. When he died in 1994, he left his grandson an old trunk full of memorabilia. In the trunk was a 1937 newspaper clipping from Jefferson County, New York, welcoming Stevens as the new lighthouse keeper for Charity Light. Part of the article reads, "Altho this is his first duty on Lake Ontario, Charity Shoal Light is an old friend. The tower was under Stevens's charge at Vermilion. Victim of an ice shove, it was salvaged and taken to Buffalo, where it was assigned to Charity."

The grandson of Olin Stevens visited the Vermilion Museum shortly after discovering the article in the trunk to inform people in the town about what he had found. And after years of disappointment, museum members were given new hope that the mystery might be solved. Excited museum members drove to Tibbetts Point, New York, and chartered a boat to the isolated lighthouse. East Charity Shoal Lighthouse sits alone, five miles from shore, over a dangerous, rocky shoal near the shipping lane. Years ago, a passing ship had rammed the original Vermilion Lighthouse, and repair work left an identifying scar on the inside of the lighthouse. Museum members entered the lighthouse, and there was the telltale scar that proved it could only be the Vermilion Light.

A full 65 years later, the secret journey of the traveling lighthouse was revealed. Leading a useful life, the structure was certainly special, having the rare distinction of flashing its beacon and warning ships and seafarers on two of the Great Lakes.

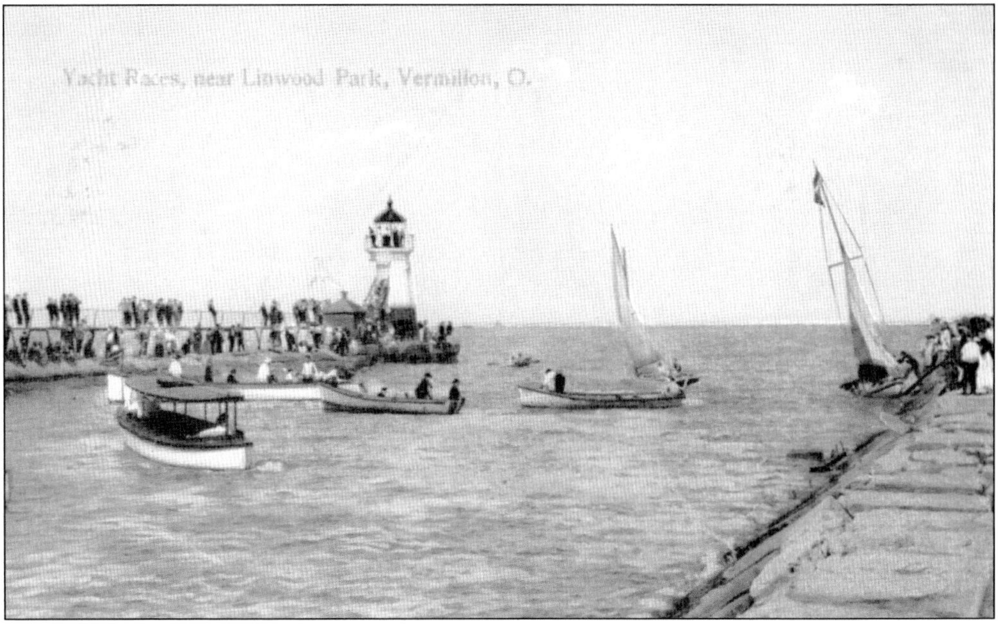

With the lighthouse to guide the way (pictured), Vermilion was the perfect place for bootleggers during Prohibition. Having a good harbor with little activity and only one policeman, one night watchman, and about 1,500 residents, Vermilion was an obvious choice for landings to store bootlegged whiskey. At night, boats brought the illegal liquor up the river to be unloaded at farms. When this became risky, nightly rumrunners would have someone onshore light a fire on a beach or near a creek so the skipper could meet a rowboat or find his way into an inlet. Fishing boats brought cheap beer and speedboats brought whiskey from Leamington and Kingsville, Ontario, directly across Lake Erie. (Both, AC.)

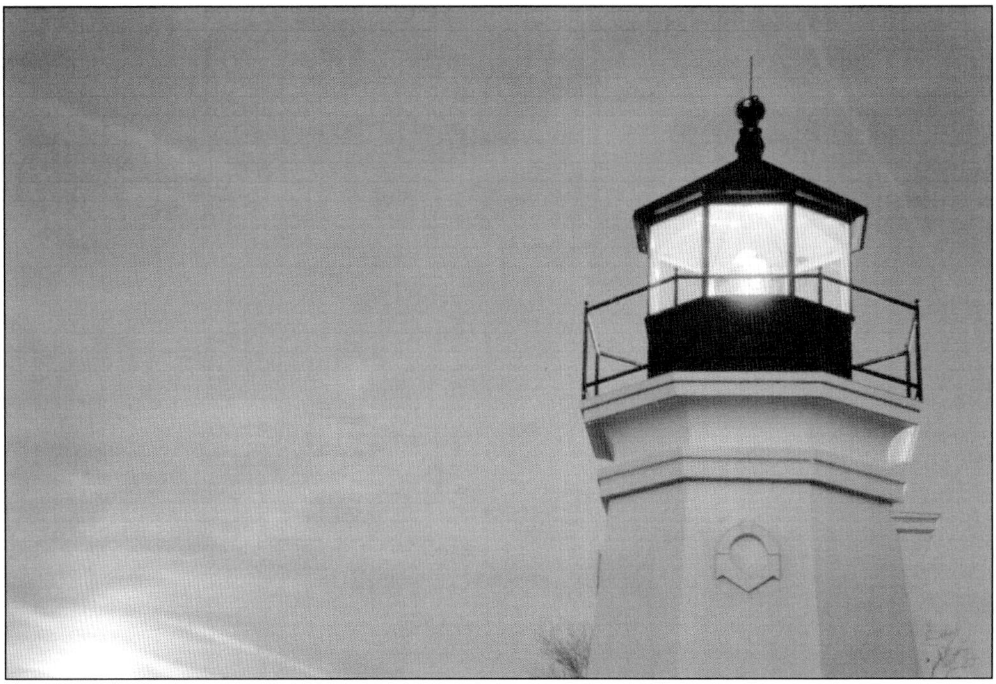

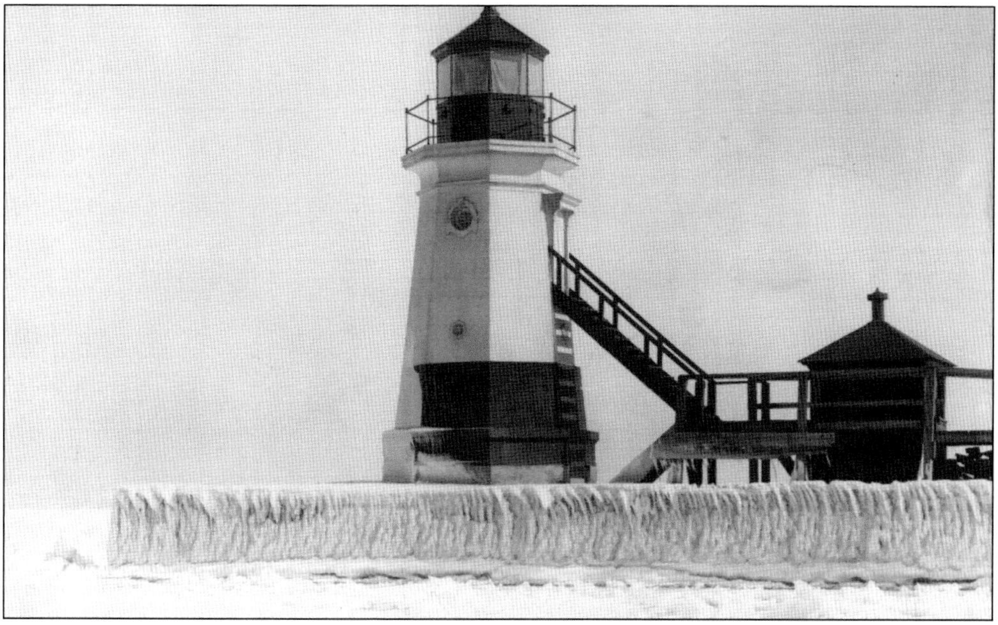

Many people wanted to make money fast during Prohibition. Old-timers said that nearly every barn near the lake in Vermilion was filled with whiskey from Canada. An icehouse that was normally used for storing fish in the summer was filled to the top with liquor and covered with insulation mats of sawdust and straw. While none of the fish companies in town was involved in rumrunning, the owners were not against renting their storage barns to bootleggers. Pictured in winter is the Vermilion Lighthouse of 1877 to 1929. (GLHS.)

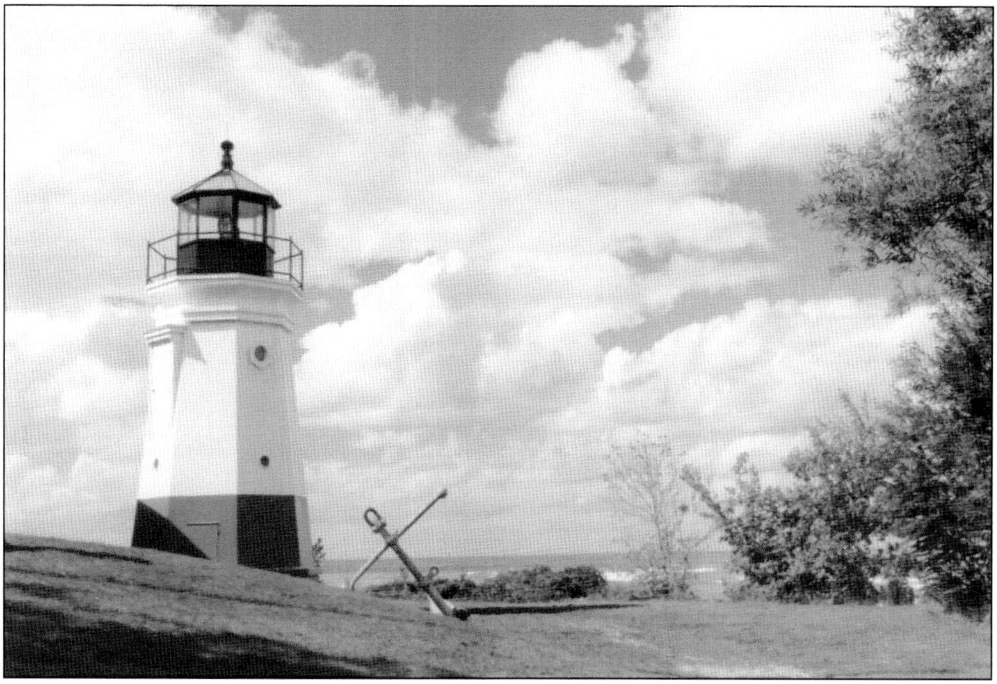

This replica of the Vermilion Lighthouse, made in 1991, sits near the Great Lakes Historical Society Museum, which will be moving to Toledo in 2012. (AC.)

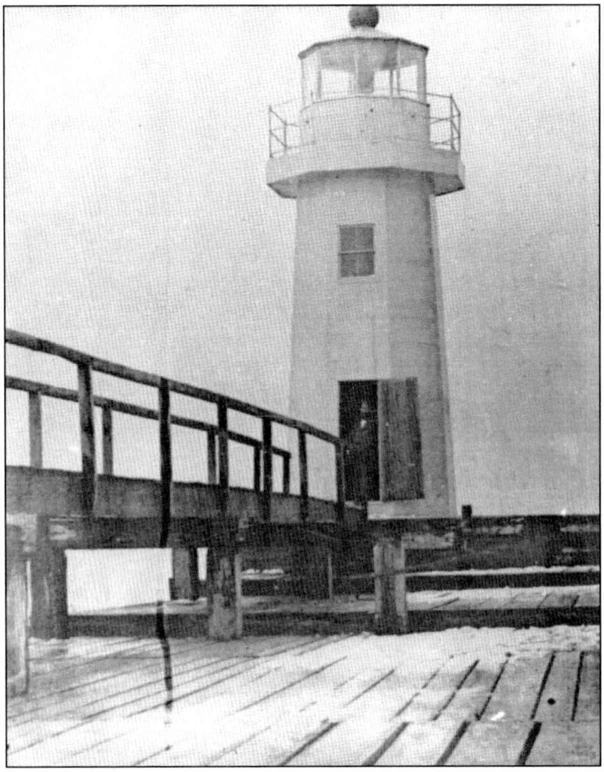

The first Vermilion Lighthouse was built in 1847 on the west pier of the Vermilion Harbor entrance. By an act of Congress in 1844, $3,000 was appropriated for its construction. The light was severely damaged by a spring storm in 1854, rebuilt, and rebuilt again in 1859. (GLHS.)

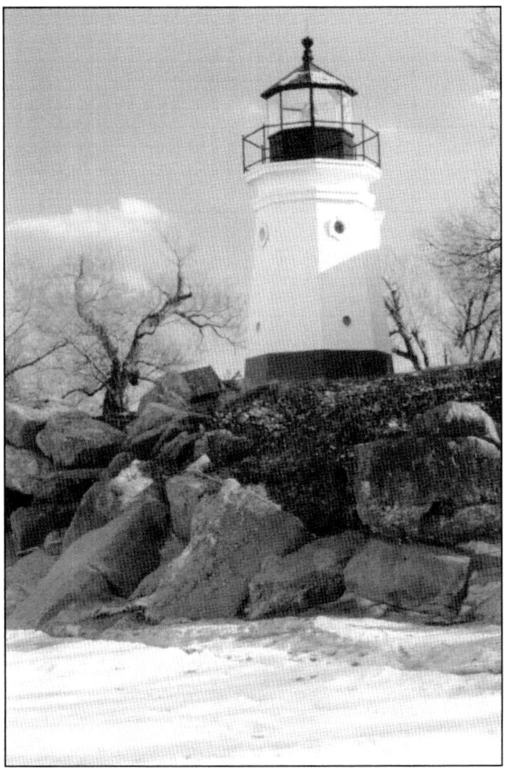

The Vermilion Lighthouse replica stands guard during the winter season. (AC.)

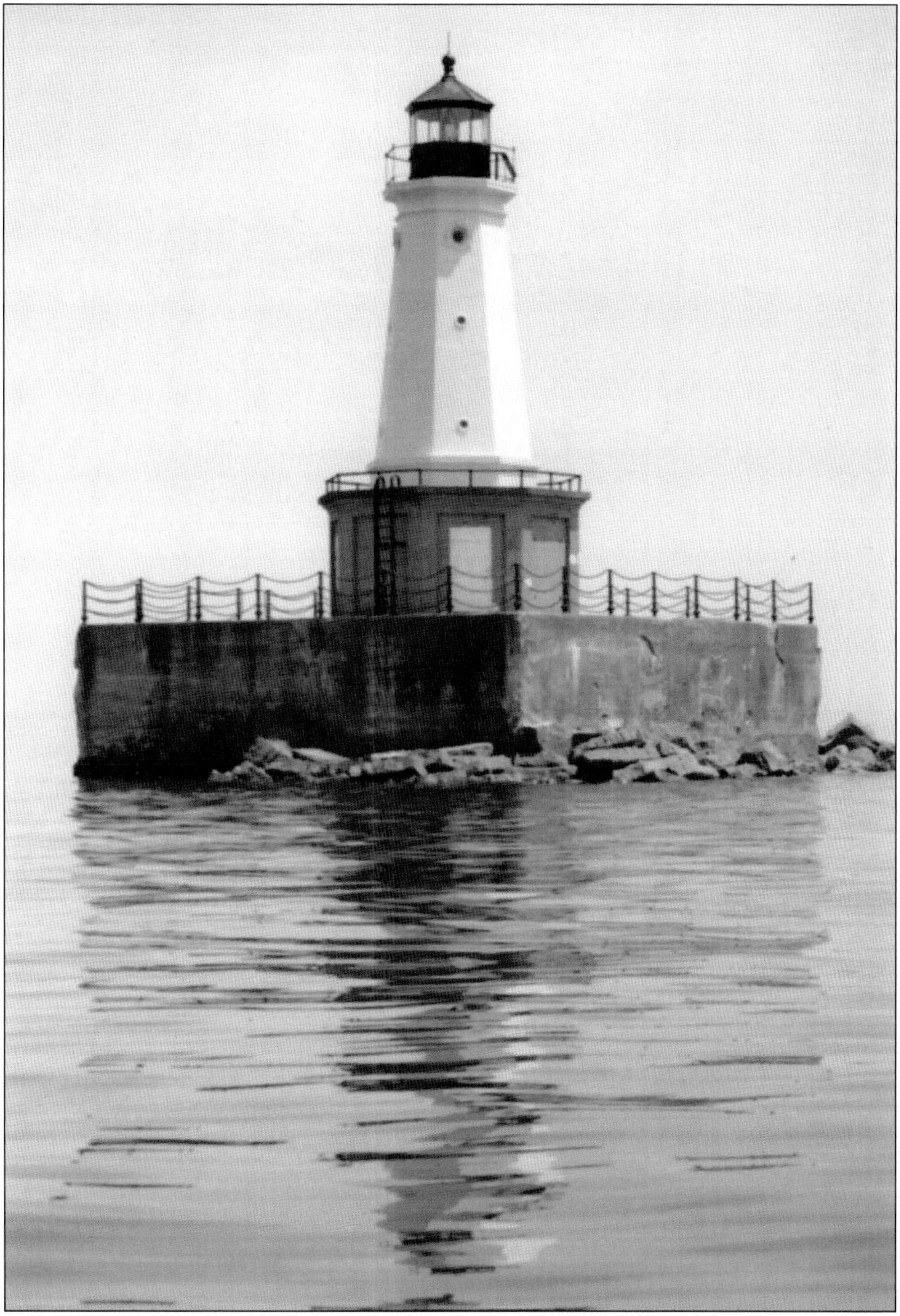

At the eastern end of Lake Ontario, the East Charity Shoal Lighthouse sits alone over a shallow reef near the middle of the lake. Only big freighters and seagulls see the lighthouse that was once in Vermilion. (AC.)

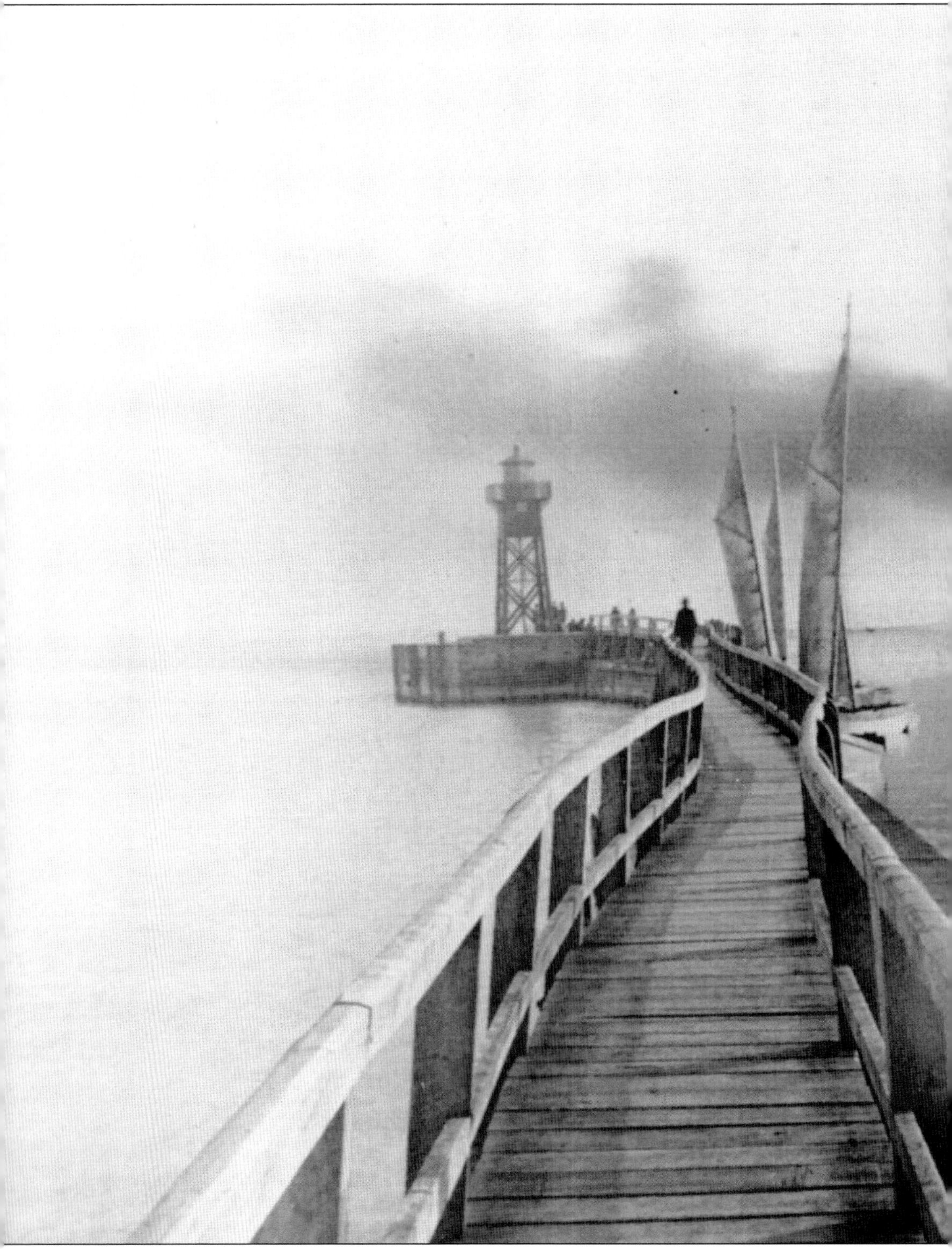

A steamer is pulled from a sandbar at the mouth of the Huron River by another steamer in this image from 1880. The old channel light and breakwall (breakwater) are on the left. The steamers

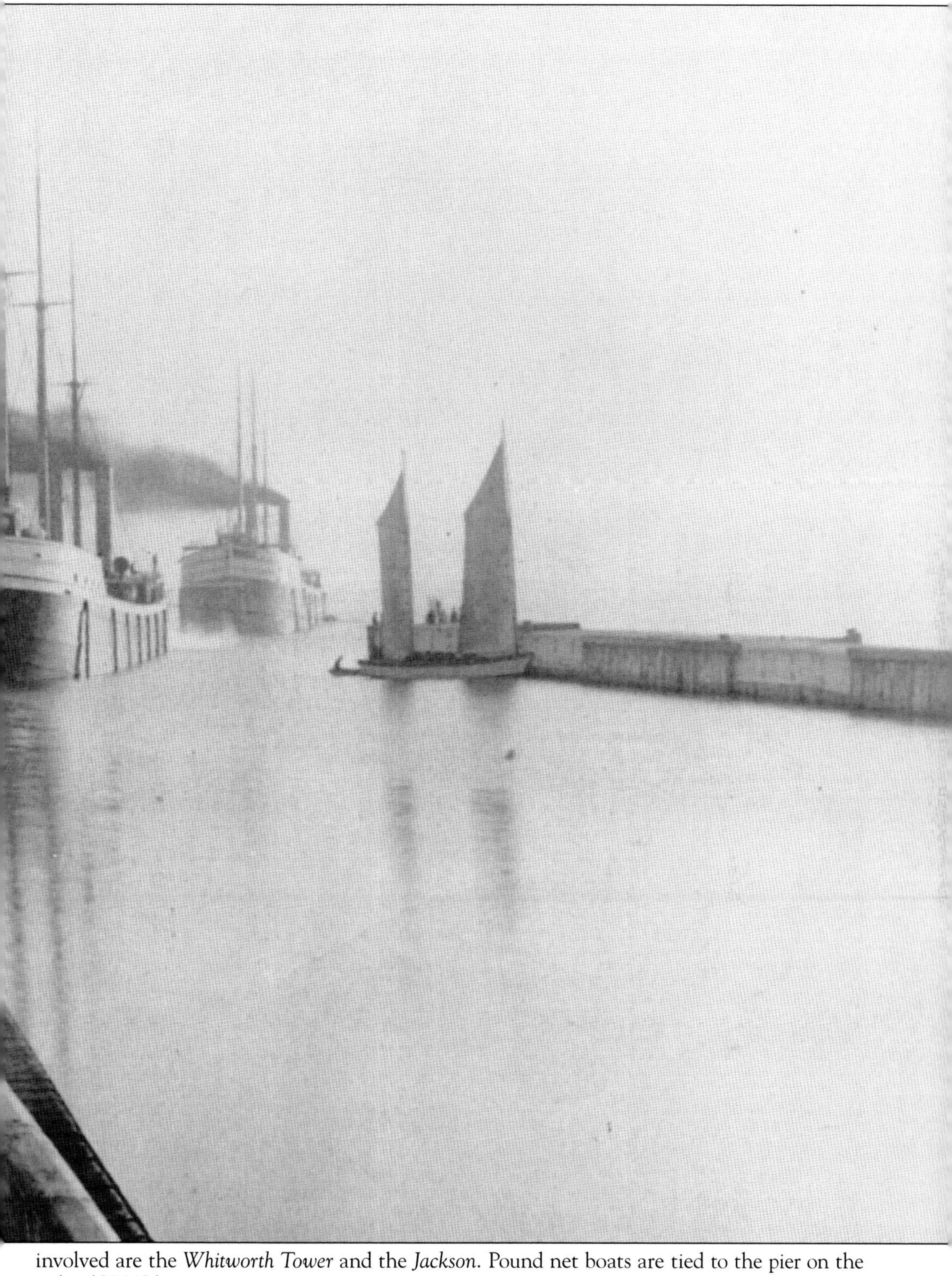

involved are the *Whitworth Tower* and the *Jackson*. Pound net boats are tied to the pier on the right. (GLHS.)

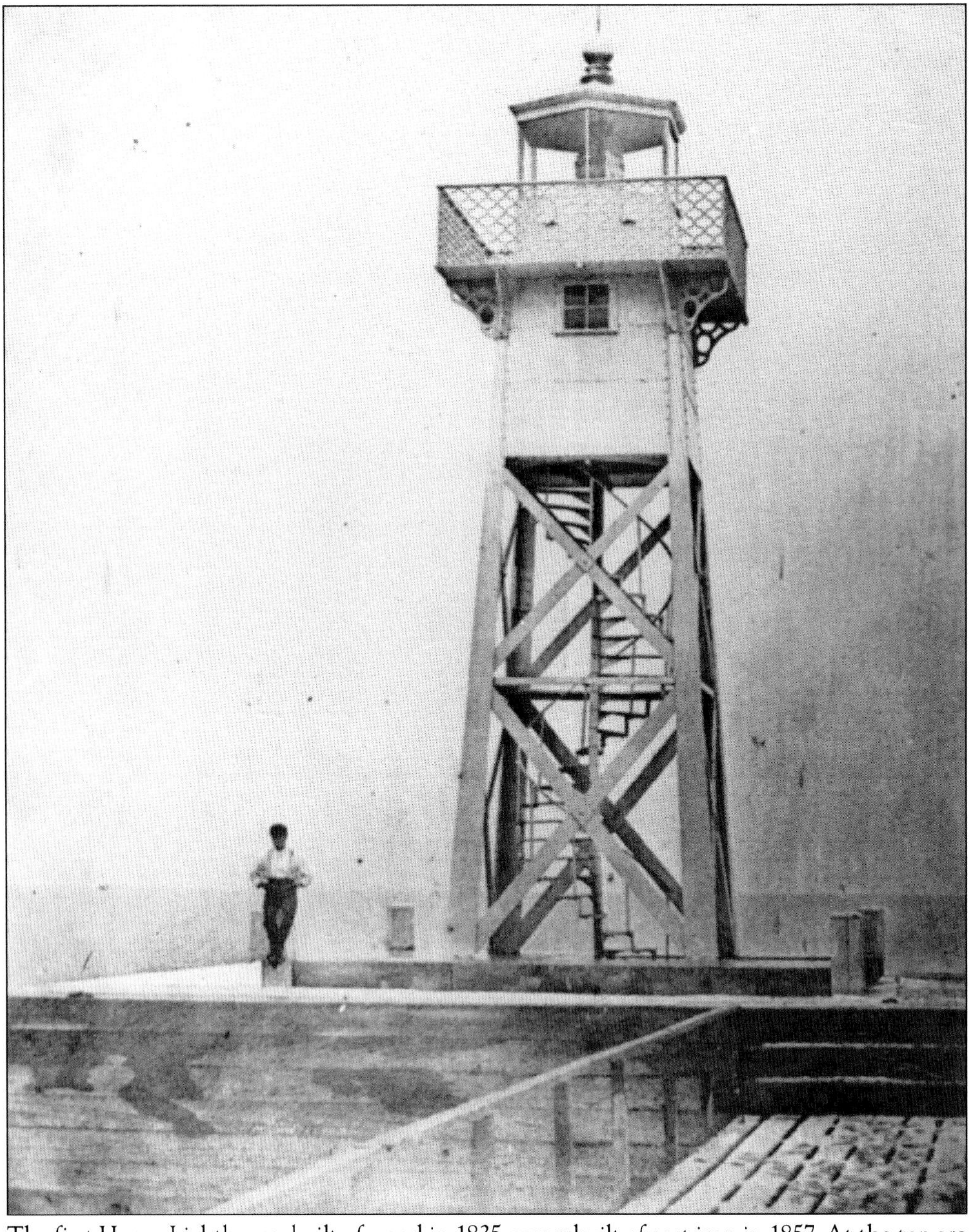

The first Huron Lighthouse, built of wood in 1835, was rebuilt of cast iron in 1857. At the top are the foghorn and light. Keepers kept eight oil lamps burning, a job requiring many trips up and down the stairs, which were doubtlessly precarious during a storm. The Huron Harbor project initiated in the mid-1820s included the completion of two piers extending 1,552 feet and 1,560 feet into the lake and standing 140 feet apart at the entrance and the building of a lighthouse at a cost of $2,600. The removal of sand at the mouth of the river cost $20,707. (GLHS.)

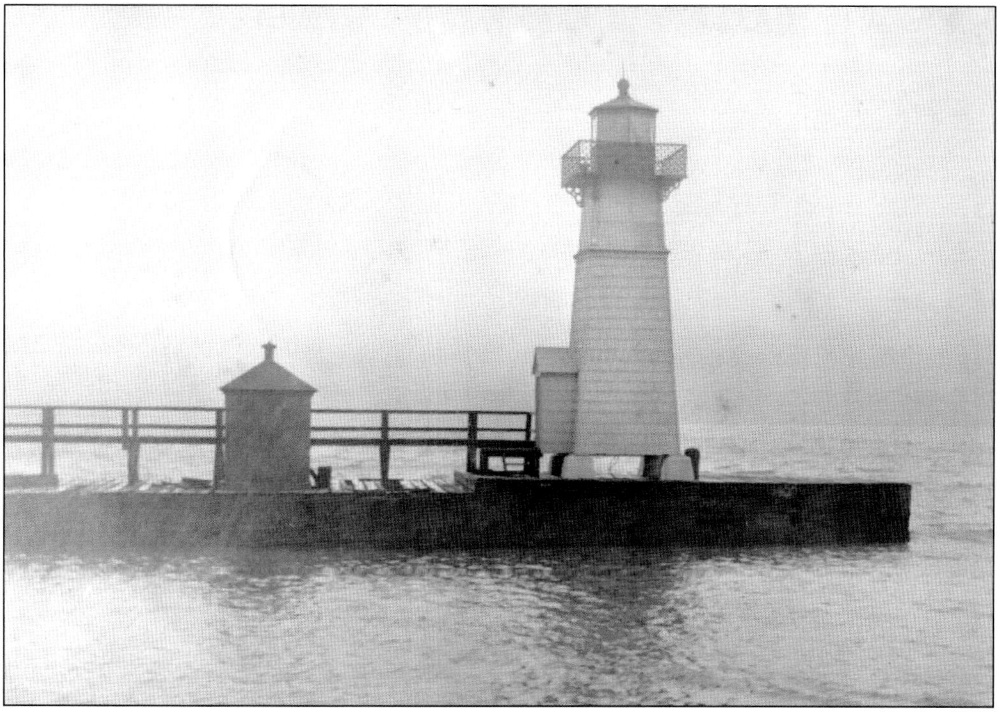

This photograph of the second Huron Lighthouse was taken before the wooden pier was replaced and extended around 1900. Notice that this pier has a few planks missing. (GLHS.)

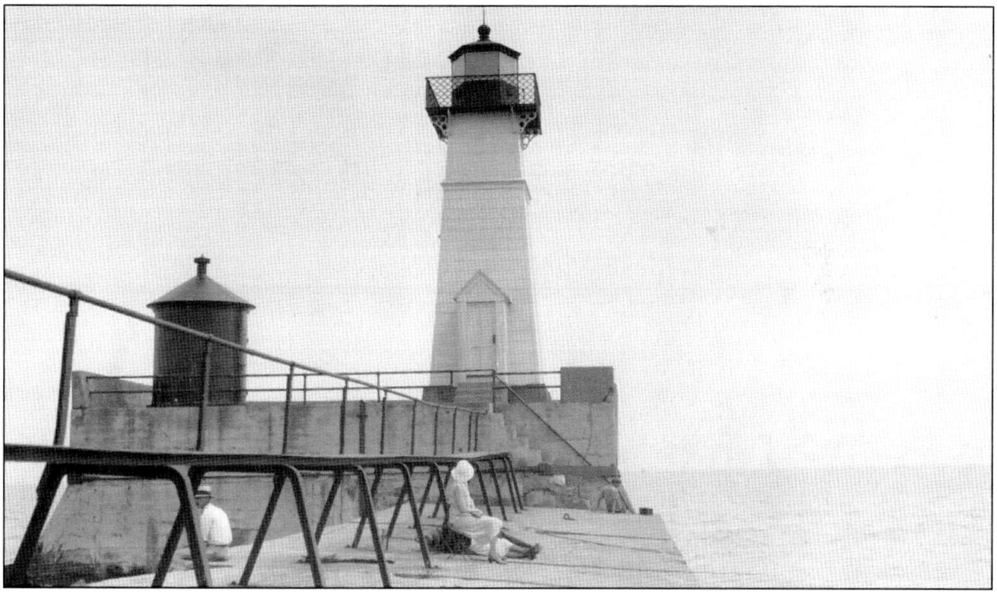

Richard Tonge, Huron keeper from 1923 to 1933, was attempting to reach the lighthouse to light the beacon in a storm when huge waves tore him from the safety of the narrow, elevated walkway and carried him into the lake. An observant Coast Guard crew saw the accident and used its boat to rescue him. This second Huron Lighthouse was moved a mile to its final position when the pier was extended around 1900. Sperm whale oil, lard, and then kerosene illuminated the light until electricity was installed. This photograph was taken by R.C. Smith in 1933. (USCG.)

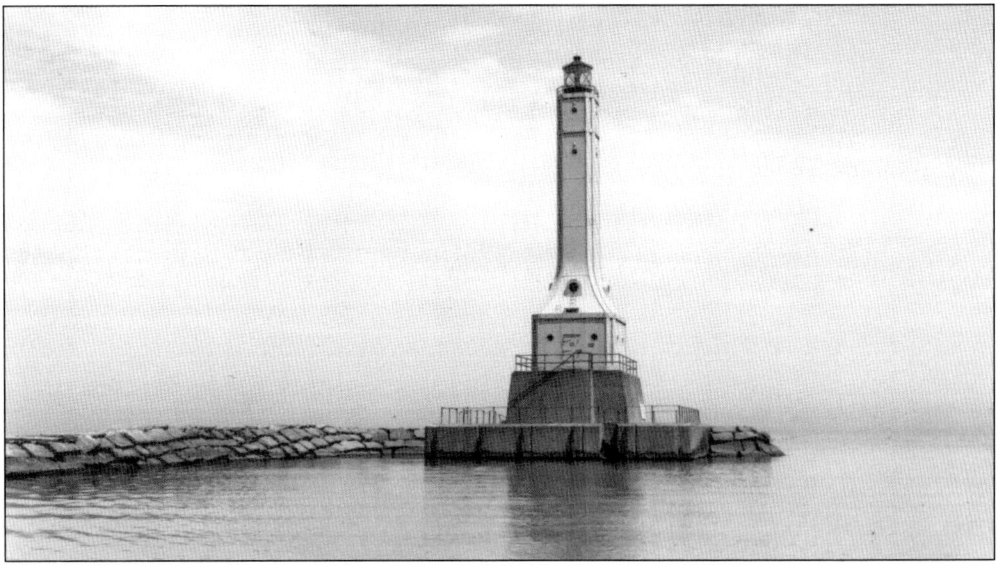

Some readers may think that they have seen this lighthouse before, and they are right. The 1936 Huron Lighthouse is a counterpart of the following lighthouses: Conneaut and Gravelly Shoal, Lake Huron; Keweenaw Waterway Upper Entrance Light, Lake Superior; and Indiana Harbor East Breakwater Light and Port Washington Breakwater Light, Lake Michigan. The Art Deco–style lighthouse was built in 1936 with a black lantern room at the top. Rising 65 feet above its concrete pad, the lighthouse had a fog detector and a horn, and its beacon was visible for 18 miles. In 1972, the lighthouse was automated and the lantern room dismantled. A 1930s harbor project costing $471,519 included deepening and widening the river, extending the west pier for the new lighthouse, and eliminating the east pier. (USCG.)

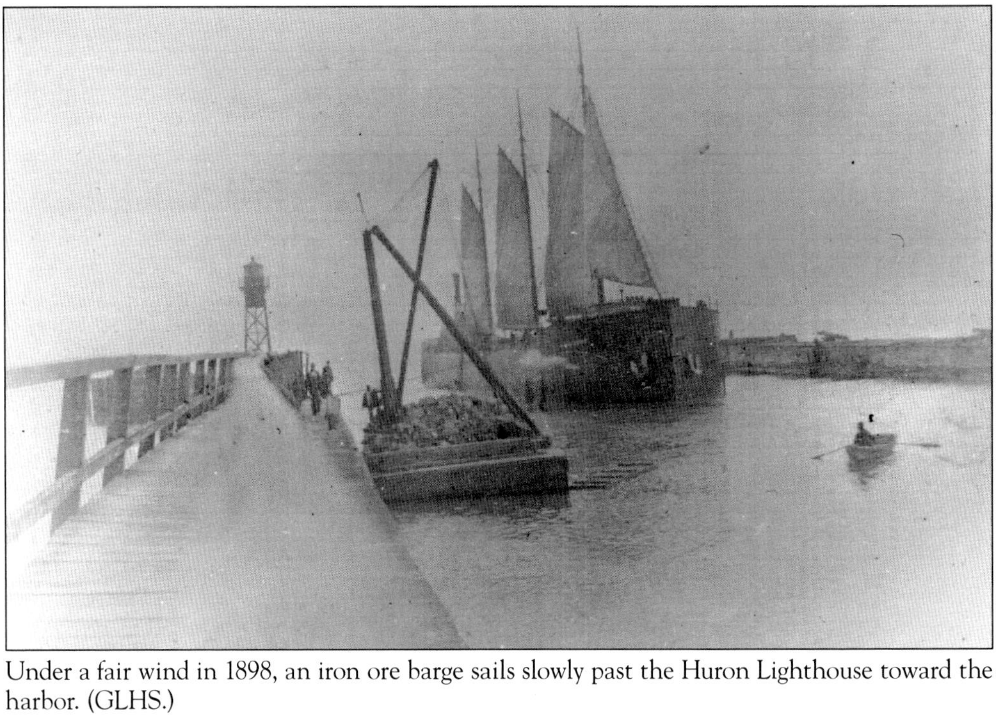

Under a fair wind in 1898, an iron ore barge sails slowly past the Huron Lighthouse toward the harbor. (GLHS.)

Eight

The Most Beloved Lighthouse

Designers and builders wanted the Lorain Lighthouse to last forever. Those who planned the construction went way over the top when they built walls of concrete 10 inches thick over steel. They must have suspected that ships would batter it, for unusual steel doorjambs, baseboards, and window frames scream permanence. The structure is like a fortress resting on a rock.

The Lorain Lighthouse of 1917 did, however, have things that could destroy it: people, politics, and money. In 1965, the government decided to save money and tear it down, replacing it with cheaper navigational lights. Lorain citizens were outraged but could do nothing. A date was set for the demolition. In October 1965, the wrecking ball would smash it forever. Locals wondered if anything could change the fate of this historical symbol that meant so much to captains and sailors entering the harbor. Loyal Lorain citizens who loved their lighthouse, their "Jewel of the Port," petitioned and fought to save it but were told it was too late, that nothing could change the scheduled demolition.

The lighthouse, though, had friends, and it was lucky. Fate temporarily intervened. Bad weather prevented the scheduled destruction in the fall of 1965, and the date was rescheduled for the spring of 1966. This opened a window of opportunity for worried citizens. They wrote letters to their congressmen. Public concern could be heard as far away as Washington, DC. With pressure from Congressman Mosher's office, the Coast Guard decided to keep the lighthouse, citing community interest and historical value. The people of Lorain had won. In 1977, the Lorain County Historical Society paid $1 for the deed to the Lorain Lighthouse, with the stipulation that it be maintained as a historic landmark.

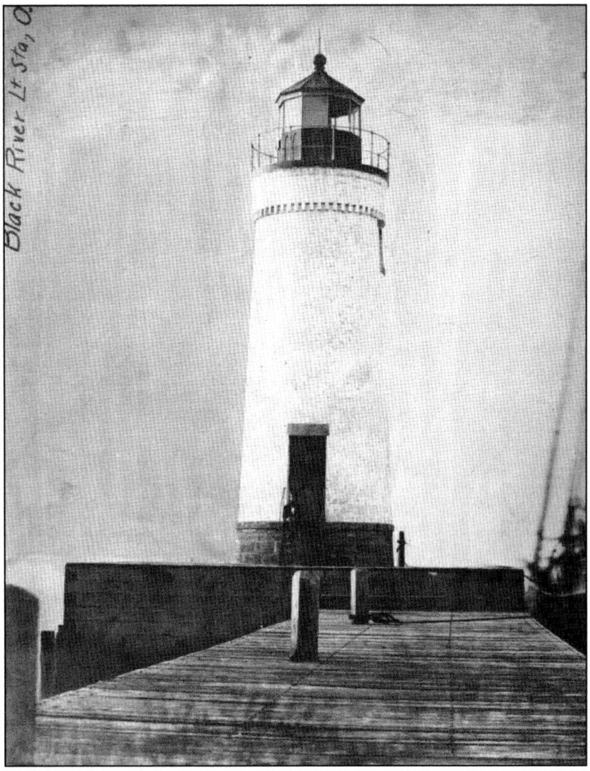

The first lighthouse at Lorain was built in 1836. Oil lit the lamps, and the keeper made daily trips to the light during the shipping season. (NARA.)

The second Lorain Lighthouse, photographed in 1885, was a wooden structure built on a 680-foot pier. The keepers had to carry oil to the lamp every day. Storms blowing from the northeast sent waves pounding the pier, and at three different times keepers were washed off that pier, with one drowning. A three-foot-high catwalk was constructed so the keepers would be safe. (NARA.)

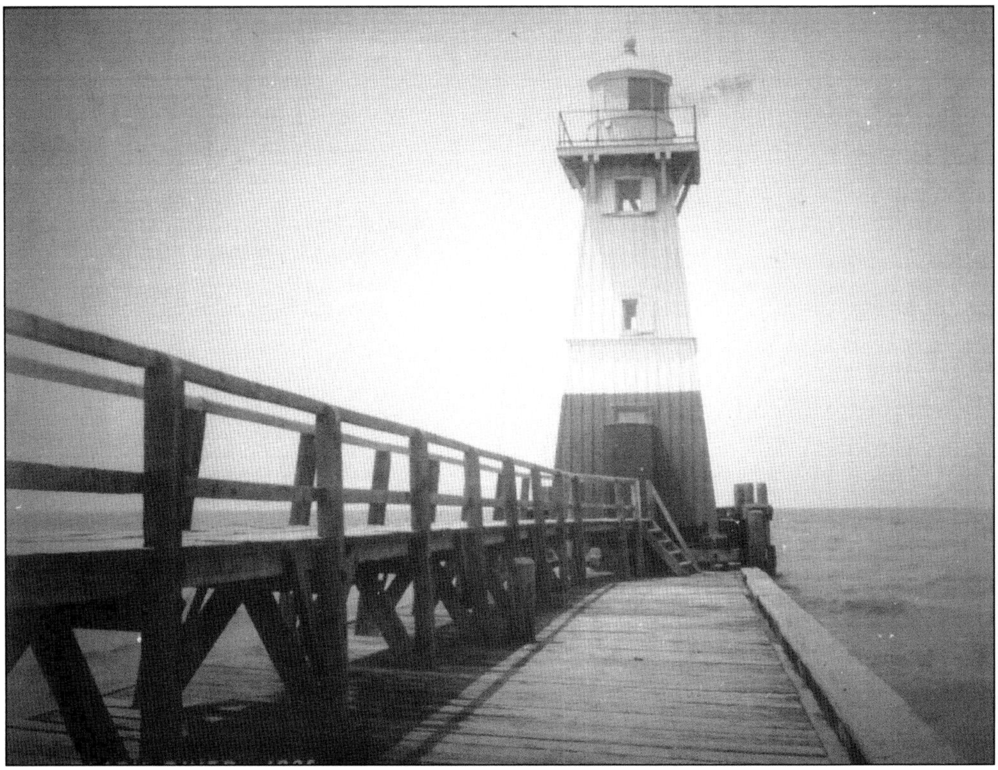

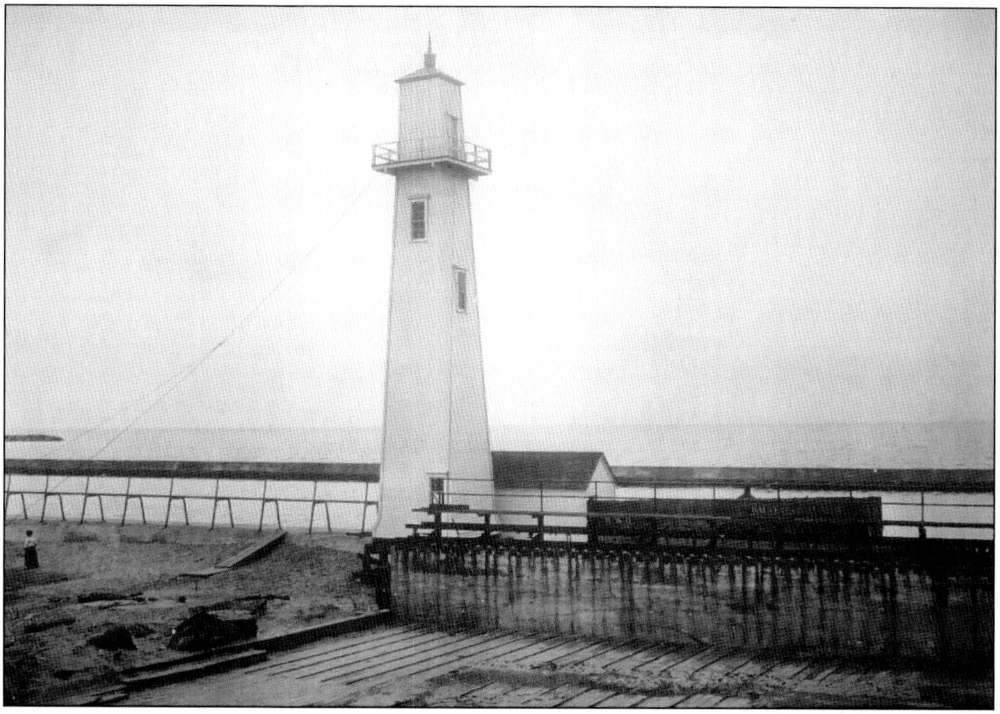

A few years later, a range light was built at the base of the pier, pictured in June 1911, so captains could line up the two lights and sail directly into the harbor. (NARA.)

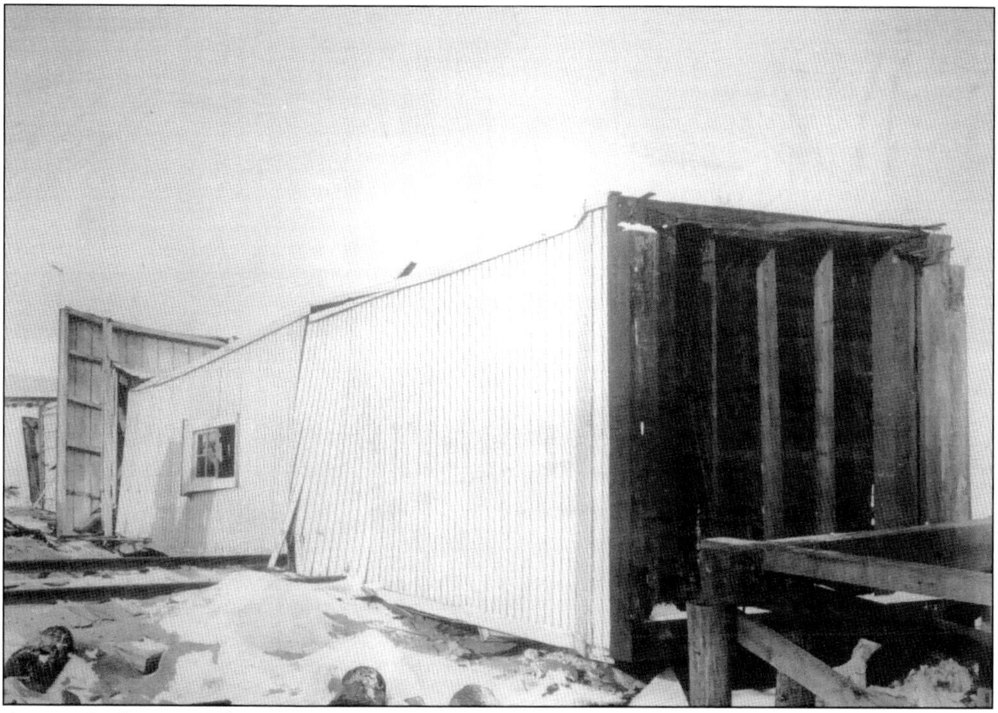

A tornado destroyed the Lorain Range Rear Light on the West Pier on February 21, 1912. (NARA.)

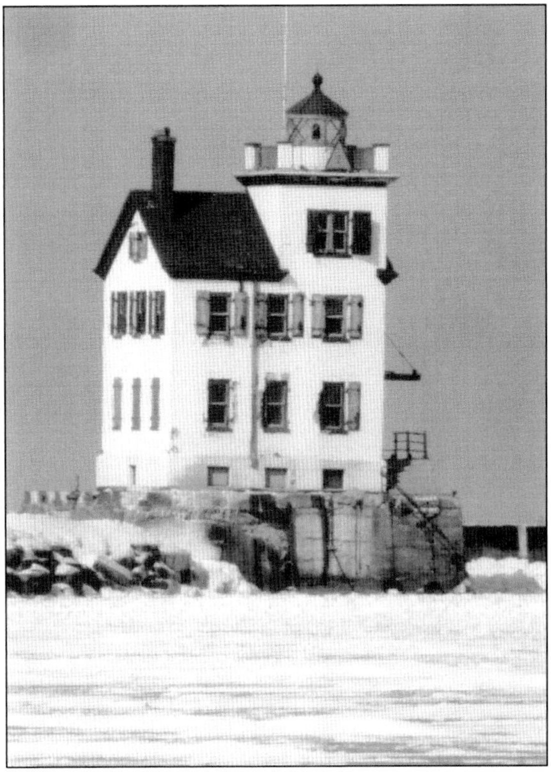

In a 1923 interview, keeper Olin Stevens mentioned that engines on the floor below pumped oil for the light and the foghorn. "A steady pressure must always be maintained. He said that an odd feature about the engines is that they have no ignition system like gasoline engines. This type of engine is commonly known as a log or hothead engine. It runs with oil and water. Everything was in duplicate at the lighthouse because no chance could be taken with machinery or any other apparatus that might keep the light from burning or the foghorn from blowing. In thick, foggy weather, the keeper wants a whistle and wants it quick," Stevens commented to the *Lorain Journal* in 1923. (AC.)

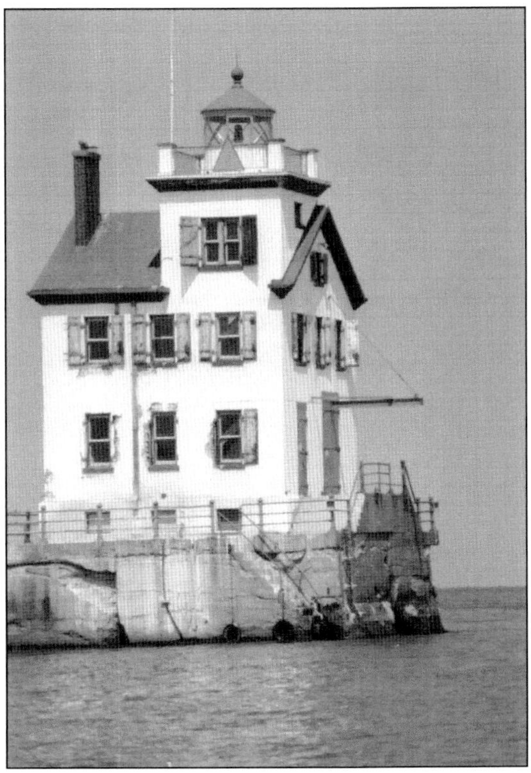

The 1917 Lorain Lighthouse is an imposing sight in this photograph. (AC.)

Olin Stevens, lighthouse keeper from 1920 to 1937, commented that during heavy storms spray washed over the top of the lighthouse. He said that a heavy nor'easter once smashed the thick wire-braced windows on the third floor and put the engines out of commission. Keepers maintained a daily log of the wind and weather, along with barometer readings. (GLHS.)

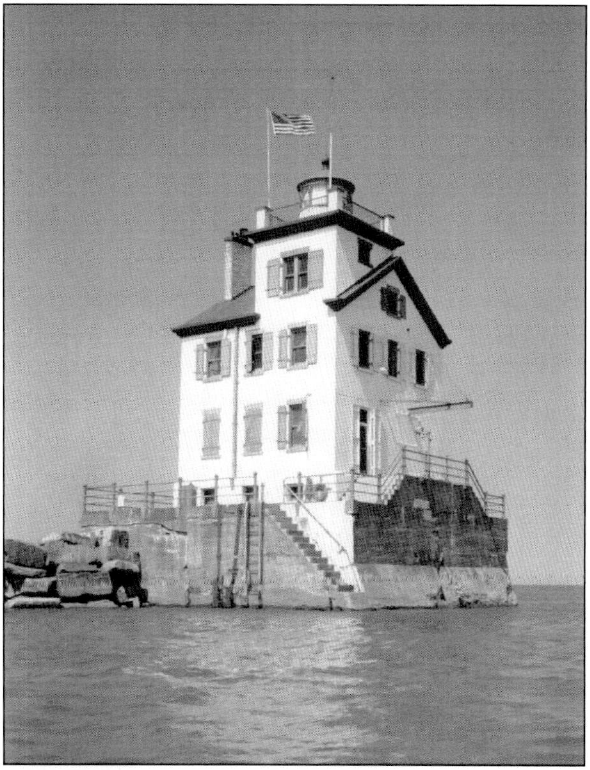

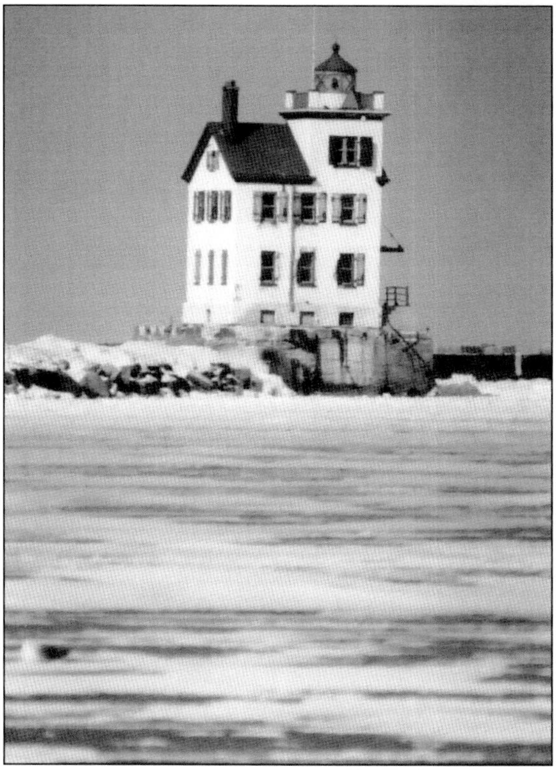

In 1923, the light was an oil-vapor lamp with 7,400 candlepower, 63 feet above the water, with a five-second flash at five-second intervals, making a complete revolution every 30 seconds. It was turned by a huge clockwork arrangement at the base of the light. If this mechanism stopped or the light went out, an electric bell in the living quarters rang a warning. The beacon could be seen 18 to 25 miles away. (AC.)

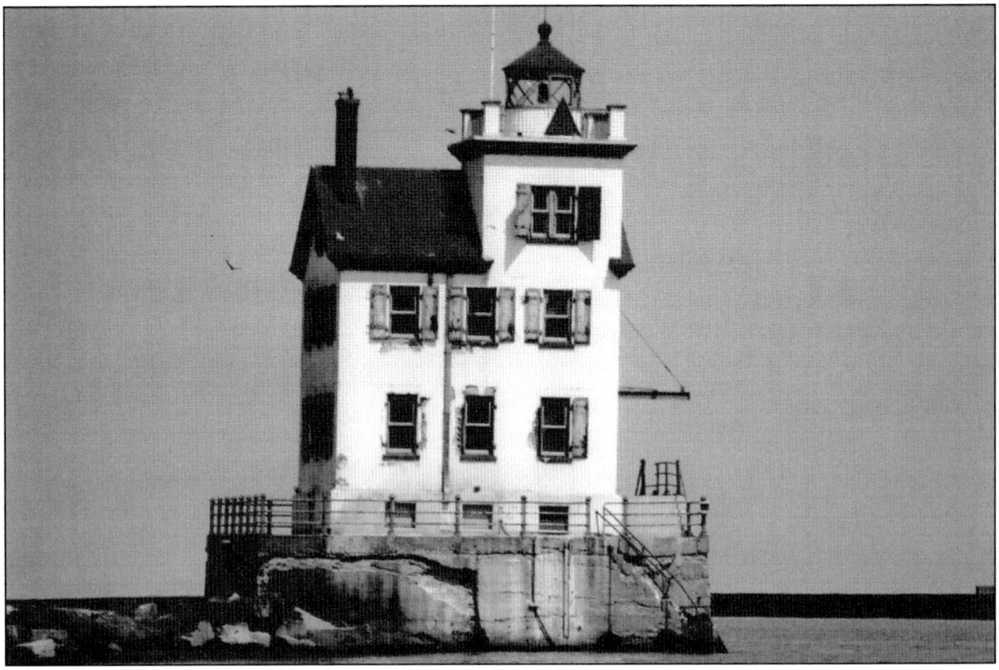

Harry Siegfied, former Lorain Lighthouse keeper in 1947 at age 19, describes the living conditions inside this special residence in a 1995 interview, when he was 67: "A raised basement holds a water pump, oil tanks, and a paint locker. On the first floor are the foghorn, auxiliary power generators, and engine room. The living area is on the second floor, with gorgeous views of the red sunsets." (AC.)

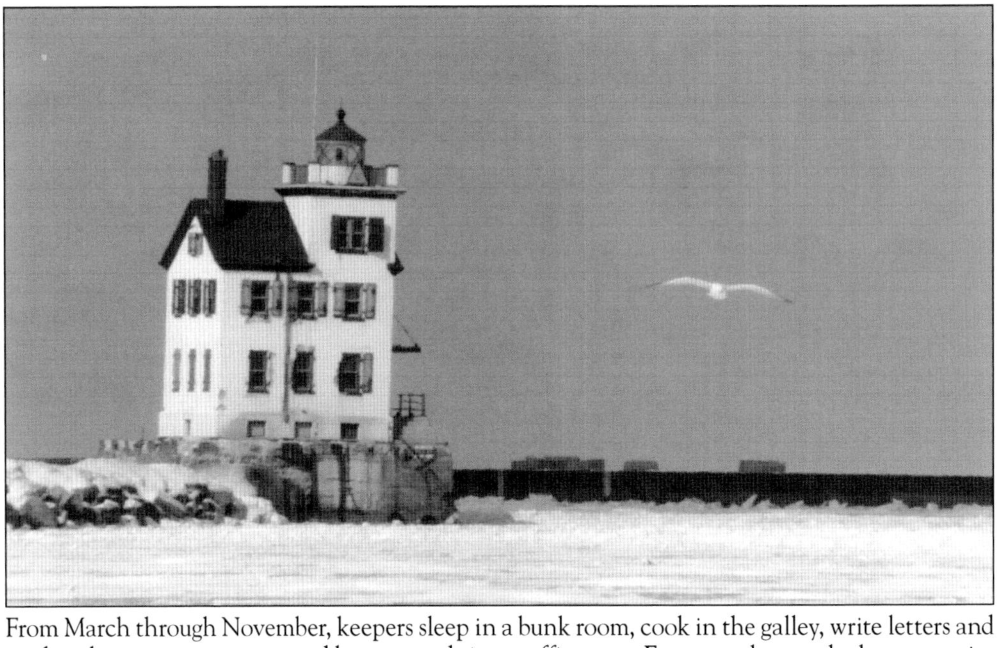

From March through November, keepers sleep in a bunk room, cook in the galley, write letters and read in the recreation room, and keep records in an office area. Every two hours, the keepers write a description of the clouds, lake conditions, wind direction, and wind velocity. A freshwater tank, an equipment storage area, and the mechanism for the foghorn are on the third floor. (AC.)

Harry Siegfied remembers when he was 19 and the Canadian freighter *Bayton* ran into the lighthouse twice, cutting the electric and telephone wires. The lighthouse leaned a little when the vessel hit it but righted itself. No one was injured, and the backup generators kept the beacon flashing, but the vessel was damaged. (AC.)

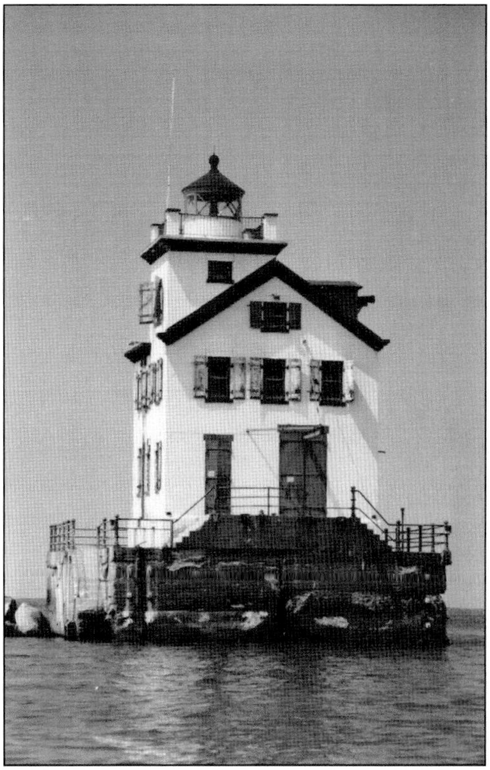

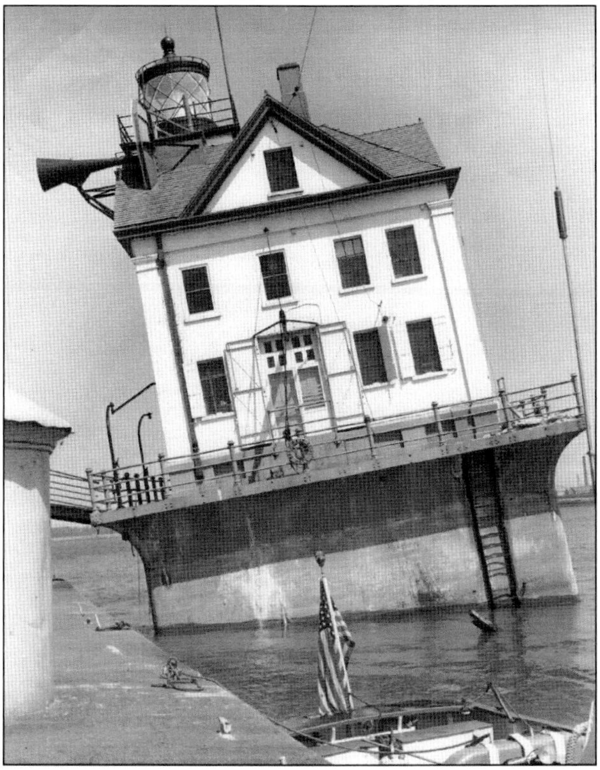

The Lorain Lighthouse could take any Lake Erie gales, but how did the men take the storms? Harry Siegfied said that anyone on watch could hear the waves splashing onto the windows and feel a slight vibration, but otherwise he would sleep through it. When Siegfied visited the lighthouse and looked at the 14 steps that spiral to the top floor holding the beacon 58 feet above Lake Erie, he commented that he could not imagine running up and down those steps like he did at 19. The leaning Buffalo Lighthouse (pictured) was hit by a freighter in 1958. It was not built as well as the Lorain Light and had to be demolished. (GLHS.)

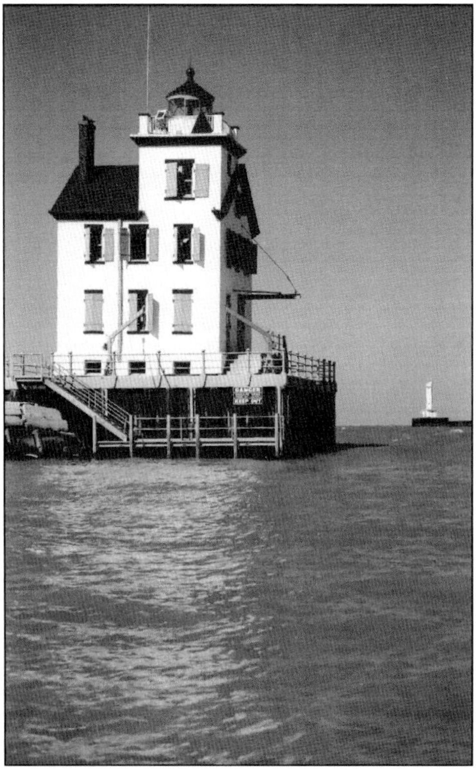

After many years of hard work by numerous volunteers, the Lorain Lighthouse has been restored to its former glory. The organization responsible was the Port of Lorain Foundation, whose president is John R. Malanowski. Frank and Carolyn Sipkovsky and other volunteer members of the Black River Historical Society in Lorain helped promote the renovation of the lighthouse. (AC.)

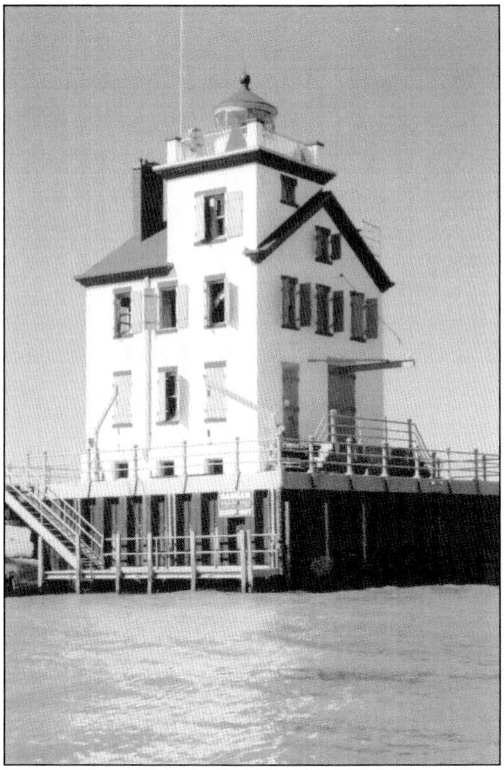

This photograph shows the restored Lorain Lighthouse. (AC.)

Nine

Heroes at Cleveland Lighthouses

"When men talk to me of courage in time of battle, I think of lifesaver Hatch's leap in the darkness from the swaying main boom of the *Sophia Minch*, stranded in a northwest gale east of the piers at Cleveland, that he might save the lives of two sailors on October 31, 1883," John R. Spears writes of Frederick Hatch in 1914.

It was 7:00 p.m. when the three-masted schooner approached the Cleveland harbor. Although a furious northwest gale was blowing, the captain attempted to bring the ship into the port. Just as it reached the narrow entrance between the two piers, a heavy sea smashed the rudder, and the ship drifted toward the rocks. The captain decided to sink the ship to keep it from being destroyed.

The lifesavers rescued all the sailors at the bow of the ship, but two men were stranded in the stern. Waves washed over the decks, and the only way to reach the stranded men was leaping from mast to mast and hanging onto the icy lines in the gale. Hatch managed this nearly impossible feat, reaching the weakened men and lifting them into a breeches buoy.

The lifesavers also rescued sailors from the *John B. Merrill* on November 1 and the *John T. Johnson* on November 11. Each rescue was at night and during a terrific gale. Hatch and eight others, including keeper Charles C. Goodwin, received a Gold Lifesaving Medal. A few years later, Frederick T. Hatch became the first lighthouse keeper at the new Cleveland West Breakwater Lighthouse, where he would earn another gold medal.

The schooner *Wahnapitae* wrecked on a pier during a gale on October 26, 1890. The ship began to break up, and the crew of eight, including the captain's wife, jumped to the pier. Hatch rescued the captain's wife, who could not swim, and put her into his lifeboat. When his boat overturned, he swam with her to safety.

In all, 500 medals had been distributed by 1914, but Frederick Hatch alone was decorated with gold twice.

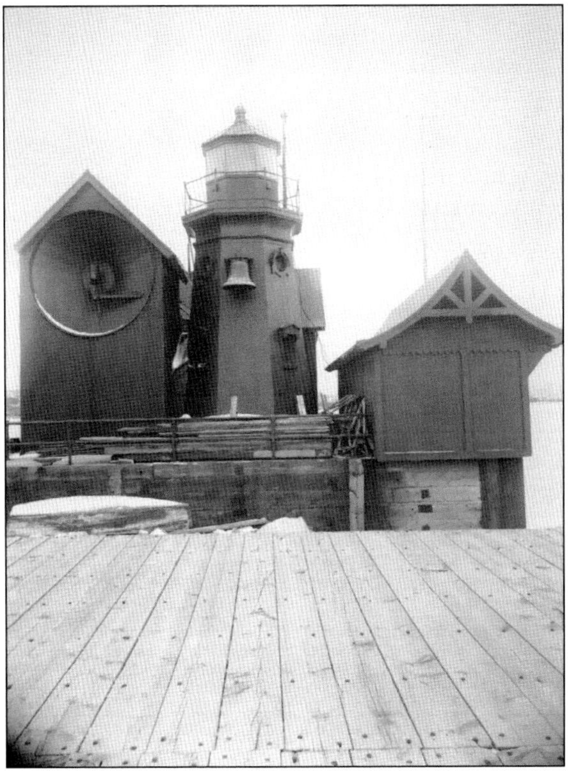

Hero and lighthouse keeper Frederick T. Hatch served the Cleveland West Breakwater Lighthouse, pictured around 1890. A steam-fog signal was added in 1889. People thought the low-pitched sound would not be audible, but the cow-like tone was actually very successful; it could be heard 12 miles into the lake and all over Cleveland. It was so loud that people in Cleveland complained, and a deflector was positioned behind the siren to direct the sound toward the lake. Regardless of the foghorn, ships kept hitting the lighthouse, weakening the crib's stability and causing the lighthouse to sway during storms, at which point the rotating mechanism would stop. Hatch used to add weights to keep the light turning, or he would rotate the lens by hand. The octagonal lighthouse, built for the Genesee River Harbor near Rochester, New York, was relocated here and placed on top of the crib, which was built in 1884. (NARA.)

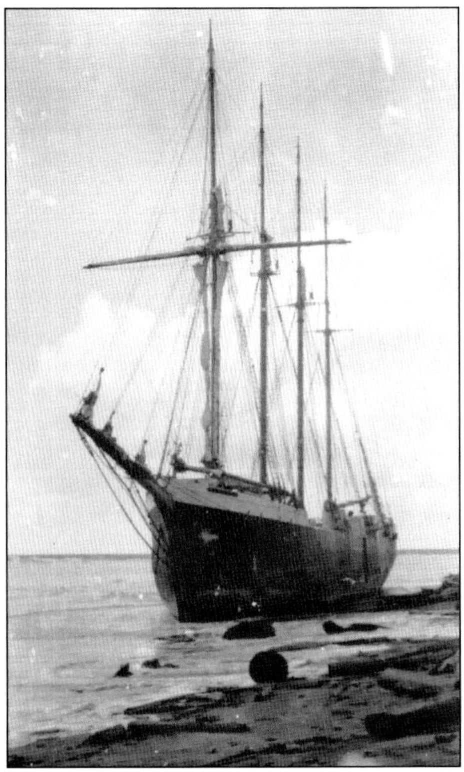

This shipwrecked schooner is similar in appearance to those that wrecked in Cleveland when Frederick T. Hatch was lighthouse keeper. (AC.)

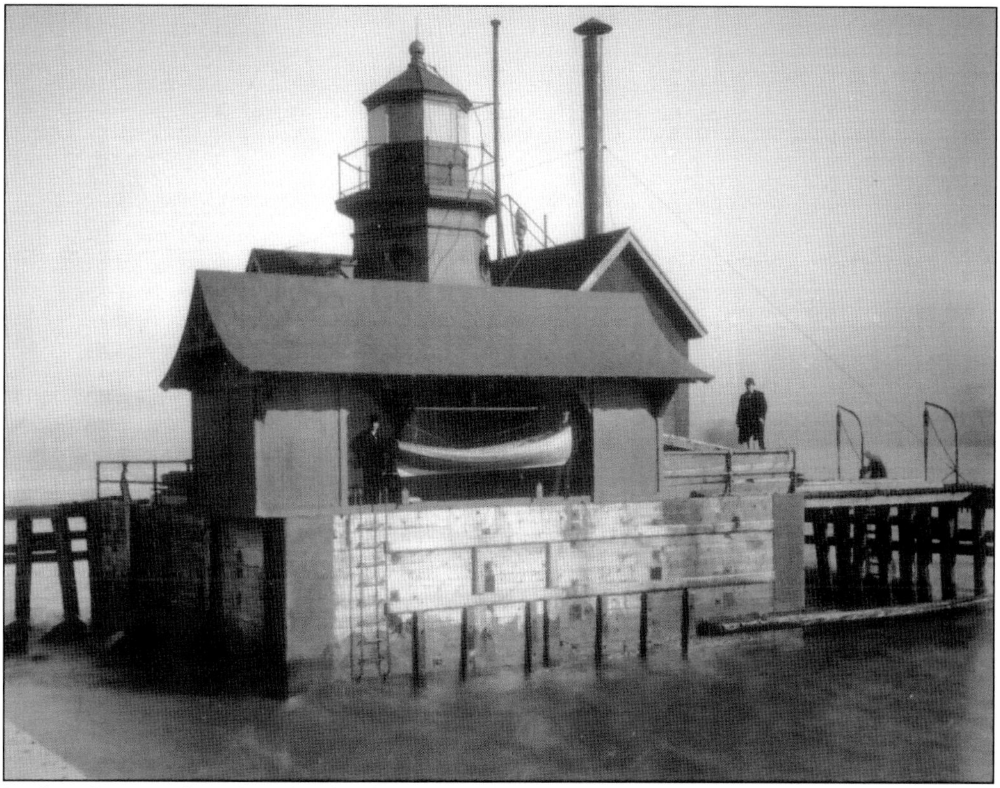

In this photograph is the Cleveland West Breakwater Lighthouse after it was raised to increase the visibility of the light. (NARA.)

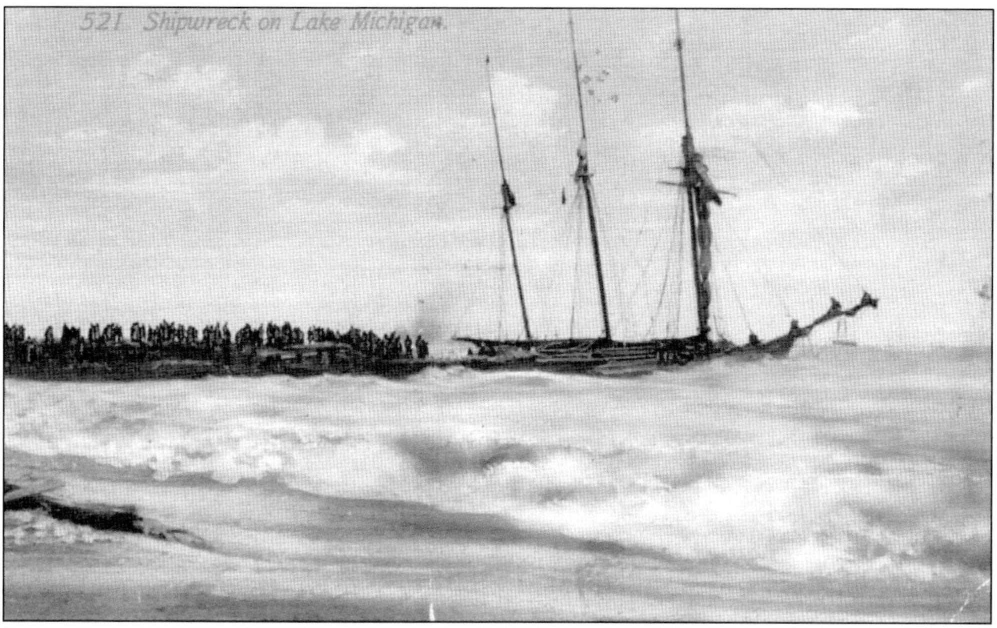

Pictured is an unidentified shipwrecked schooner during the 1800s. (AC.)

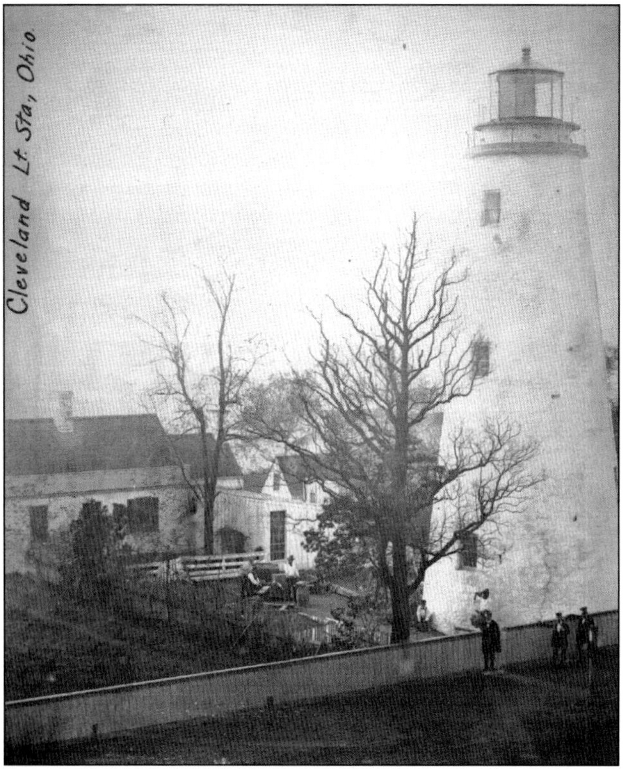

The first Cleveland Lighthouse was built in 1830 on the hill of Water Street (West Ninth). Levi Johnson was the builder of the 67-foot rubble masonry lighthouse and nearby two-room keeper's house. The iron lantern burned whale oil and held 13 patent lamps and 14-inch silvered reflectors. (NARA.)

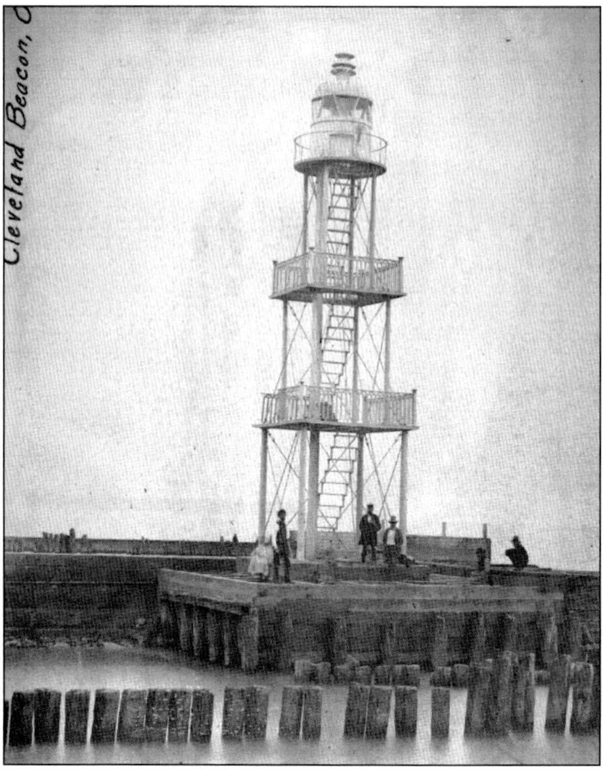

From 1831 to 1832, a scaffold-type tower was built on a pier east of the Cuyahoga River. Steven Woolverton, lighthouse keeper, serviced both the main light on the hill and this structure on the pier. (NARA.)

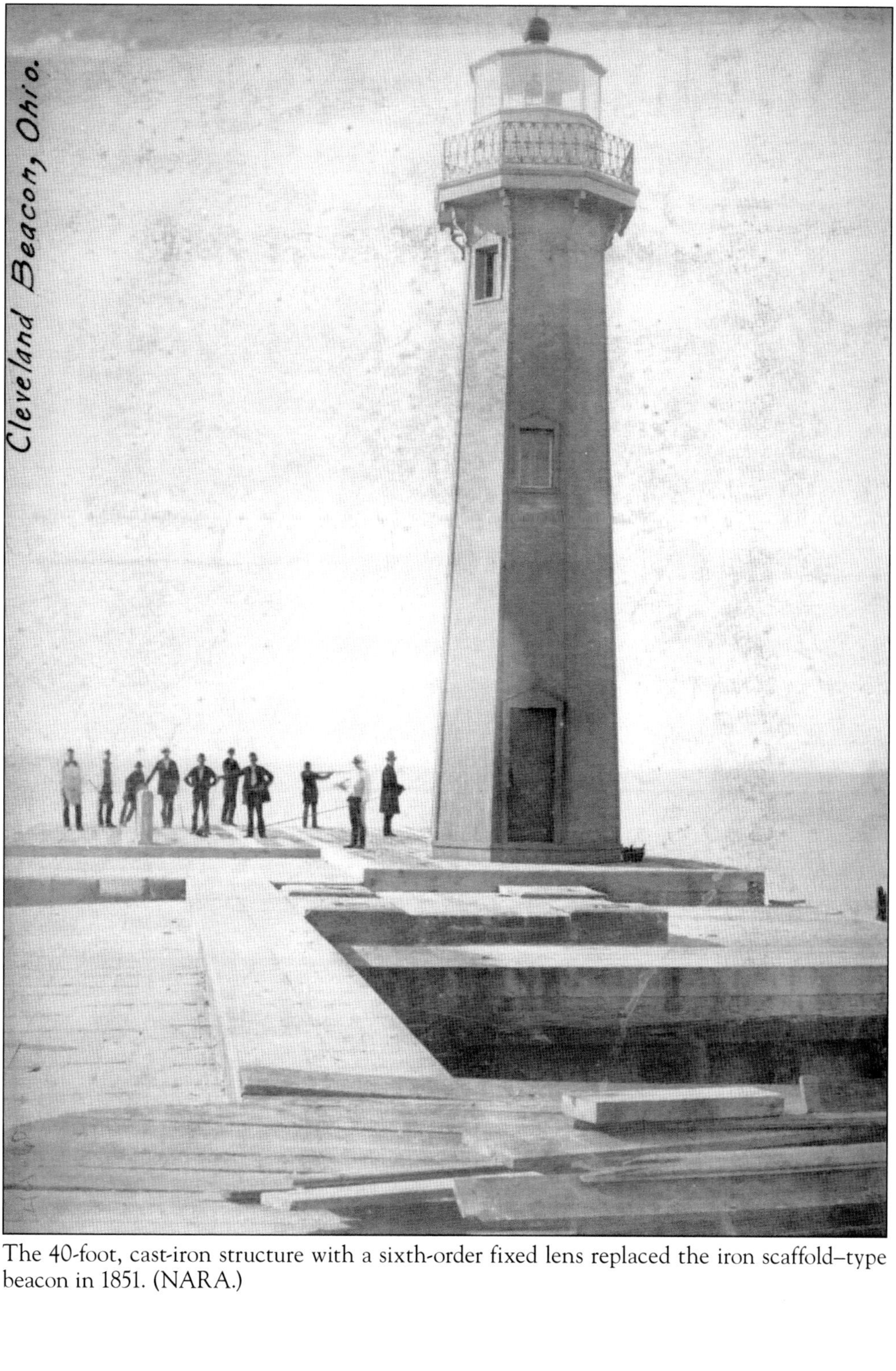

The 40-foot, cast-iron structure with a sixth-order fixed lens replaced the iron scaffold–type beacon in 1851. (NARA.)

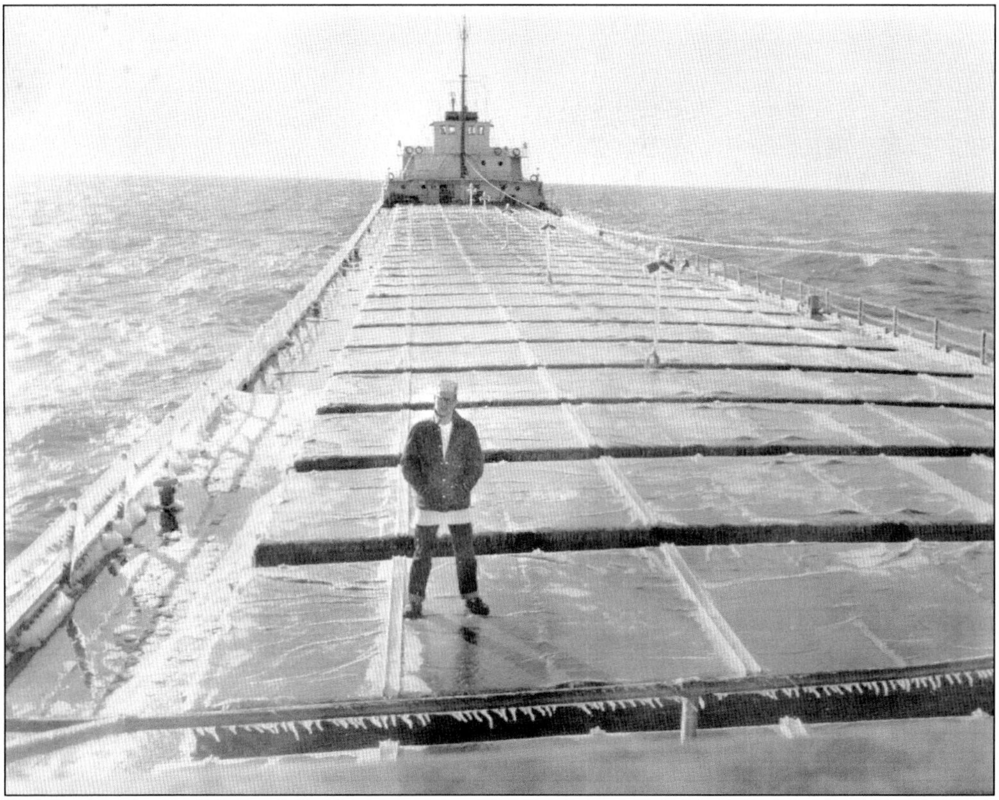

Danger rides the waves, and sailors tell the tales. In this c. 1954 view from the bridge of the iron-ore freighter *Ireland*, there is a small line on each side of the deck. In rough seas when waves constantly roll over the deck, sailors must grip this line when walking to the rear or they will be swept overboard. (AC.)

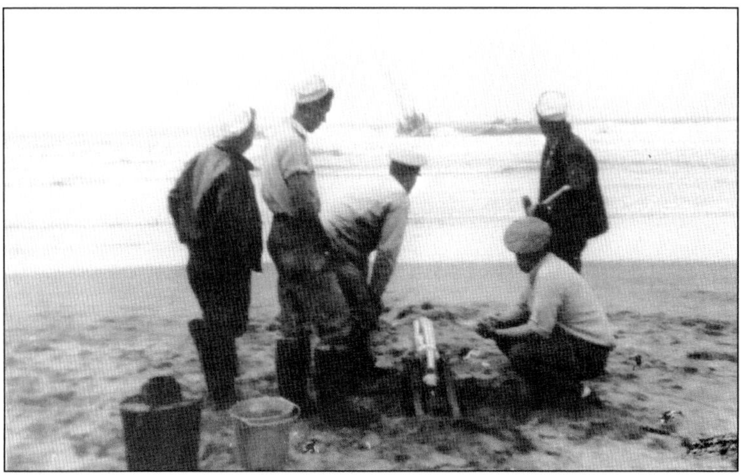

Unidentified US Coast Guardsmen prepare to shoot a line to a wrecked ship by using their Lyle gun. (AC.)

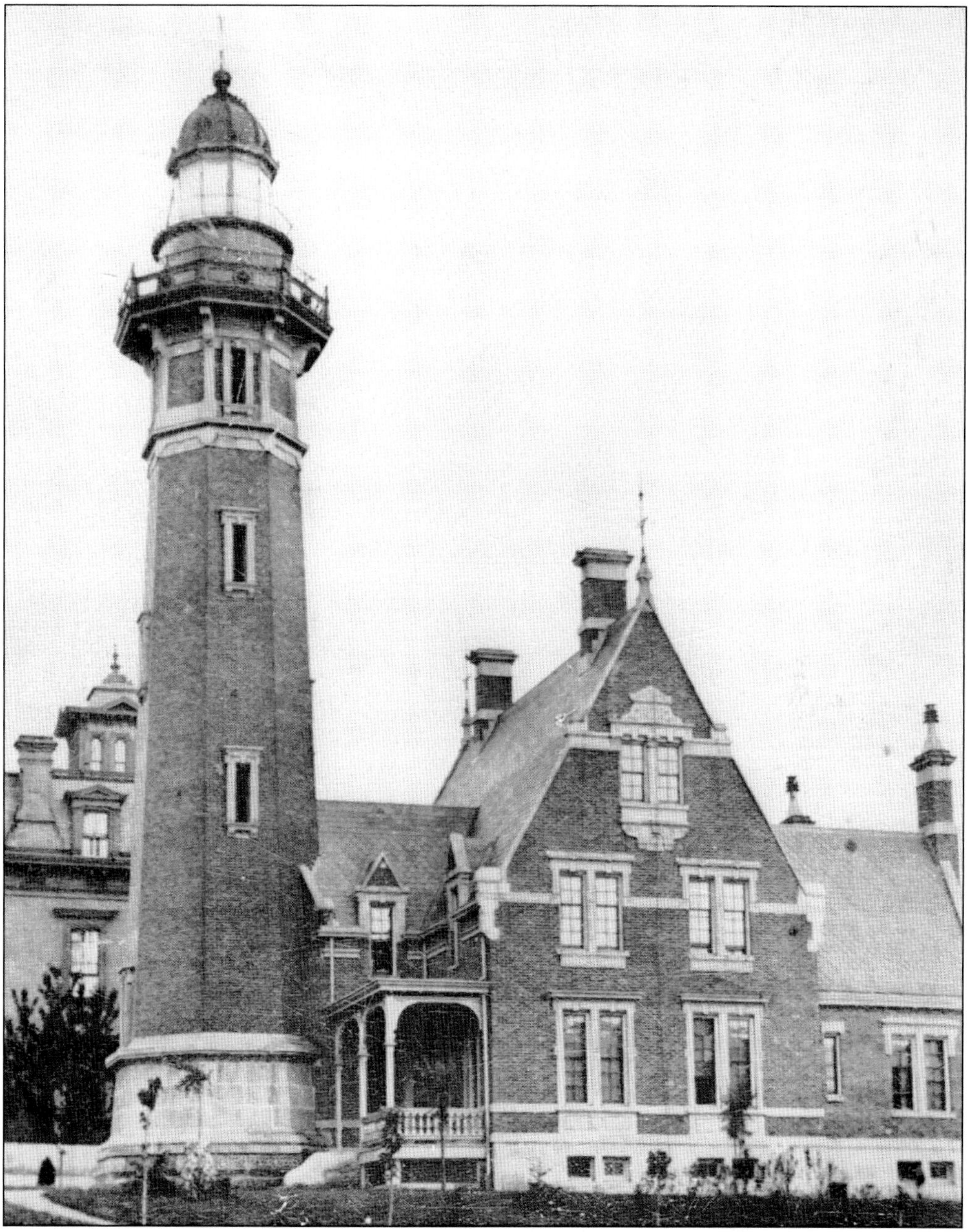

Being in the wrong place at the wrong time might best describe the destiny of this attractive, 84-foot tower built on Water Street in 1872. One of the most elaborate lighthouses in the country, this Victorian Gothic lighthouse in Cleveland was destined for a short life. The lantern room held a three-and-a-half-order lens with a fixed white light, but captains coming into the harbor could not see the beacon due to fog and industrial smoke. By the fall of 1892, the tower had been demolished. The lantern and lens were installed in an identical lighthouse on Lake Ontario at Braddock Point, New York. The keeper's house in the background was enlarged and renovated, with the four keepers' families continuing to live there until 1927. But when the Main Avenue High Level Bridge was built in 1937, this lighthouse was also demolished. (GLHS.)

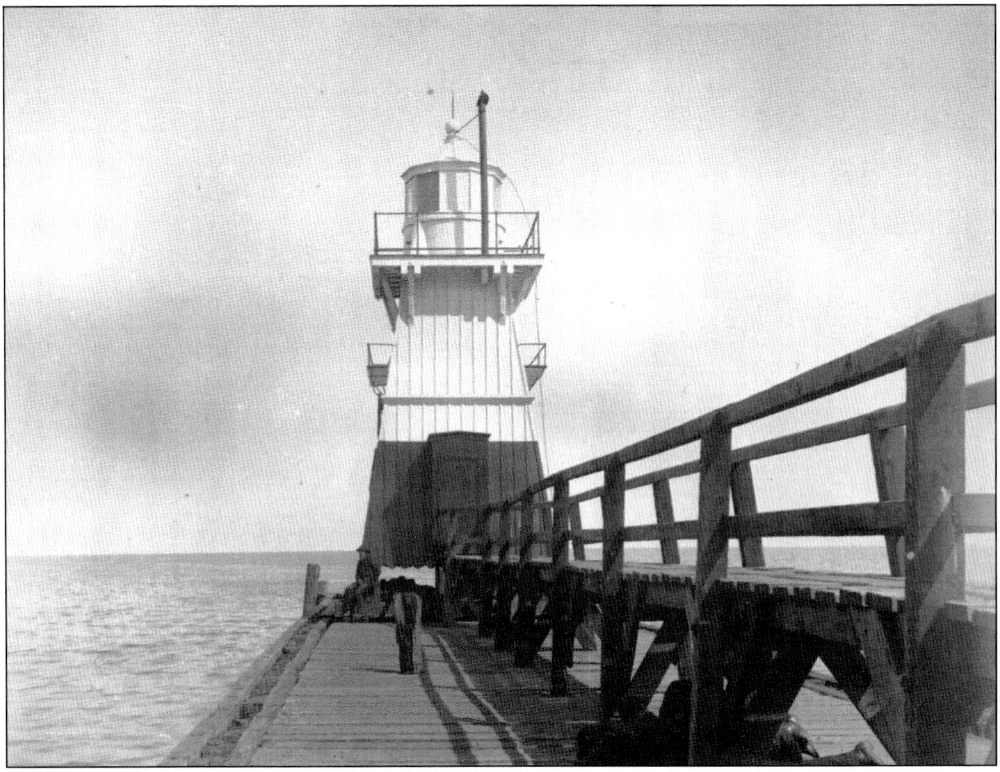

Walking on the raised catwalk at night during a gale would have been challenging and not for the fainthearted. The Cleveland East Pier Lighthouse is pictured in 1885. The pier was 575 feet long. (NARA.)

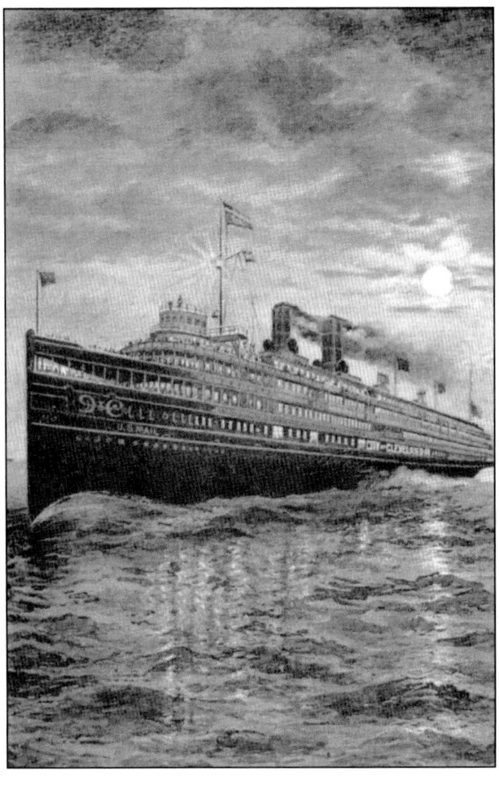

The *City of Cleveland* took passengers on nightly cruises. It was a treat to dance under the stars while the band played romantic tunes. (AC.)

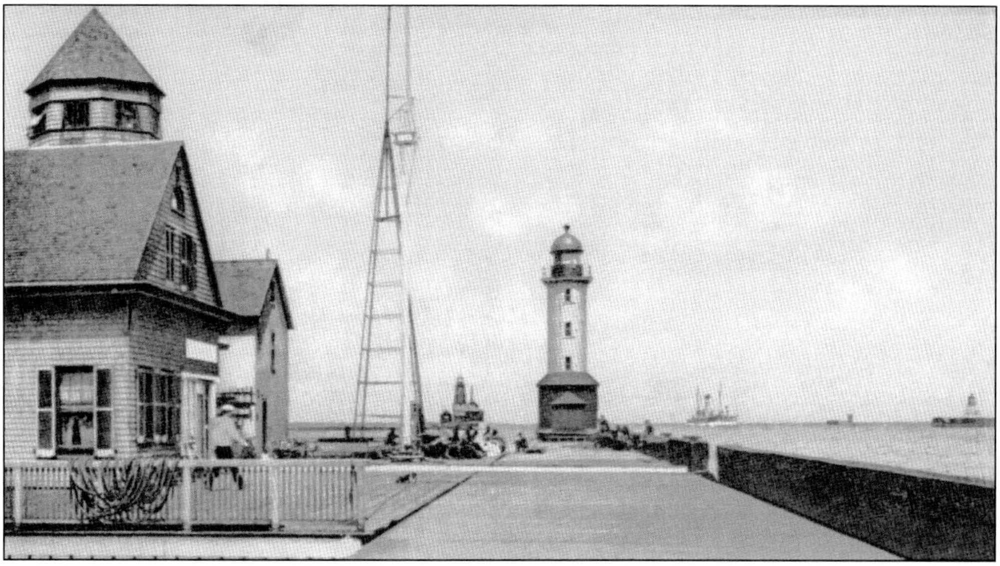

Cleveland West Pier Lighthouse and the Cleveland US Life-Saving Service Station are pictured in 1905. The Life-Saving Service became a part of the Coast Guard in 1915, and the US Lighthouse Service was absorbed into the Coast Guard in 1939. The Cleveland West Breakwater Lighthouse can be seen between the lighthouse and the lifesaving station (above). Notice the lifeboat on the side of the station (below). (Both, AC.)

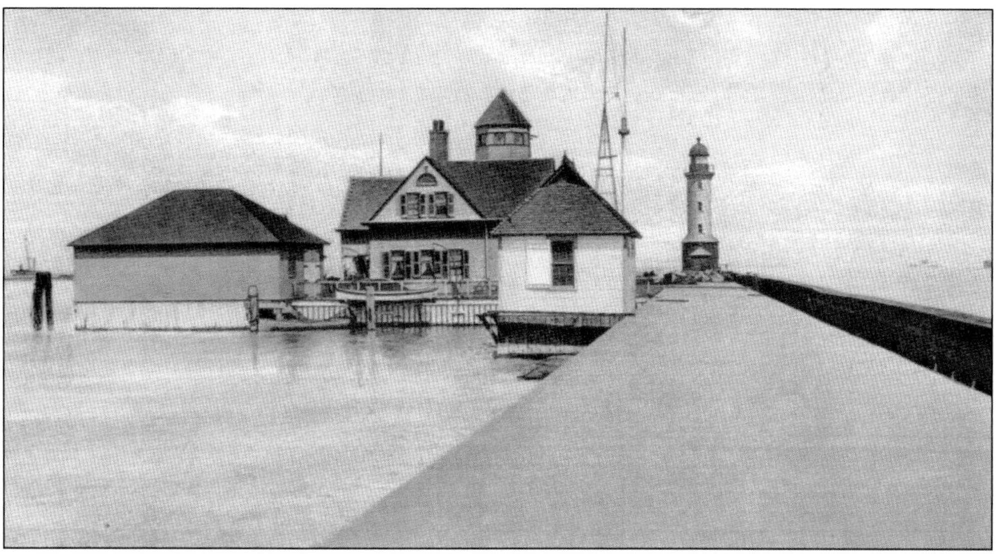

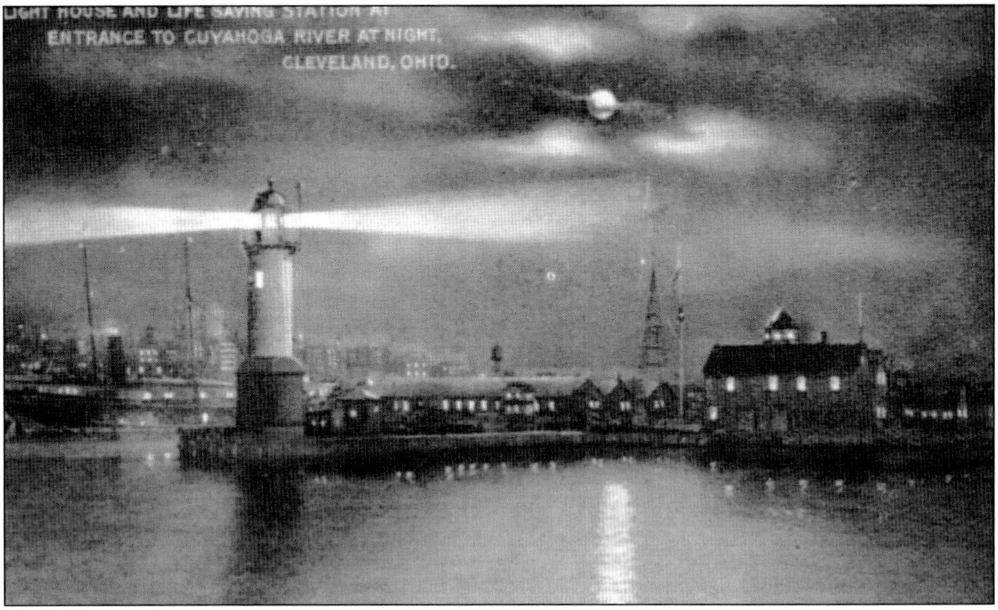

The Cleveland West Pier Lighthouse and Life-Saving Station are pictured in the moonlight around 1900, with Cleveland in the background. (AC.)

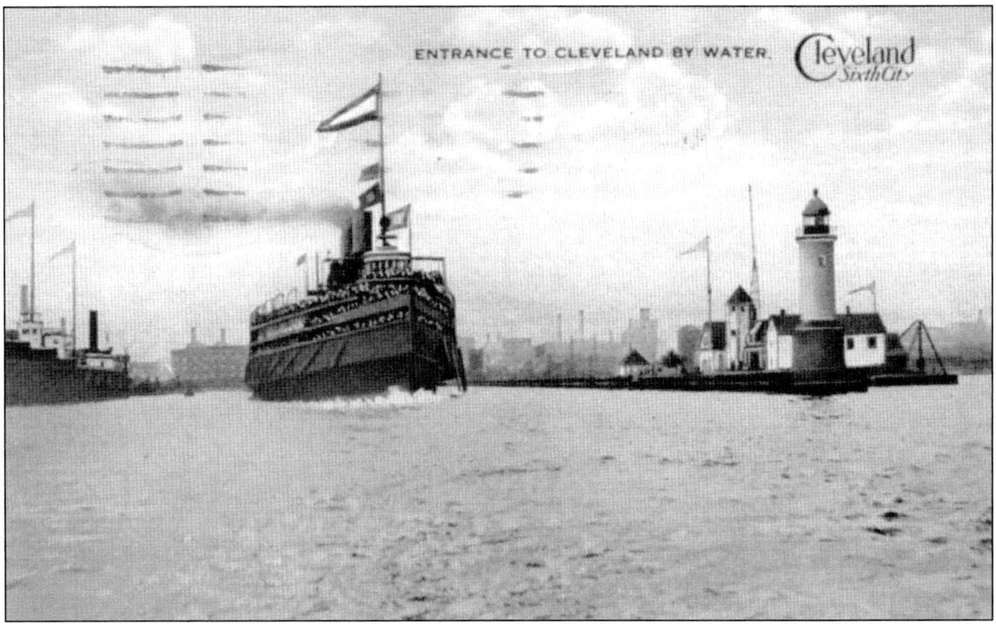

An excursion ship leaves Cleveland Harbor and passes the West Pier Lighthouse and Life-Saving Station. (AC.)

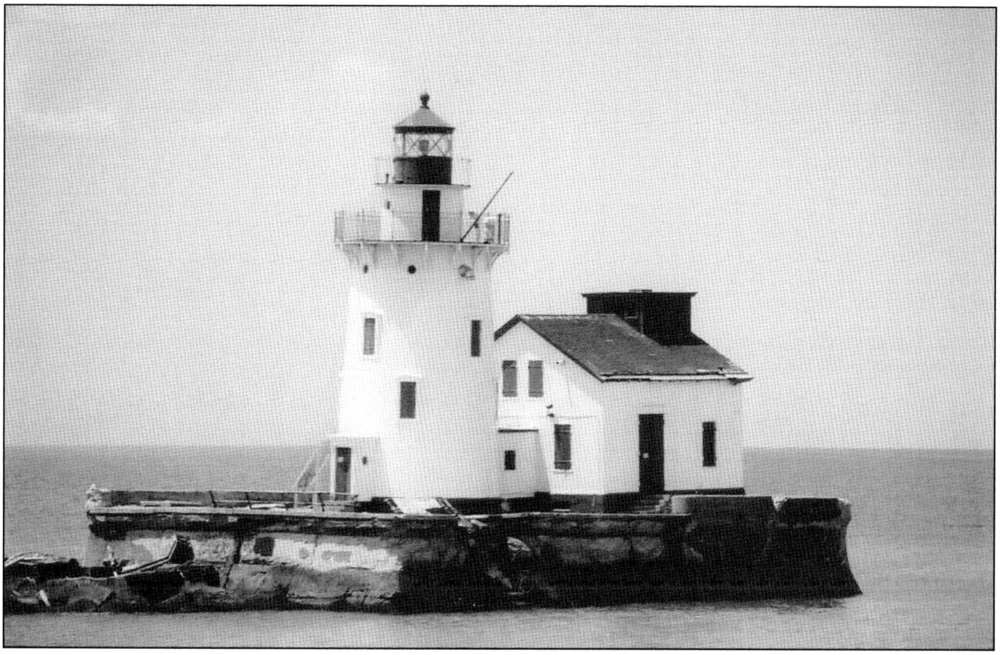

The Cleveland West Pierhead Light, built from 1910 to 1911, was fitted with a fourth-order Fresnel lens taken from the 1885 West Breakwater lighthouse. In 1995, a solar-powered, flashing red-and-white light replaced it. Today, the 55-foot tower is named the Cleveland Main Entrance Lighthouse. The rectangular building housing the foghorn was built in 1916. (AC.)

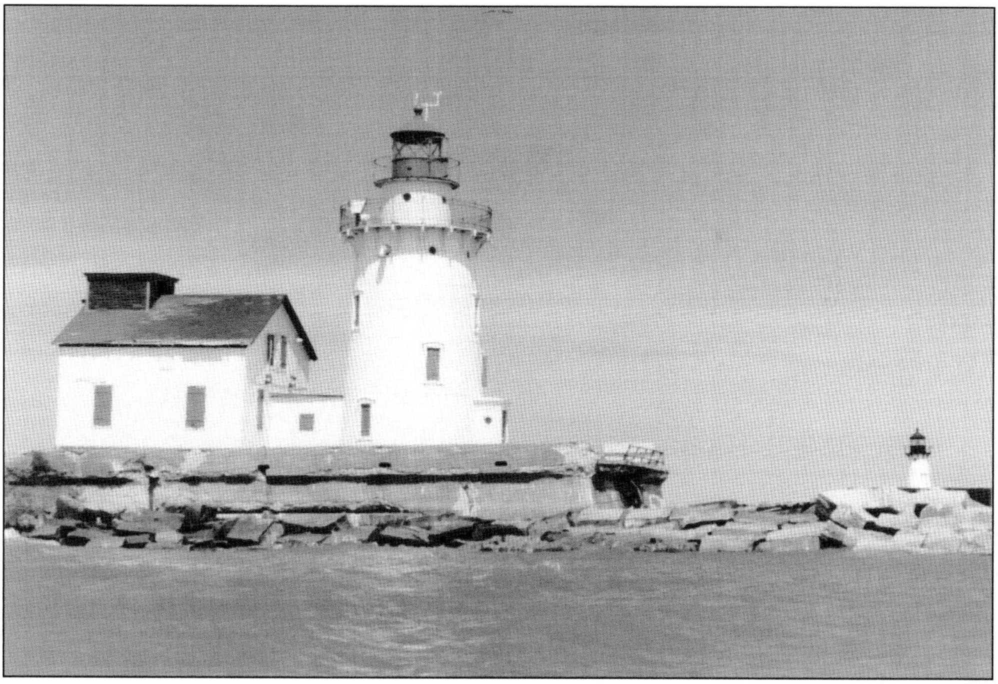

The 25-foot Cleveland Harbor East Pierhead Lighthouse, visible across the channel on the right, was also built from 1910 to 1911. Its green light was automated in 1959 and is currently solar-powered. (AC.)

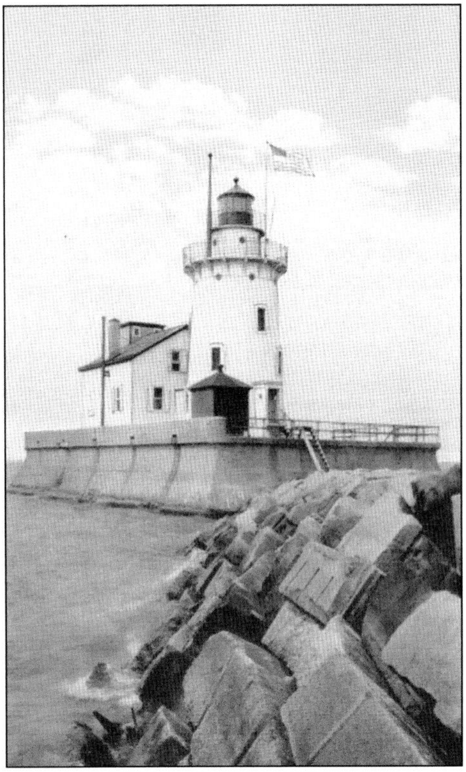

Cleveland Harbor West Pierhead Lighthouse is pictured around 1921. (AC.)

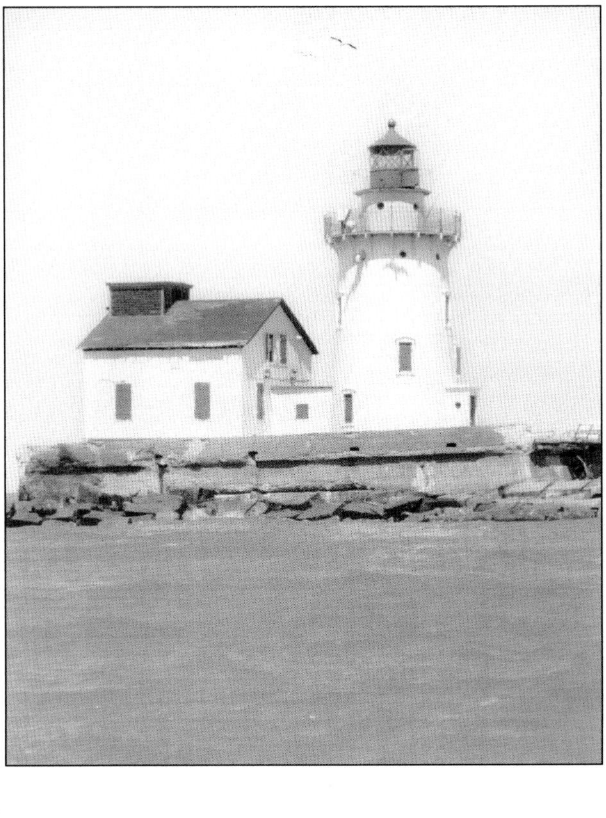

Seagulls cast shadows on the Cleveland Harbor West Pierhead Lighthouse. (AC.)

Ten

A Haunted Lighthouse and Entombed Keepers

It was late fall in November 1928. Two lighthouse keepers were getting ready to leave the Ashtabula Lighthouse for the winter when a blizzard struck. For three days, waves washed over the lighthouse in subzero temperatures, the water freezing as it fell. The sun finally came out on the fourth day, but the men were unable to open the door; they were trapped. The two spent hours trying to thaw the door, their only means of escape. When it finally opened, they discovered a mountain of ice five feet thick blocking them. Using a small, sharp knife, they took turns flaking off little bits of ice. Days later, their tunnel was finally wide enough, and each crawled through it to a life he had thought lost.

The Fairport Harbor Lighthouse was decommissioned in 1925, and only intense public outcry prevented the tower from being demolished. In 1945, the Fairport Harbor Historical Society was formed to save the lighthouse. It would become the first marine museum on the Great Lakes.

On January 10, 1922, six men were stranded on the Conneaut Breakwater Pier and about to freeze in a winter storm. The tugboat *Oregon* had been towing the barge *Newman* when the cable snapped. When their barge drifted close enough to the breakwater pier, the men jumped onto it. But as waves covered them in ice, they realized that without help they would soon freeze. Lighthouse keeper Edward A. Pfister and his assistant Joseph Lasko saw the men jump. Pfister and Lasko immediately lowered their skiff into the water and rowed toward the pier. In the blizzard, Pfister helped the stranded men down the side of the icy pier and into the boat. The men survived, and they stayed at the lighthouse for two nights and a day before the storm passed. In 1922, Pfister was officially congratulated by the US government for his rescue.

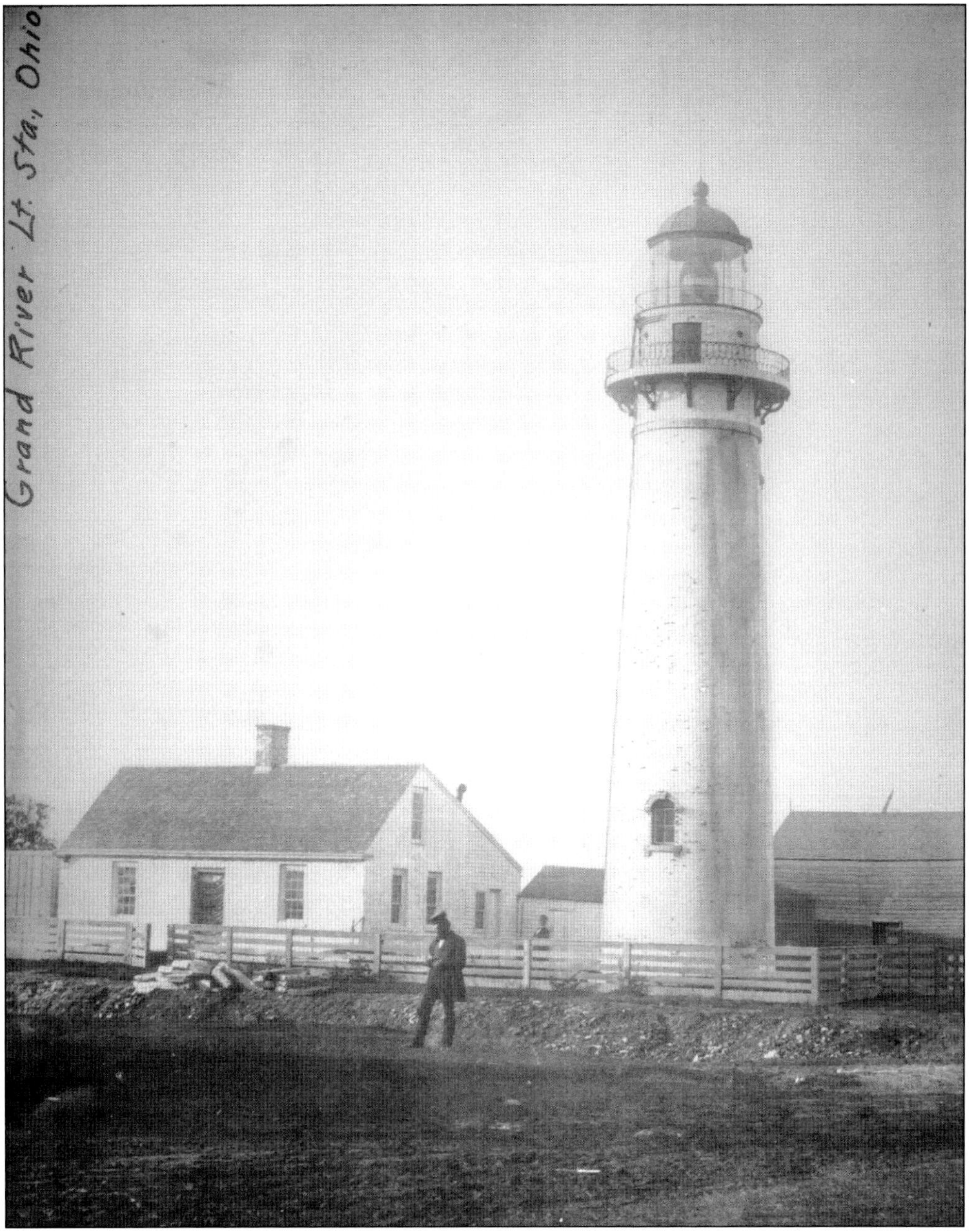

Prior to the Civil War, the 1825 Grand River Lighthouse (or Fairport Harbor Lighthouse) was a guiding light along the Underground Railroad, with the keeper assisting those fleeing the South on boats to Canada. The first keeper at the lighthouse was a colorful character and active abolitionist named Samuel Butler. By 1868, the lighthouse was badly deteriorated, the two-foot foundation inadequate for supporting the heavy brick tower, and the structure was demolished. (GLHS.)

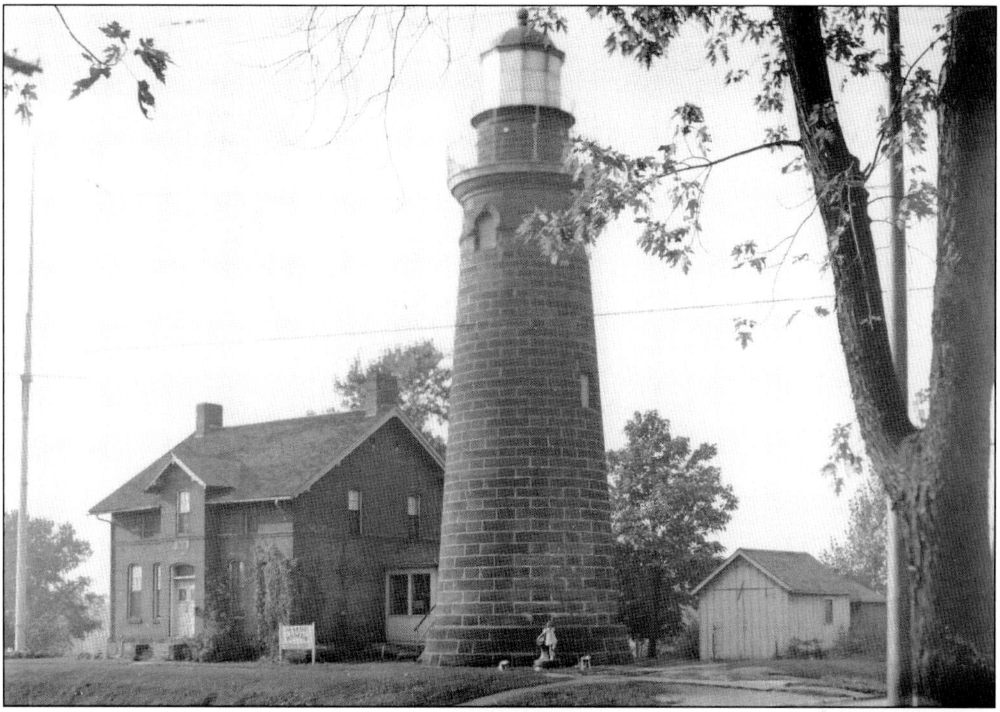

A second Fairport Lighthouse was built in 1871 on a foundation 11 feet, four inches deep. The gray Berea sandstone tower, 102 feet above lake level, had a third-order Fresnel lens with a fixed white light that shone for 18.5 miles. The first keeper was Joseph Babcock, a Civil War veteran. His son Daniel was the assistant from 1901 to 1919. Daniel became the main keeper and served until 1925, when the lighthouse was replaced with a pier lighthouse. (USCG.)

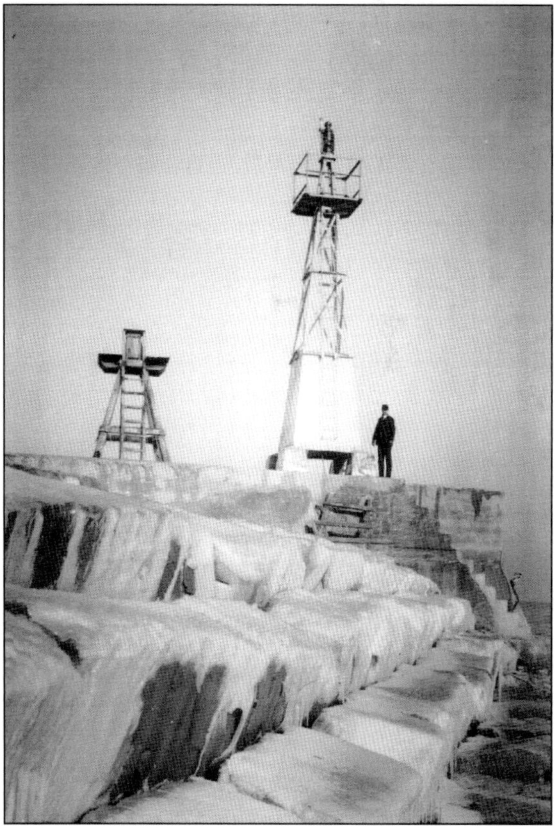

The Fairport West Breakwater Pierhead Lights are pictured on December 7, 1911, along with the lighthouse keeper. (NARA.)

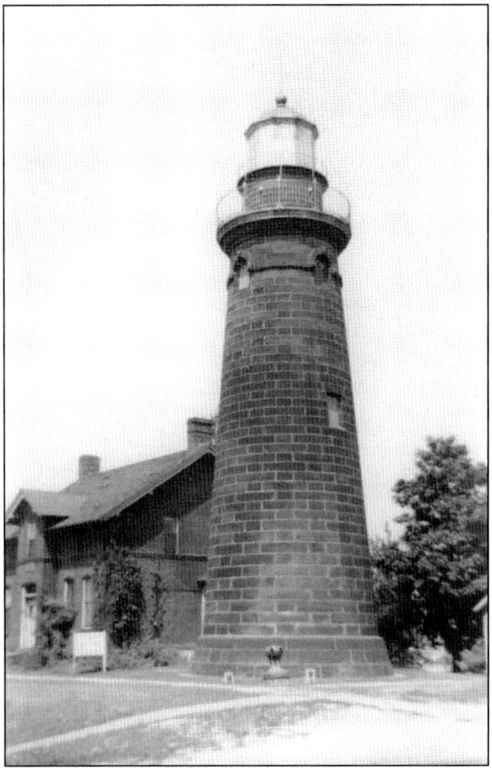

This haunted lighthouse became famous for its ghosts, but they were known as "spirits that did not represent people." In 1945, residents formed the first marine museum on the Great Lakes at the Fairport Lighthouse and the curator, Pamela Brent, began living at the lighthouse for the next four years. Haunting and the supernatural came to her mind when she saw ghostly cats skittering from the rooms. The scariest incident happened at night, when she was in bed and one of these spectral felines jumped up next to her. Perhaps this was the ghost of one of the cats kept by Mrs. Joseph Babcock, the first lighthouse keeper's wife. Mrs. Babcock was bedridden and kept cats for company. Whether there are spirits or not, a mummified cat was found in a crawl space in the basement in 2001. (GLHS.)

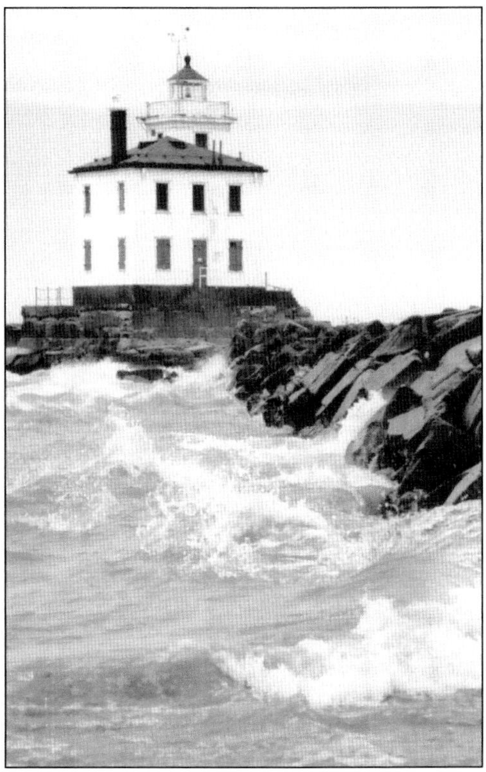

On June 21, 1921, a pier lighthouse was built in Buffalo, New York, and ferried to Fairport Harbor on the steamer *Wotan*. The US Coast Guard claims it saved $10,000 by not building the lighthouse at this location. The 65-ton structure, clad with steel plates painted white, was secured on the ship by steel cables. The lantern room and tower were built on-site and completed in 1925. (AC.)

Fairport West Breakwater Light, after being removed from the *Wontan*, is captured in this photograph. The lantern is a fourth-order Fresnel lens with a range of 15 miles; it was automated in 1965. (AC.)

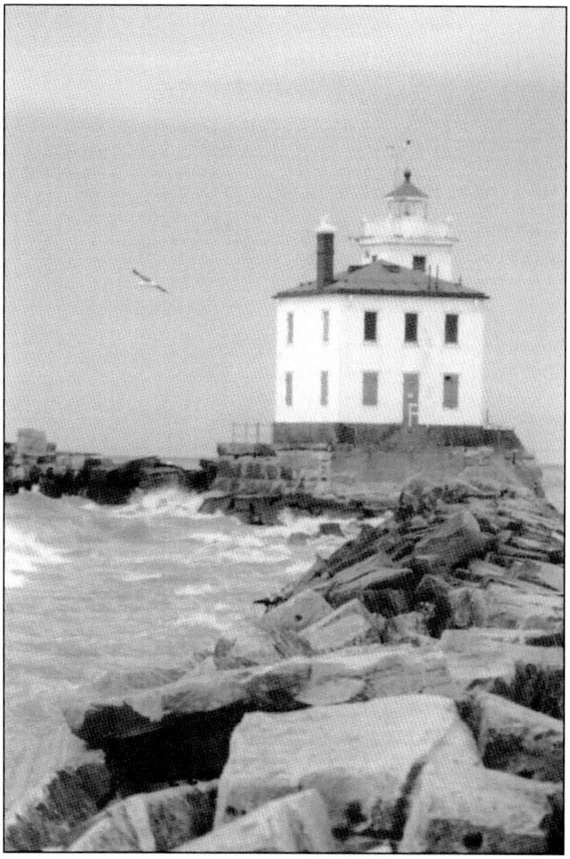

An unidentified couple walks along the beach near the Fairport Harbor West Breakwater Lighthouse. (AC.)

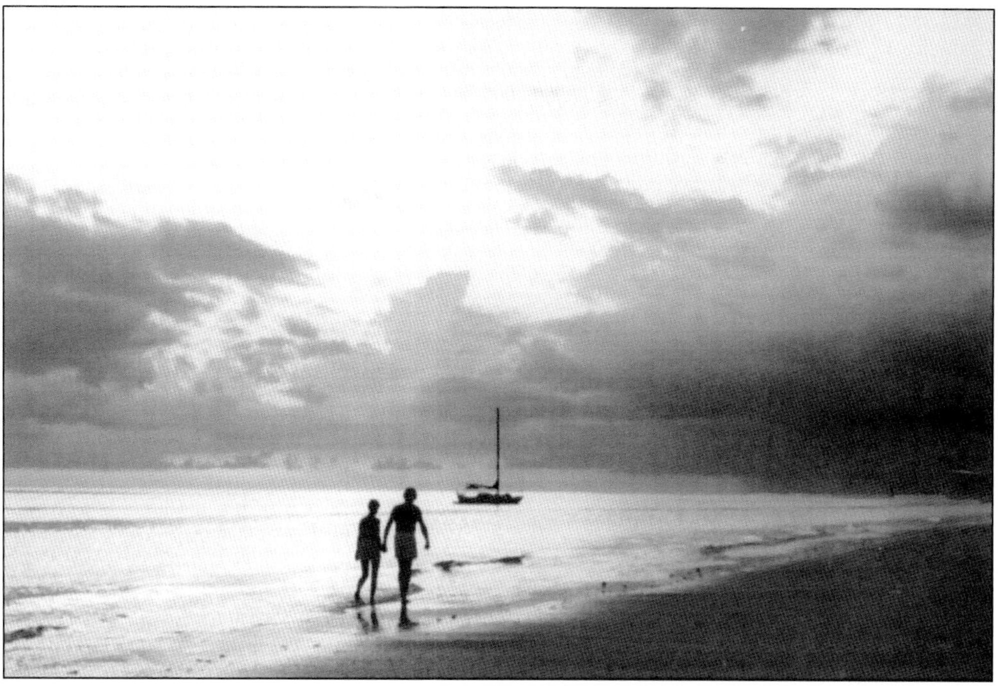

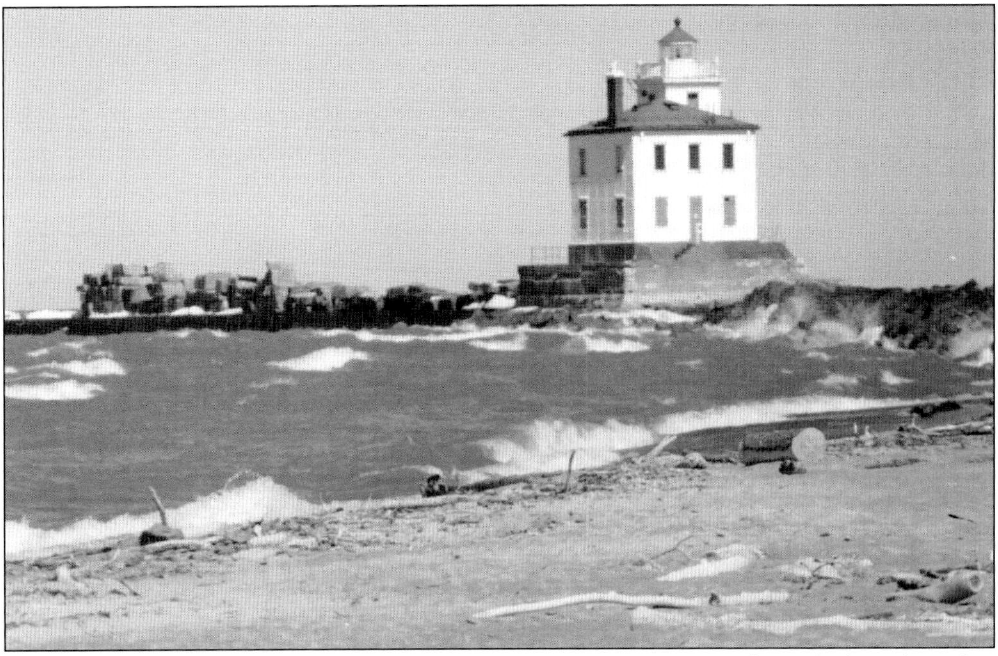

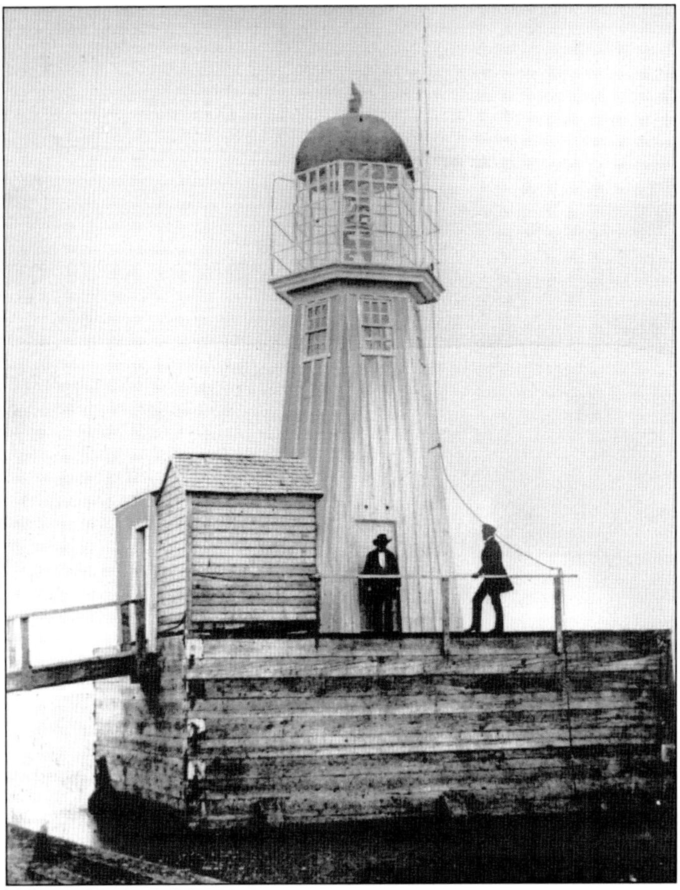

At the end of a wide, mile-long beach is the Fairport Harbor West Breakwater Lighthouse. Gray driftwood lies scattered about the lonely shore, perhaps from a wrecked ship with a story to tell if only it could talk. There are no names or letters etched in the cut planks that were surely shaped by humans. Perhaps these mysterious pieces of driftwood were from the wreckage of the *Queen of the West*, which sank offshore in 1903. (AC.)

The first Ashtabula Lighthouse was built from 1835 to 1836 on an east pier. The light consisted of seven lamps that burned sperm oil. The hexagonal board-and-batten tower was three stories high. (GLHS.)

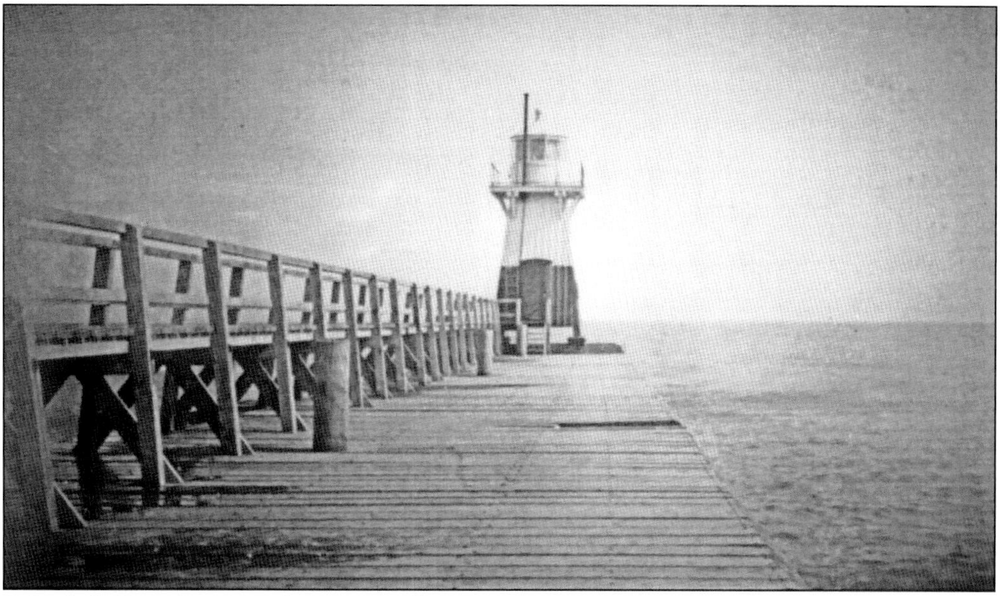

Ashtabula Front Range Light is pictured in 1885. In 1896, a keeper's house was built on a hilltop not far from the lighthouse. This residence would become the home of the Great Lakes Marine and Coast Guard Memorial Museum (Ashtabula Maritime Museum) in 1984. (NARA.)

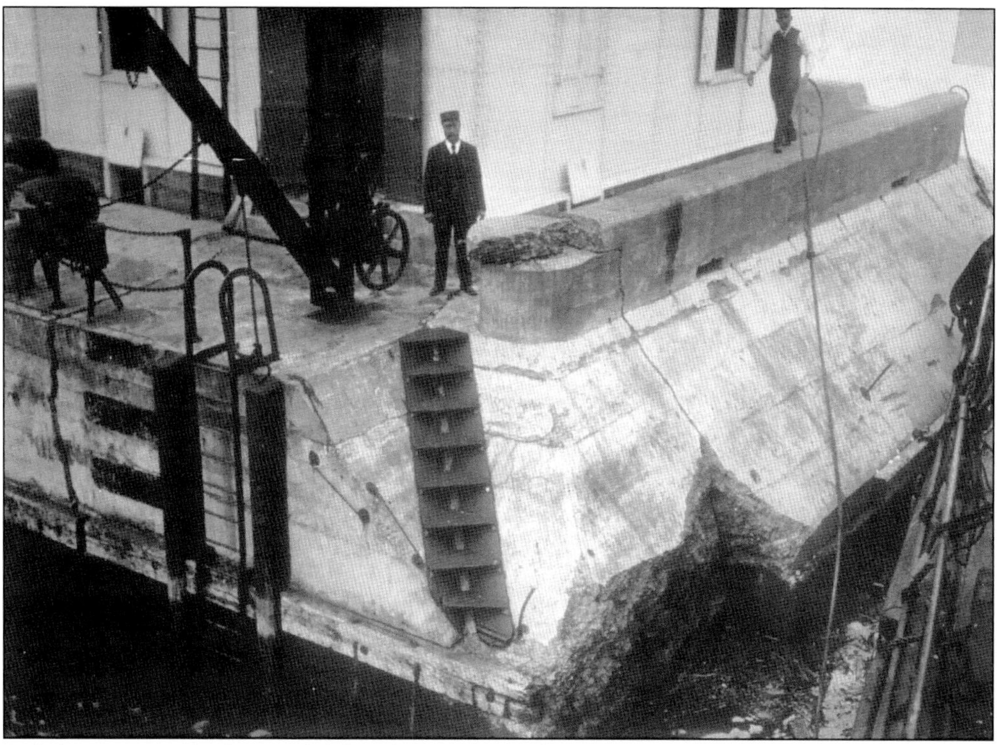

Lighthouses were built on solid foundations not only to withstand the storms of Lake Erie but also collisions with large freighters. Ashtabula Harbor Front Light Station is showing damage from a collision on the southerly corner in this image from 1911. In 1905, the river was widened, and a new lighthouse was built at the end of a breakwater pier. (NARA.)

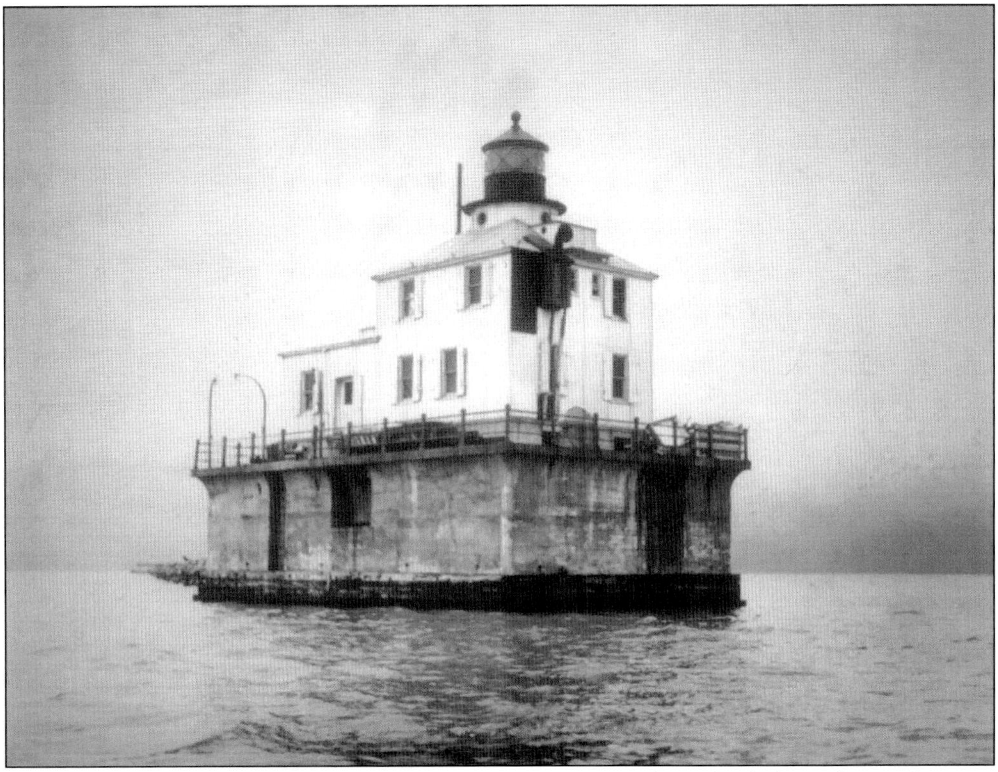

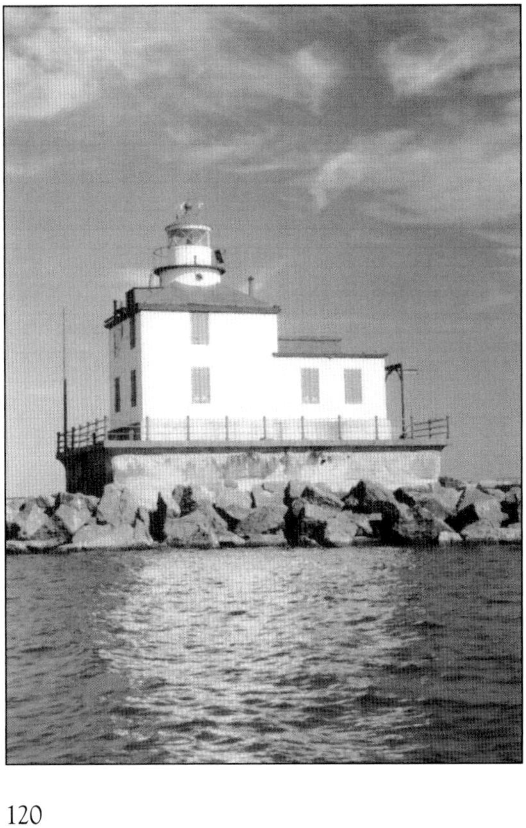

In 1916, the Ashtabula Harbor Light Station was put on a barge and moved 1,800 feet north-northeast and placed at the west end of a new breakwater pier. A one-story addition was added for the air-operated diaphone (fog signal). The Ashtabula Lighthouse Restoration and Preservation Society formed in 2000 to obtain ownership of the last Ashtabula Lighthouse in order to restore and preserve it for future generations. (NARA.)

In this photograph, Ashtabula Lighthouse shines its beacon. (AC.)

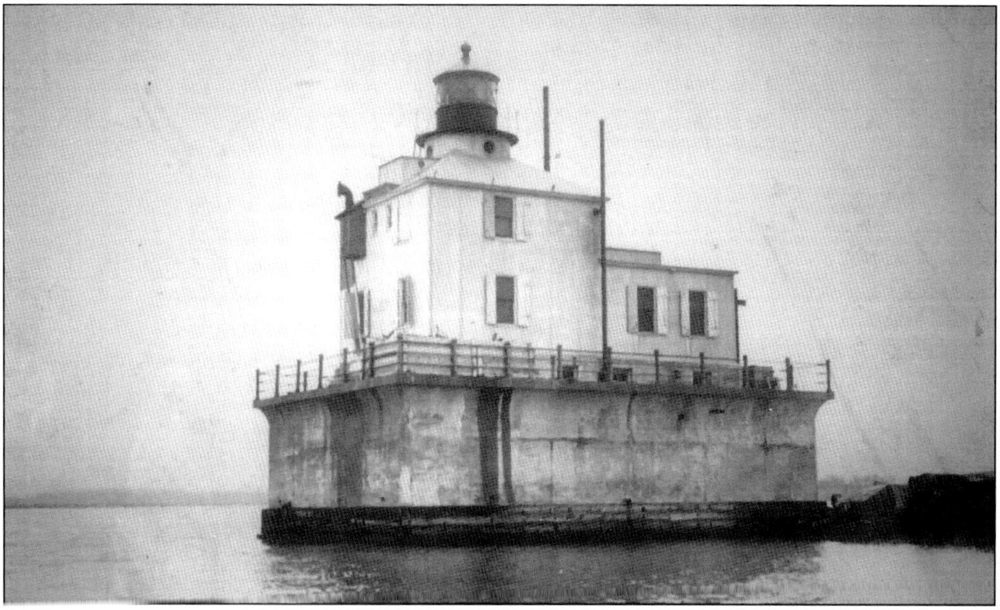

In 1959, a new fourth-order Fresnal lens was installed in the Ashtabula Harbor Light Station. It flashed every five seconds and had a visibility of 17 miles. In 1973, the light was automated. The fourth-order Fresnal lens was replaced in 1995 by a new light made of plastic, fiberglass, and aluminum with a 300-millimeter lens. It is powered by 12-volt solar batteries. A 35-watt solar panel recharges the batteries. The fourth-order lens was put on display in the Ashtabula Maritime Museum, located in the old lighthouse keeper's house on the hill. The lighthouse is only accessible by boat and is not open to the public. (NARA.)

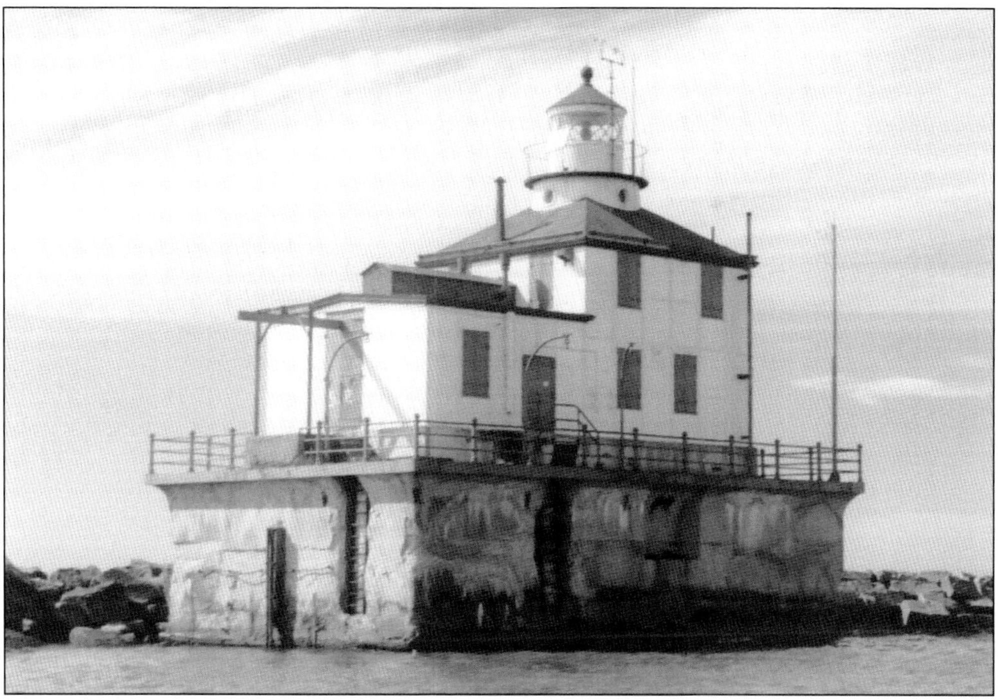

This is the Ashtabula Lighthouse, where the keepers were once entombed in ice. (AC.)

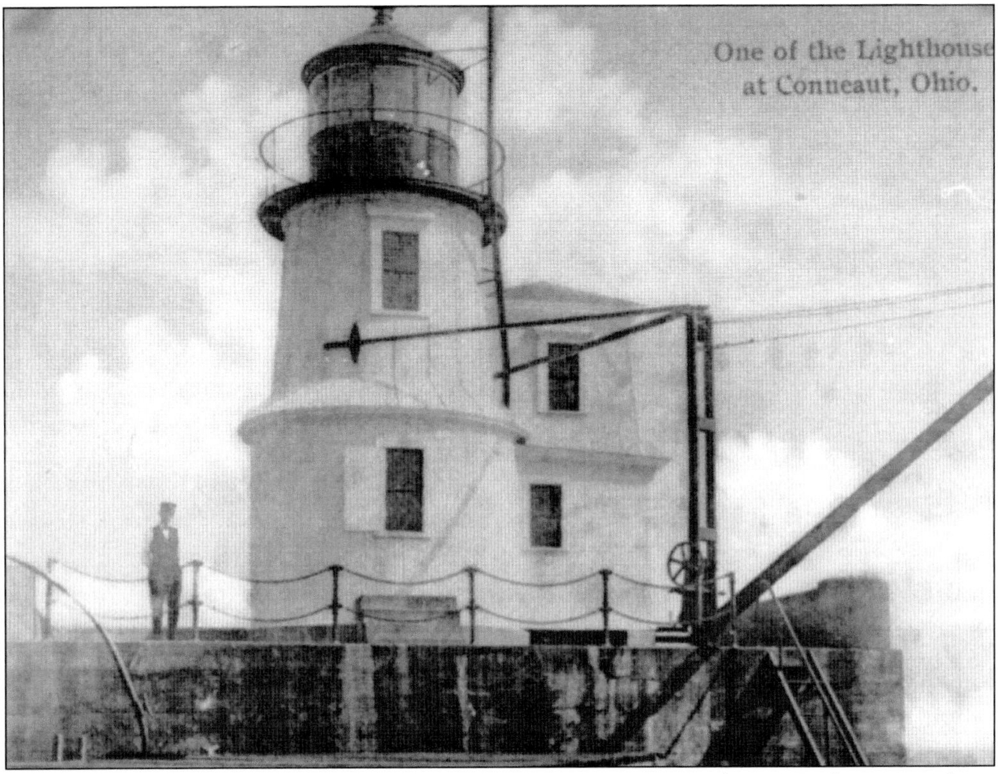

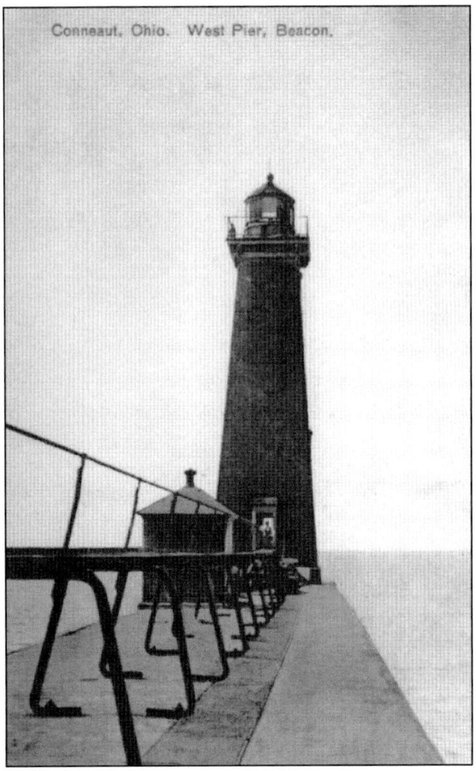

Conneaut West Breakwater Light, pictured around 1918, was an impressive sight, with the lighthouse keeper on the left. This second pierhead light at Conneaut was built in the 1890s on the old 500-foot wooden seawall. The bell-tower lighthouse had a bell on the north side. The first beacon at this site was installed in 1835. A keeper's house was built in 1873 on a bluff overlooking the harbor. Shipments of grain, whiskey, and forest products made Conneaut a busy port in the 1880s. (CL.)

The lighthouse keeper can be seen standing at the top near the lantern room in this image of the Conneaut West Pier Beacon. Another lighthouse keeper, perhaps an assistant, appears in the doorway at the bottom. (CL.)

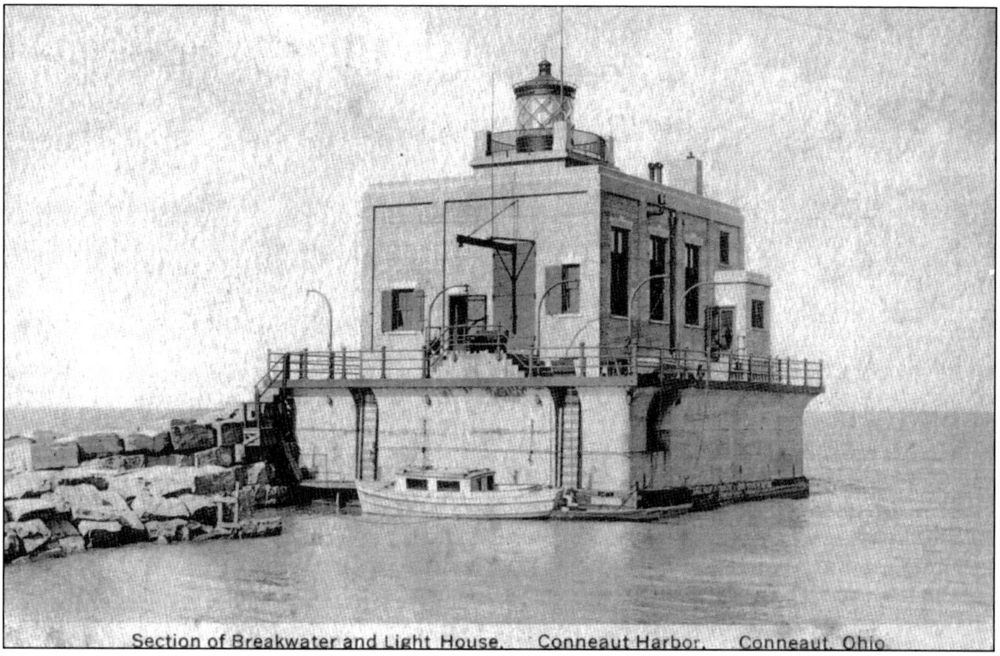

Looking like a modern administration building in the city, this 1917 Conneaut Lighthouse cost a whopping $125,000. Built on a cement crib, this square building of concrete and brick could withstand the vicious storms of Lake Erie, but it was no match for dynamite. A massive federal project in the early 1930s extended the east and west breakwater piers and made the indestructible lighthouse obsolete. By 1933, it was gone, and a new concrete crib was built for the 1936 lighthouse, which cost only $70,000. (Both, CL.)

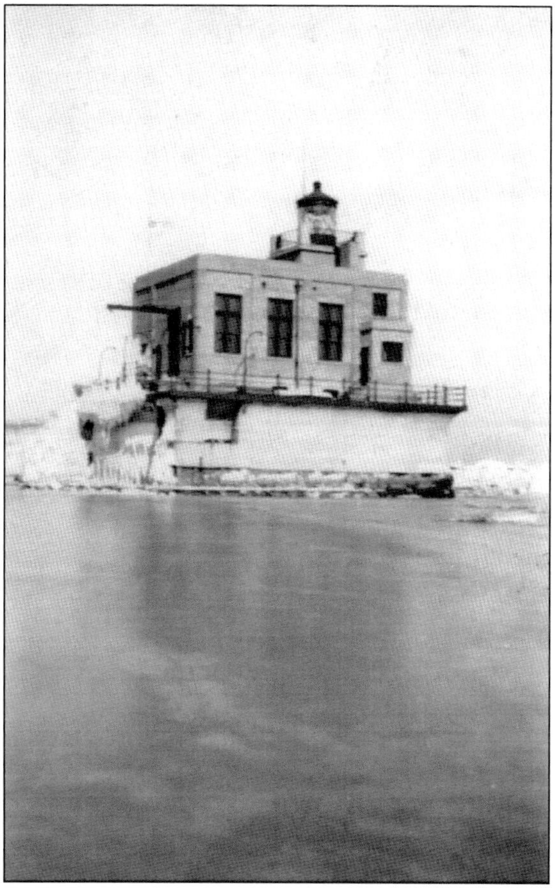

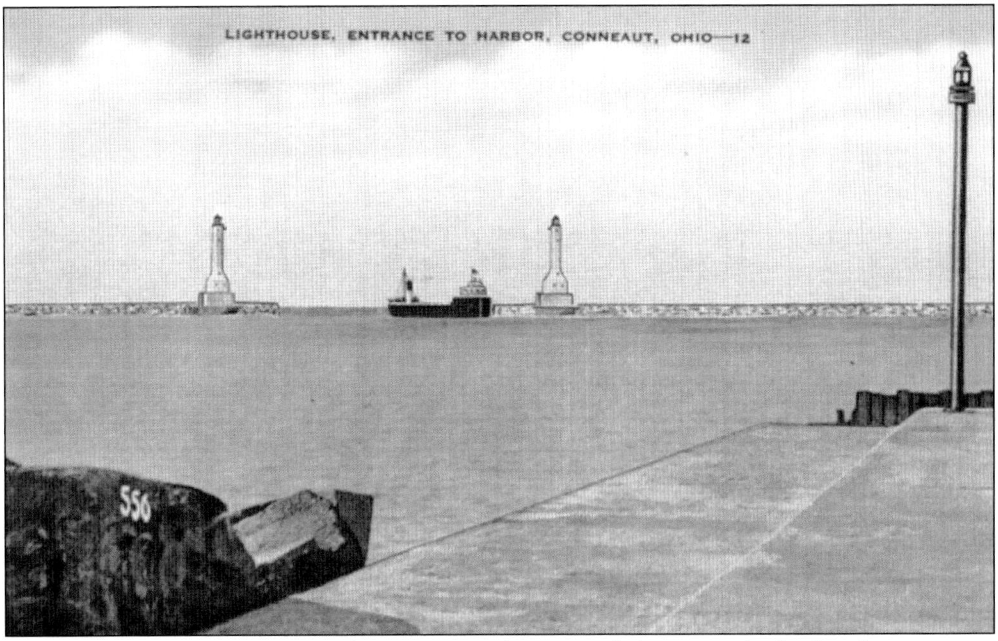

There is only one Conneaut Harbor West Breakwater Lighthouse in the harbor, but someone placed two Conneaut Lighthouses in this postcard. A prankster working in the printing office in 1936 was having some fun creating this image. The real lighthouse is on the left. (CL.)

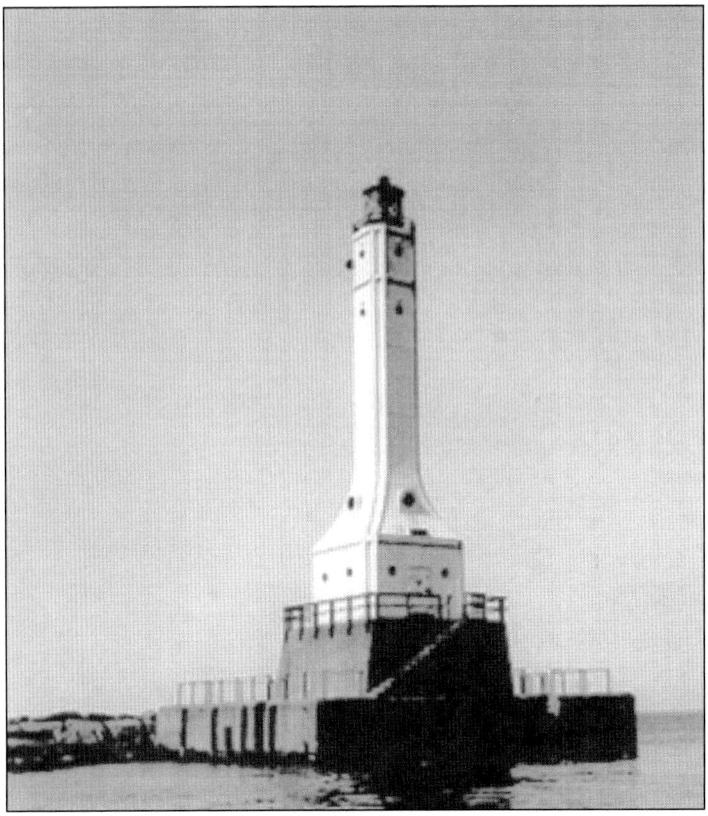

The Conneaut Harbor West Breakwater Light, with lantern room, was built in 1936. Huron Lighthouse is its identical twin, and four other lighthouses on the Great Lakes are similar. (USCG.)

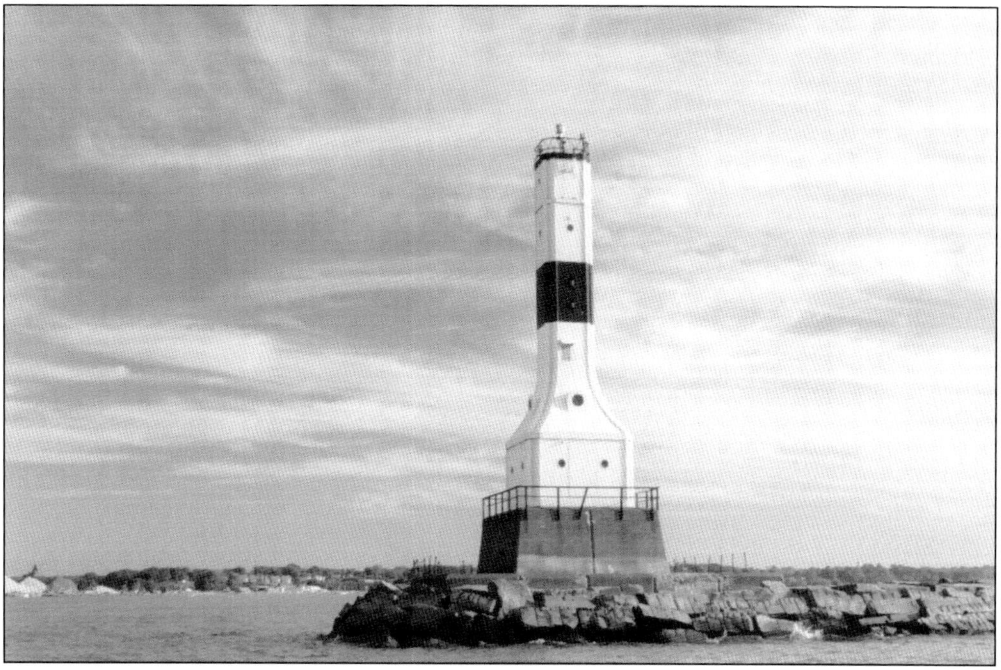

This 1936 Conneaut Lighthouse was once painted all white and had a circular black lantern room at the top. Later, a horizontal black band would distinguish it from the Huron Lighthouse. One keeper was on duty during the day, and two keepers manned the light at night. In 1949, it was updated to a plastic beacon with an alternating red-and-white flash. The light was automated in 1971, and the lantern room was removed in 1972. (AC.)

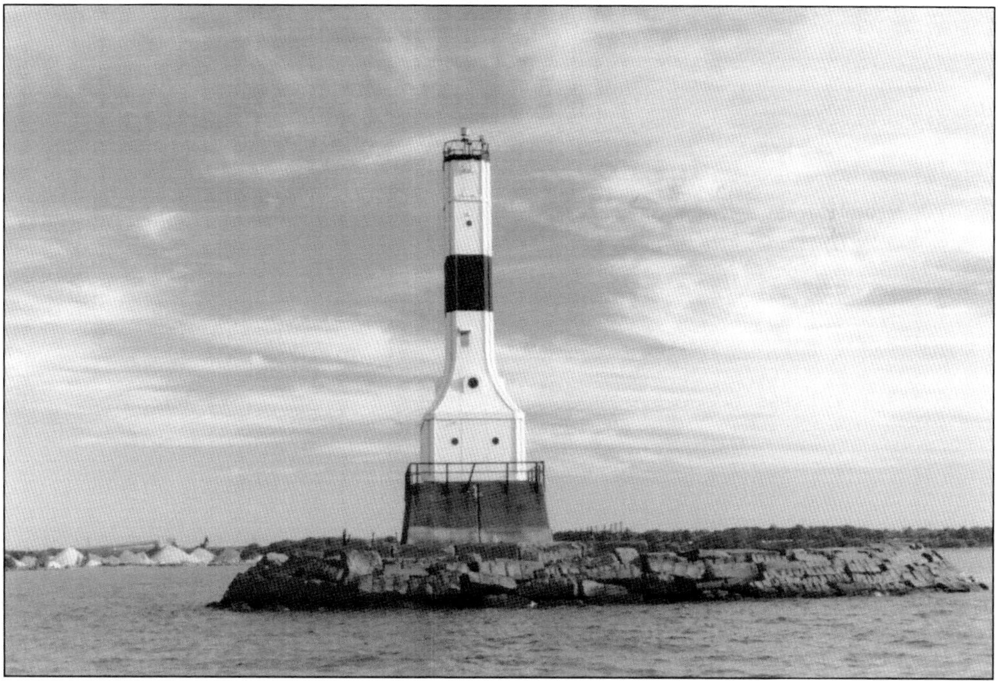

Conneaut Lighthouse is pictured without the lantern room at the top. (AC.)

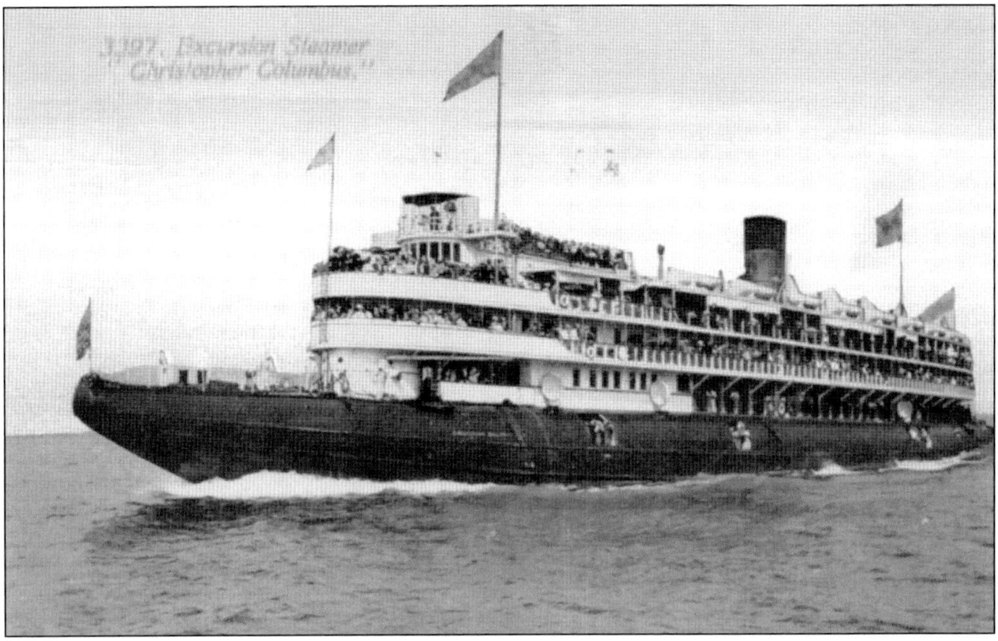

People thought these round, steel ships looked like whales with pig noses, hence the name whalebacks. *Christopher Columbus* was built for Chicago's 1893 Columbus Exposition. This rare ship is the only whaleback excursion ship built, and it carried more passengers than any other excursion ship during its years of operation (1893 to 1936). Between 1888 and 1898, before the design became obsolete, 44 cargo whalebacks were built. Alexander McDougall, from Duluth, Minnesota (1845–1923), was the designer. (AC.)

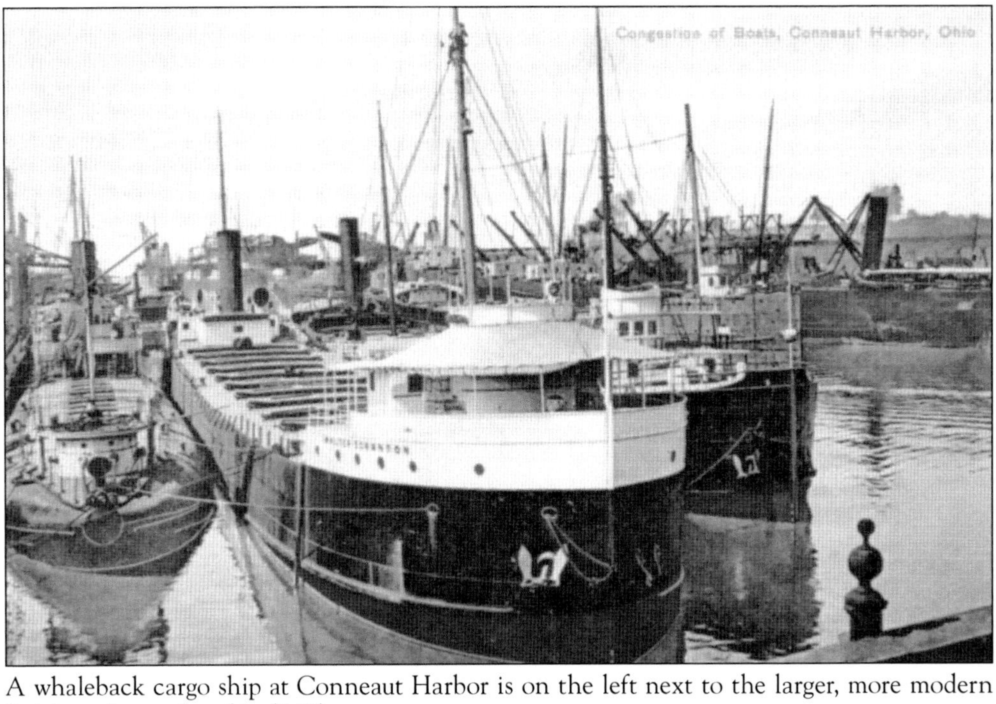

A whaleback cargo ship at Conneaut Harbor is on the left next to the larger, more modern freighter that replaced it. (AC.)

BIBLIOGRAPHY

Adamson, Hans Christian. *Keepers of the Lights*. New York: Greenberg, 1955.

Annual Report of the United States Life-Saving Service, 1876–1914. Historical Collections of the Great Lakes, Bowling Green State University, Bowling Green, OH.

Butts, Edward. *Outlaws of the Lakes: Bootlegging and Smuggling from Colonial Times to Prohibition*. Toronto: Lynx Images, Inc., 2004.

Cantrell, Charles. "Remembering Rum Runners Roaring Rampant," *Vermilion Bugle*. 1985.

Frohman, Charles E. *Sandusky's Yesterdays*. Columbus, OH: Ohio Historical Society, 1968.

Gardner, Barbara and B. Ellen Gardner. *Turtle Island Lighthouse: The Darkened Light*. Cornwall, NY: Hawks Cry Publications, 1997.

Gora, Michael. *Lake Erie Islands–Sketches and Stories of the First Century After the Battle of Lake Erie*. Put-in-Bay, OH: Lake Erie Islands Historical Society, 2004.

Gutoche, Andrea and Cindy Bisaillon. *Mysterious islands: Forgotten Tales of the Great Lakes*. Toronto: Lynx Images, Inc., 1999.

Kohl, Cris. *The Great Lakes Diving Guide*, second edition. Chicago: Seawolf Communications, 2008.

Neidecker, Betty and Rose Kernan. *The Marblehead Lighthouse: Lake Erie's Eternal Flame*. Ohio: Betty Neidecker, 1995.

Patterson, Janice B. *Cleveland's Lighthouses*. Charleston, SC: Arcadia Publishing, 2009.

Stonehouse, Frederick. *Wreck Ashore: The United States Life-Saving Service on the Great Lakes*. Duluth, MN: Lake Superior Port Cities, 1994.

Thay, Edrick. *Ghost Stories of Ohio*. Edmonton, AB: Lone Star Publishing, 2001.

Wright, Larry and Patricia Wright. *Great Lakes Lighthouse Encyclopedia*. Erin, ON: Boston Mills Press, 2006.